STAYING HUMAN
DURING RESIDENCY TRAINING

The ultimate survival guide for medical students, interns, residents, and fellows, *Staying Human during Residency Training* provides time-tested advice and the latest information on every aspect of a resident's life – from choosing a residency program to coping with stress, enhancing self-care, and protecting personal and professional relationships.

The book features hundreds of tips on how to cope with sleep deprivation, time pressures, and ethical and legal issues. Updated to reflect the latest research and resources, the seventh edition provides new emphasis on virtual practice, gender, diversity, and accountability in the context of medical education. It offers practical strategies learned from new technologies and new insight on the COVID-19 pandemic regarding public health, virtual appointment protocols, and AI developments. Presenting practical antidotes regarding cynicism, careerism, and burnout, the book also offers guidance on fostering more empathic connections with patients and deepening relationships with colleagues, friends, and family.

Acknowledged by thousands of doctors across North America as an invaluable resource, *Staying Human during Residency Training* has helped to shape notions of trainee well-being for medical educators worldwide. Offering wise, compassionate, and professional counsel, this new edition again shows why it is required reading for medical students and new physicians pursuing postgraduate training.

ALLAN D. PETERKIN is a professor of psychiatry and family medicine at the University of Toronto.

DEREK PUDDESTER is an associate professor of psychiatry at the University of Ottawa and a clinical instructor at the University of British Columbia.

Praise for Previous Editions

"Through most of this century physicians have looked back on their internship and residency years as a painful but necessary maturation ritual. Once out of residency, they quickly forget or at least deny, how much damage – depression, burn-out, marriage breakdown, alcoholism and suicide – was wrought during the process. Allan Peterkin and Derek Puddester ... provide a useful guide for self-preservation and well-being. It should be required reading for all graduating medical students."

Bruce P. Squires, MD, PhD, former editor-in-chief,
Canadian Medical Association Journal

"This guide should be required reading for each intern beginning residency and also for each and every residency program director in North America."

Aliye Runyan, Medical Education Team Chair,
American Medical Student Association (AMSA), and Sonia Lazreg,
AMSA/Committee of Interns and Residents Health Justice Fellow

"*Staying Human during Residency Training* is an important reminder: that humane treatment – of oneself and fellow residents, as well as our patients – is what makes a good doctor, and that one cannot have empathy without good self-caretaking. That is a lesson we can all afford to review."

Sonya Rasminsky, MD, *CIR News*

"An excellent resource for residents at any stage in their training."

The Canadian Association of Internes and Residents

"There is no area in a resident's life that Drs Peterkin and Puddester don't tackle: finances, substance abuse, fellowship options, foreign, gay, and disabled students, ethical and legal considerations, study tips and support groups. It's the ultimate how-to book for all apprentice doctors and its commonsense approach makes it a mandatory trouble-shooter."

Elaine McNinch, *Family Practice*

"This catalog of indispensable advice can help residents at all stages of training. Read it today, and pass it on!"

Wayne M. Sotile, PhD, author of *Letting Go of What's Holding You Back!* and *The Resilient Physician*

ALLAN D. PETERKIN, MD
DEREK PUDDESTER, MD

STAYING
HUMAN

DURING RESIDENCY TRAINING

*How to **Survive** and **Thrive** after Medical School*

SEVENTH EDITION

UNIVERSITY OF TORONTO PRESS
Toronto Buffalo London

© University of Toronto Press 2024
Toronto Buffalo London
utorontopress.com
Printed and bound by CPI Group (UK) Ltd, Croydon, CR0 4YY

ISBN 978-1-4875-5547-4 (paper)
ISBN 978-1-4875-5549-8 (EPUB)
ISBN 978-1-4875-5548-1 (PDF)

Library and Archives Canada Cataloguing in Publication

Title: Staying human during residency training : how to survive and thrive after
    medical school / Allan D. Peterkin and Derek Puddester.
Names: Peterkin, Allan, author. | Puddester, Derek, author.
Description: Seventh edition. | Includes bibliographical references and index.
Identifiers: Canadiana (print) 20230578225 | Canadiana (ebook) 20230578233 |
    ISBN 9781487555474 (paper) | ISBN 9781487555498 (EPUB) |
    ISBN 9781487555481 (PDF)
Subjects: LCSH: Residents (Medicine) — Canada — Life skills guides. |
    LCSH: Residents (Medicine) — United States — Life skills guides.
Classification: LCC R840.P48 2024 | DDC 610.71/55—dc23

Cover design: Val Cooke
Cover image: Katsiaryna yuralaits/Alamy Stock Photo

We welcome comments and suggestions regarding any aspect of our publications –
please feel free to contact us at news@utorontopress.com or visit us at utorontopress.
com.

Every effort has been made to contact copyright holders; in the event of an error or
omission, please notify the publisher.

We wish to acknowledge the land on which the University of Toronto Press
operates. This land is the traditional territory of the Wendat, the Anishnaabeg, the
Haudenosaunee, the Métis, and the Mississaugas of the Credit First Nation.

University of Toronto Press acknowledges the financial support of the Government
of Canada and the Ontario Arts Council, an agency of the Government of Ontario,
for its publishing activities.

 **Canada Council
for the Arts** **Conseil des Arts
du Canada**    ONTARIO ARTS COUNCIL
CONSEIL DES ARTS DE L'ONTARIO
an Ontario government agency
un organisme du gouvernement de l'Ontario

Funded by the   Financé par le
Government   gouvernement
of Canada   du Canada | Canadä

Contents

Foreword

Residency training has always been a challenging time in the life of a physician. There may be no other comparable rite of passage that compresses so much into a short, finite period of three to six years. The acquisition of knowledge, technical skills, clinical confidence, and professional maturity is exciting and galvanizing. But there can be a downside – a cost that accompanies the inevitable stress and an assault to one's bearings and equilibrium. For generations residents were expected to cope, to endure, to not complain, and to, in the vernacular of today, simply "suck it up."

Enter Dr. Allan Peterkin. In the first edition of *Staying Human during Residency Training* (penned while he was a resident), he wrote, "On the day I wrote this preface, I heard of a resident who by chance left call early to find her husband walking out of the door with packed bags. I have witnessed three divorces, one paranoid reaction, three cases of depression needing treatment, as well as miscarriages and catastrophic illness among my friends and classmates." Thousands of residents around the world, their families, their teachers, and their patients have benefited from this landmark book and all its updated editions. Anecdotal comments of readers highlight the insights, wisdom, suggestions, and survival tips contained within – and always, gratitude for Dr. Peterkin's thoughtfulness and humanity.

Now enter Dr. Derek Puddester, noted expert in physician health, medical education, and executive coaching. Thanks to the rich collaboration of these two talented physicians, *Staying Human during Residency Training* is now in its seventh edition. And it soars! The breadth is encyclopaedic yet not ponderous. The hands-on, humane touch is preserved as they address many of the contemporary realities and trials of training: cultural awareness, sensitivity and humility, anti-oppression training, violence in the workplace, microaggressions, disruptive behavior in fellow residents and faculty, climate change, social determinants of health, physician impairment, LGBTQ2S+ patients and peers, international medical graduate (IMG) hurdles, neurodiverse residents, virtual care and telemedicine, artificial intelligence, self-care, healthy boundaries, narrative medicine, social justice, and many more. The resources contained within the pages of this book are bountiful and international in scope.

Graduating medical students, residents, and early-career physicians will be enriched and comforted by this book. It is a validation that you can not only thrive as a physician in training but also preserve and strengthen your humanity. I highly recommend it.

– Michael F. Myers, MD
Professor of Clinical Psychiatry
SUNY Downstate Health Sciences University
Brooklyn, NY
Author of *Becoming a Doctors' Doctor: A Memoir,*
The Physician as Patient, Doctors' Marriages, and
other books on physician health

Acknowledgments

Many thanks to all my students, residents, former teachers, current colleagues, and all the readers of previous editions of *Staying Human* over the last thirty years. Many of them took the time to write or speak to me about edits, critiques, and personal anecdotes, which have helped to keep the book relevant. Thanks also to my co-author of this seventh edition, Dr. Derek Puddester, who knows the literature on physician wellness so well, and who brought to the book his own lived experience of leadership and of working effectively with residents and medical governing bodies and institutions.

I completed the book as a resident myself for an elective project at McGill University. I co-wrote this last edition as a full professor of psychiatry and family medicine at the University of Toronto, where I have had the pleasure of helping to create opportunities for arts-based reflective learning and have helped promote the medical humanities as a way of keeping us all creative, critical, and accountable.

Thanks to my editors at the University of Toronto Press, who have shepherded each edition with academic rigor, generosity, and good humor.

As I approach retirement, I also want to thank all of my patients and their families, who have taught me so much about healing, humility, and what it is that makes each of us so uniquely human.

– Allan Peterkin, MD

I dedicate this work to my co-author, Dr. Allan Peterkin. What a joy it has been to collaborate with him, and on the very book that inspired me to pursue a career in physician health when I was a resident! Dr. Peterkin has been a compassionate, courageous, and caring advocate for our profession for his entire career. Thank you, Allan, for taking such good care of us.

Changing culture is something best done in partnership and community. I am deeply grateful to many learners, physician-patients, physician health program colleagues, physician association leaders, and physician-health scholars for their inspiration, encouragement, and insights over the past twenty years. There is still much good work to do, and I am excited to see how our profession will carry on evolving. May we continue to learn how to take good care of ourselves so we can provide the best possible care for patients, families, communities, and each other.

Thanks also to the team at University of Toronto Press, learners who provided feedback on this edition's drafts, my dear friend and colleague Dr. Michael Myers, and to my family for their endless love and support.

– Derek Puddester, MA, MD, MEd, FRCPC, PCC

STAYING HUMAN
DURING RESIDENCY TRAINING

1

Body, Mind, and Soul

The Opportunities, Risks, and Challenges of Resident Training

Congratulations on finishing medical school and welcome to residency! Residency (or postgraduate medical) training will provide many opportunities for great personal and professional development. While these years pass quickly, you will be faced with complex and demanding challenges that will shape you both as a person and as a professional. Yes, there will be times your limits of endurance will be tested, and there will also be times where your ability to have a positive impact on the lives of others will be limited. However, there will be many more times where you will absolutely thrive. Remember, you have already faced and mastered many challenges in your life and career path to this point, and you know that residents are not fragile people. In fact, your intelligence, compassion, desire to learn, and commitment to service and social justice are your biggest strengths. Although residency presents multiple challenges and stressors, it also affords you the opportunity to develop resilience and coping skills that will serve you throughout your career.

Along with medical students, residents make up approximately 30 per cent of the physician workforce in the United States and Canada. It is striking, however, that some of the character traits that lead many people towards a career in medicine are also predictors of possible struggles and impairment.[1,2,3] High levels of responsibility, intense contact with people, time restrictions, role uncertainty and transition (i.e., from student to neophyte professional), sleep deprivation, and social isolation are linked to stress in any profession. Although residency today is a much better place to be than when the first edition of this book came out, significant stressors are still present in postgraduate medical education. In addition, residents must deal directly with suffering, fear, death, uncertainty, and problem patients and staff.[4] In these circumstances, it is not surprising that they suffer varying degrees of stress-related symptoms, however healthy they may be upon entering residency.

What's different today is that burnout is not seen as an inevitable by-product of training. Resilience and compassion for self and others are its antidotes, and you'll learn how to cultivate both throughout the chapters in this book. Recent research, such as the National Academy of Medicine's clinician well-being study, has identified specific traits that reduce the risk of burnout, including being easy-going, having a receptive personality, enjoying an internal locus of control, leaning into a strong sense of self-efficacy, protecting time to be with loved ones, openly talking about challenges and emotions, and engaging in active learning strategies that enhance resilience (e.g., the American Medical Association's STEPS Forward open-access modules).[5]

Readers of previous editions of *Staying Human during Residency Training* have pointed out that providing endless lists of health risks for learners seemed discouraging considering the book's role in emphasizing resident resilience and well-being. The book's original title, *Staying Human*, conveyed that residents, thirty years ago, often felt dehumanized by their experiences as persons due to unexamined power differentials reflected in unfair working and teaching conditions that often incorporated elements of shame and humiliation. This newest edition encourages residents to develop as fully realized and happy human beings first and foremost as they pursue their shared passion for medicine.

We are happy to report that things have improved significantly since the first edition of *Staying Human* came out in 1989, balanced by some new trends emerging in recent years:

- Residents show significantly higher resilience scores than the general employed US population.[6]
- Residents with higher skills of resiliency are less likely to experience emotional exhaustion and depersonalization, with resident-led initiatives becoming more common and more effective in reducing burnout and improving wellness.[7]
- Residents are now more aware of self-care and are more insistent on achieving balance and resilience in their personal and work lives.

- Work-hour restrictions exist in both Canada and the US and continue to be monitored and fine-tuned.[8,9]
- Most residency programs in North America offer wellness initiatives and resources, and up to 80 per cent of physicians report being aware of the services available from physician health programs.[10]
- There has been a significant shift away from a study of physician impairment to looking at physician wellness and sustained well-being as key ingredients for fostering the practice of humanistic care. (See chapter 6 for more on humanism in medicine.)
- A growing literature actually looks at definitions of physician happiness (and more on that, shortly).

These are all welcome developments. Nonetheless, residency does present some unique challenges and stressors, and recent studies have identified that physicians in the early years of practice may have particularly higher rates of burnout and lower rates of resiliency when compared to those in later phases of their careers.[11] Many organizations are now looking at ways to support "early career physicians" as they make the transition from residency to practice.

Table 1.1 summarizes the top stressors as identified by residents in 1987, 2008, and 2012. This last table reflects current concerns as well.

As of the writing of this current edition, some additional stressors are being identified or amplified:

- Impacts of COVID-19, including the risk of infection, vaccine hesitancy, impacts on education, and isolation[12,13] (Of note, anecdotally, over two-thirds of residents reported leaning into their pre-existing resiliency skills to cope with these stressors, including accessing wellness programs and services.)
- Finances, including inflation, housing costs, health insurance and other insurability, and management of debt
- Climate change[14]
- Violence towards physicians[15]
- Workload volume, complexity, and uncertainty
- Both subtle and overt racism (micro/macroaggressions) and other forms of discrimination (more on this below)

Although most Canadian and US resident physicians have and maintain a positive outlook, residents still experience significant stressors, and a significant portion may be at risk for emotional and mental health problems.

Table 1.1. **Top stressors over time**

In 1987:
- Insufficient sleep, less than 3 hours
- Frequent night calls every third night or more often
- Uncompromising attending physicians
- Large patient load
- Too much scut work
- Too much medical records work
- High rates of death among patients
- Little or no contact with fellow residents
- Inadequate sexual activity
- High peer competition to impress staff

In 2008:
- Work load
- Sleep deprivation
- Difficult patients
- Fear of litigation
- Death load
- Information overload
- Social isolation
- Fear of infection (HIV, SARS, hepatitis)
- Dying patients
- Lack of personal time

In 2012:
- Time pressures
- Finances
- The Affordable Care Act aka Obamacare (in the US)
- Assisted suicide legislation (in Canada)
- Needle sticks
- Abusive, inappropriate house officers
- Requests to do inappropriate procedures
- Competitive classmates
- Patient death
- Sexual harassment
- Difficult /violent patients
- Difficult family members
- Fatigue
- Personal family illness

Source: Aminazadeh, N., Farrokhyar, F., Naeeni, M., Reid, S., Kashfi, A., & Kahnamoui, K. (2012, Aug). "Is Canadian surgical residency training stressful?" *Canadian Journal of Surgery*, 55(4): S145–51.

The "happy docs" study[16] surveyed residents across all medical schools in Canada and was administered through CAIR, the Canadian Association of Internes and Residents (now called Resident Doctors of Canada). One-third of residents reported their life as "quite a bit to extremely stressful," with time pressure being the most significant factor associated with stress. More than half of all residents experienced intimidation and harassment, most often based on training status (as related to seniority or gender), and 18 per cent of residents reported their mental health as either "fair" or "poor." The two top resources that residents wished to have available were career counseling and financial counseling. These areas have been surprisingly neglected but are now offered in many programs.[17]

"Haiku of Residency" by Emily R. Transue[18]

1. **Please**
   Please do not code now;
   I have just found a warm spot
   in this cold hard bed.

2. **Identity**
   Who am I to you?
   White-coated figure folds cold hands,
   calls in scripts by phone.

3. **Hematemesis**
   We each have five pints
   of blood. I counted your five
   in the red basin.

4. **Eight A.M.**
   You say good morning
   but does it count as morning
   if I did not sleep?

5. **Alarm**
   My pager goes off
   Searing explosion of noise
   – No, that's a fire drill.

   Seven flights of stairs
   Run breathless in double steps
   My heart fast; yours, still.

Risk Categories

Here are some sample results of other recent studies on resident health in both Canada and the United States, according to risk categories. These statistics are not meant to be discouraging but rather to serve as a reminder, or an ounce of prevention, for you to take good care of yourself and of each other.

Burnout, Anxiety, and Depression

- 76 per cent of a sample of first-year internal medicine residents met criteria for burnout.[19]
- 65 per cent of ER residents met criteria for burnout.[20]
- Overall, more than one in four residents report high levels of burnout.[21]
- Depression and anxiety symptoms were reported to be three to four times more common in a sample of family medicine residents compared with the general public.[22]
- 40 per cent of residents reported impaired performance as a result of anxiety and depression lasting four weeks or longer.[23]
- Of a sample of ER residents, 30 per cent reported post-traumatic stress disorder symptoms.[24]
- A meta-analysis concluded that the prevalence of depression in resident physicians was 28.8 per cent.[25]

Substance Abuse

- 7.6 per cent of 1,555 interns self-prescribed medications.[26]
- A sample of 3,000 third-year residents revealed higher past-month rates of alcohol and benzodiazepine use compared to the general public.[27]
- 15 per cent of the profession may meet criteria for alcohol use or dependence.[28]

Abuse and Harassment

- 46.4 per cent to 96.5 per cent of medical trainees experienced some form of abuse (verbal, sexual, or physical) during their training.[29]
- Two-thirds of emergency/ER residents worry about their own safety while working shifts.[30]

- In spite of many changes in the culture of medical education and training, over 45 per cent of medical residents report some form of workplace mistreatment, frequently from patients or patients' families.[31]

Residents are now increasingly calling for anti-oppression training. An anti-oppressive framework is the method and process by which we understand how systems of oppression such as colonialism, racism, sexism, homophobia, transphobia, classism, and ableism can result in individual discriminatory actions and structural/systemic inequalities for certain groups in society and within health care. A good example of resident-created "Guidelines for Inclusivity" can be found in chapter 6.

It Happened in First Year

I never liked presenting at Grand Rounds. One false move and you were humiliated.

I was on my cardiac rotation in first year medicine, up on the stage presenting on mitral valve prolapse, when my beeper went off.

I kept talking – only five minutes left to go. It went off again.

Then the phone in the auditorium rang. The Chief wanted to speak to me.

I asked them to take a message.

"No, now!" was the answer.

They passed me the portable phone.

I explained I was in the middle of presenting and would call him back right away, but the yelling wouldn't stop.

I had "inadequately diuresed" one of his VIP patients in (cardiac) failure when I was last on call.

I'm pretty sure everyone in the audience heard the tirade word for word.

I blushed. I stuttered. I shook a bit. My body was hunched and deflated. A heart attack of my very own would have been welcome.

I hung up the phone.

Nobody said anything.

I don't even remember presenting my last three PowerPoint slides or how I walked down the stairs off the stage.

Suicide

- A landmark study of the causes of resident death during the period from 2000 to 2014 concluded that suicide was the most common cause for male residents, and the second-most common cause for female residents. Resident death by suicide was observed to be less frequent than that reported among the general population. The greatest proportion of residents who died by suicide were PGY-1s, with a peak in incidence in academic quarter 1 and 3.[32]
- Physicians under forty years of age have three times the suicide risk of the general population.
- Suicide is the second-greatest cause of death in medical students.[33]

The good news is that residents can be trained to recognize suicide risk in their colleagues.[34,35]

Relationships

- A significant proportion of residents – 37 to 40 per cent – report problems with their intimate partner.[36]
- Of 1,805 residents and interns, 59 per cent believed that role conflict was always or often a problem and that work interfered with their family and social lives.[37]
- While rates of divorce among physicians are less than the general population, women physicians are substantially more likely to divorce than male physicians.[38]

Job Satisfaction

- Of doctors under age forty surveyed by the American Medical Association (AMA), 31 per cent said they would not have gone to medical school if they had known what they know now.[39]
- An unfavourable balance between effort and reward is significantly linked to stress (high effort with low reward is a predictor of distress).[40]

Stressors

- Many residents have concerns about job prospects.
- Many residents fear the prospect of litigation (e.g., 96 per cent of a sample of US obstetrics and gynaecology residents were afraid of

being sued),[41] and there is an increasing rate (~94 per cent/year) of residents involved in regulatory complaints and litigation.[42]
- Training hospitals in the US are being sold, closed, or amalgamated.
- Reportedly the average resident's salary in the US was at just below US$60,000 in 2021; for residents working 80 hours/week, that translates to below $15/hour – reportedly less than the average wage of a Starbucks barista as of January 1, 2022.
- The average debt load of a first-year resident in the US is estimated to be US$241,000 as of 2021.
- Although work-hour restrictions have been implemented in the United States and Canada, program non-compliance remains an issue.[43]
- Of graduating residents, 10 per cent feel unprepared for certain clinical challenges, such as substance abuse, domestic violence, geriatrics, and HIV care.

Other Health Risks[44,45]

- Risk of COVID-19 and other emerging pathogens like mpox.
- Increased risk of weight gain and loss of cardiovascular health.[46]
- Other infections: needle-stick injuries; hepatitis A, B, C, E; tuberculosis; SARS; Epstein–Barr virus; human immunodeficiency virus (HIV); upper respiratory tract infections; gastroenteritis; conjunctivitis.
- Chemical: radiation anesthetic agents; antineoplastic agents and agents used in pathology laboratories (e.g., formaldehyde).
- Physical: musculoskeletal stress related to lifting and prolonged standing; violence from patients; lack of security in hospitals located in dangerous areas.

Table 1.2. Sources of stress from "happy docs" study

time pressure	own personal or family responsibilities	caring for own children
work situation	own emotional mental health problem	caring for others
financial situation	employment status	discrimination
residency program issues	own physical health problem	personal family safety.
personal relationship		

Source: Cohen, J.S., Leung, Y., Fahey, M,, et al. (2008, Oct). " The happy docs study: A Canadian Association of Internes and Residents well-being survey examining resident physician health and satisfaction within and outside of residency training in Canada." *BMC Research Notes*, 1: 105.

- Fatigue leading to car accidents post-call or increased errors on the job.
- Increased incidents of preterm labor and pre-eclampsia among women who become pregnant during residency.
- Exposure to direct and vicarious trauma.
- Avoidance of medical care and follow-up, perhaps because residents are fearful of being in the patient role.

Diversity, Equity, and Inclusion (DEI)

The face of medicine has changed dramatically since the first edition of this book came out. Women often make up more than 50 per cent of med school classes nowadays, and racialized. Gender and sexual minority trainees have also increased in numbers and visibility. In the past, these residents were encouraged to "blend in" and to ignore both subtle and overt discrimination expressed towards them (and their similarly vulnerable patients) in order to "get by." The impact of these daily macro- and microaggressions was an unexamined yet huge additional stressor for these trainees.

Furthermore, we all carry multiple identities, and sometimes discrimination can become layered and cumulative. "Intersectionality" has become a significant concept for those thinking about the many ways that race, gender, and other social identities converge or combine in order to create unique forms of oppression for an individual (be it a resident or patient).

Residents now insist on "speaking truth to power" and on creating safe learning and clinical environments. Like the broader medical culture (and academia in general), the medical literature is only now catching up with the scholarly work being done within DEI and anti-oppression frameworks.

The tips and suggestions provided below have come directly from the existing literature and from actual discussions with these resident populations, but the dialogue on DEI and safety has a long way to go. We, as the authors of *Staying Human*, invite you review, critique, and enhance this section, as so much about resident experience and stigma remains unnamed, unpublished, and undocumented. We all have much to learn from those who have been overlooked, oppressed, or silenced in the past.

Gender-Based Challenges

Back in 1989, when the first edition of this book came out, 44 per cent of Canadian medical school graduates were cis-women, compared to 6 per cent in 1959 and 33 per cent in 1981.[47] Comparably, as noted in subsequent editions of *Staying Human*, in 1990, 30 per cent of all medical residents in the United States were women. By 2003, the number of women enrolled in medical school already surpassed 50 per cent in many provinces in Canada, reaching 52 per cent in 2007.[48] These numbers have continued to climb in both Canada and the United States.[49] In 2020, the Association of American Medical Colleges (AAMC) reported that the majority of US-based medical students were women.[50]

More female and female-identifying medical students of course means more female physicians in the following decades. In most countries, women have tended to choose primary care fields for specialization: internal medicine, pediatrics, obstetrics, gynaecology, family practice, and psychiatry. Several studies have shown that in residency women tend to work more hours, experience more stress, and report more personal, emotional, and relationship problems than do their male counterparts.[51] Many intentionally postpone pregnancy because of perceived threats to their careers, despite a marked drop in fertility rates after age 35.[52] Moreover, women have traditionally had higher debt loads upon graduating and tend to earn less money in medical practice than do men.

Women have also been shown to have similar academic but better communication skills than men, and to experience fewer lawsuits and higher levels of career satisfaction.[53] (Some of these findings may be attributable to the fact that women tend to show more candor in surveys on residency stress and/or may be more open to seeking help.) It is, however, important to recognize some of the unique pressures that women face during their medical careers that men do not experience or may experience to a lesser degree.

Medicine in North America has historically been and often continues to be a male-dominated field to which women have been obliged to adapt. Patriarchy and sexism persist. Historically, women residents have tended to have few female role models among teachers and administrators in their chosen career, and still only sometimes find the satisfying mentoring that all developing physicians require. They still tend to be over-represented in some fields such as obstetrics and gynaecology (OB-GYN), psychiatry, and family medicine and under-represented in other specialities such as neurosurgery and radiology.[54] The AAMC reports regularly on gender representation across the training and practice spectrum.

Women in medicine have also traditionally experienced what has been called "role strain," in that they were expected to conform simultaneously to cultural stereotypes of the feminine "caregiver," who will humanize a harsh medical technology, and of the competent, competitive physician. This often led to struggles with assertion, authority, and designatory tasks, called "role incongruity," as many leadership qualities were designated as stereotypically male.[55] Even now, the hectic schedules of female doctors often wreak havoc with the expectations they and others have of their capacity to manage the responsibilities of housekeeping, parenting, and supporting family members.

In the hospital setting, female nurses have sometimes competed with or were less tolerant of female physicians. Even now, male colleagues may expect them to carry a higher female or pediatric patient load, and patients may doubt their credibility or not address them as "doctor." Sexual harassment by colleagues and patients is also a more serious problem for women residents than for men. In a sample of 599 female doctors, 77 per cent reported being sexually harassed by patients at least once since becoming physicians (see the "Abuse and Harassment" section above for more statistics).

Pregnancy and issues related to the timing of starting a family pose logistical and personal dilemmas for couples. One older American Medical Association study found that one-half of women physicians who had children had had their first child – and one-quarter had had their second – during residency.[56] Despite these facts, some US schools and programs still do not have formal maternity leave policies. (One older study showed that only 80 per cent of US OB-GYN programs had maternity leaves and only 69 per cent had paternity leaves – and they are in the business of delivering babies!)[57] In Canada, maternity benefits are in all residents' contracts, although the length of leave may vary from program to program. However, a pregnant resident may still encounter subtle and not-so-subtle expressions of resentment from colleagues who believe they will have to carry her clinical load while she is on maternity leave.

Historical Trends among Women in Medicine[58]

The following trends were documented in previous editions of *Staying Human*:

- Within a decade of completing training, one-third of women physicians will take maternity leave, and 24 per cent take prolonged leave for other reasons. Most will have shorter work weeks than their male counterparts.[59]
- Two-thirds of practicing women physicians in the United States have children.[60]
- One University of Michigan study found that over their careers, women lose US$350,000 due to a persistent gender wage-gap (www.cirseiu.org/).
- For the most recent trends regarding women in medicine, visit the Women Physicians Section of the AMA (ama-assn.org).

SUGGESTIONS FOR WOMEN

- Apply to the residency you want to pursue. Don't let outdated practice and training trends limit your career trajectory. Speak to women leaders in your chosen field.
- Review contract issues on maternity leave and time-sharing options before applying.
- Make an effort to form links with female colleagues. If you encounter an attending physician or lecturer who appears to have managed juggling family and career life successfully, ask to keep in touch with her from time to time. Find a mentor.
- Consider forming a women's residency support group or lecture series. Nominate a person in your hospital as a contact person for women's issues or grievances. Include medical students.
- Check out the Office of Women's Programs at AAMC (aamc.org).
- Investigate the services provided by national and international medical women's groups. Here are some useful resources for assisting the process:
  - American Medical Women's Association (AMWA) Gender Equity Task Force (amwa-doc.org/our-work/initiatives/gender-equity-task-force/mission-and-position)
  - Mom MD (MomMD.com)
  - American Medical Student Association (AMSA) Gender and Sexuality Committee (amsa.org)

Pregnancy

- Where possible, plan carefully the timing of your pregnancy. Notify your residency program director of your dates (preferably after thirteen weeks) so that together you can plan a reasonable schedule (e.g., lighter rotations before delivery, outpatient rotations upon return).
- Stay safe. Watch out for radiation, chemotherapy, and infectious exposures.
- Take good care of yourself! Carry snacks. Ask for help if you're tired.
- Be open with colleagues about dates and continuing difficulties. Do not become apologetic or overcompensating.
- Maintain close ties with your obstetrician, general practitioner, or midwife in case you experience complications or need letters for sick leave or scheduling recommendations.
- Three months has been shown to be the minimum period that should be allotted for maternity leave to allow for adequate rest and reorganization and to take account of daycare regulations on the age at which infants are accepted. The Committee of Interns and Residents (cirseiu.org) has prepared a highly recommended resource packet of union ideas, proposals, and programs called "Pregnancy in Residency: A Union Perspective." Plan carefully, and well in advance, the support you need with the logistics around your delivery and childcare. Consult your own housestaff or post-graduate medical office for guidance.
- The latest AMA policy "encourages residency programs, specialty boards and group practices to incorporate into the parental leave policy a six-week minimum leave allowance, with the understanding that no parent should be required to take a minimum leave."

Racialized Residents

Special incentive programs for Indigenous and Black students in Canada and for Black, Hispanic, and Native American learners in the United States have produced an increase in their overall representation in the profession.[61] These students sometimes encounter resentment and even overt racism during residency because frequently such programs are believed to constitute tokenism or "reverse discrimination or racism": that is, they

are seen to give preferential treatment, or even exclusive access to medical training, to the participants solely because of their ethnic or racial
background. In reality, these trainees report quite the opposite; they are
often discriminated against in training and outside the hospital when it
comes to issues like housing. Some of these residents experience a socio-
economic and status shift, because they are more educated or better paid
than many of their family members but are less affluent than or socio-
economically remote from their white resident counterparts. They may
experience a unique kind of marginality that leaves them feeling suspect,
or like "impostors," both at home and at work.

Residents whose skin colour others perceive to be "similar" may be
"lumped together" racially and culturally in the minds of patients and
colleagues. As happens with international medical graduates (IMGs),
these residents encounter subtle assumptions, biases, and microaggressions along with offensive expressions of overt racism from patients,
colleagues, and support staff. Medical education is only now looking
critically at the impact of these assumptions and damaging encounters on the well-being and professional identity formation of these
individuals.

Challenge generalizations and stereotyping when you encounter
them clinically and discuss overt or persistent discriminatory behaviors
with your chief resident and program director so that your training
program, hospital, or affiliated medical school can organize seminars
on cultural safety/countering racism and anti-oppression framework
training (see chapter 6 for some excellent resources on creating a culture
of inclusivity and anti-oppression).

The resources for racialized residents below are frequently updated
and are written by trainee and physician representatives from these
organizations themselves.

Resources for Indigenous Physicians:

- Association of American Indian Physicians (aaip.org)
- Indigenous Physicians Association of Canada (ipac-amac.ca)
- National Consortium for Indigenous Medical Education (ncime.ca)
- "Stand Up for Indigenous Health," an immersive, simulation-based
  tool for teaching the social determinants of health in an Indigenous context to health care workers (cmaf-famc.org/programs/
  stand-indigenous-health)

Resources for Physicians of Other Nationalities/Ethnic Origins:

- American Association of Physicians of Indian Origin (aapiusa.org)
- Association of Chinese American Physicians (acaponline.org)
- Black Physicians of Canada (blackphysicians.ca)
- Chinese Canadian Medical Association (ccmsontario.com)
- National Hispanic Medical Association (nhmamd.org)
- National Medical Association (nmanet.org)

International Medical Graduates

Historically, it has been difficult for internationally trained physicians to obtain their license or to find residency positions in North America. Once accepted into residency, IMGs face unique pressures. These issues are addressed in detail by the Educational Commission for Foreign Medical Graduates (ecfmg.org).[62]

Not only do IMGs have to cope with the rigors of residency scheduling and high levels of responsibility, but they must also adjust to the medical hierarchy, to changed legal status as immigrants or refugees, and to a new country, culture, language, and ethical or religious system. Rules governing dynamics between men and women may differ. Dress and personal hygiene codes may be more stringent or more relaxed. IMGs tend to be older and already have families. Family members may become isolated from the new culture and thus more dependent psychologically and financially on the resident, who thus becomes a caregiver at both home and work. Adjustment and adaptation to a new culture creates significant stress for anyone and results in culture shock.[63] The social isolation of "foreign" residents caused by the absence of family or their own sensitivity about cultural differences can put them at high risk. They often experience both microaggressions and overt racism.

Foreign-trained residents who have studied in centers equipped with less technology or fewer resources than those in North America may experience particular struggles over competence, whereas those who have come from settings similar to North American centers resent the assumption by some that they are less skilled. Many IMGs have been delayed – some for ten years or more – in being accepted for an internship or supervised practice because of restrictions related to language, medical qualifying exams, and citizenship requirements. Historically, some provinces and states have imposed restrictive contracts on IMGs that oblige them on completion of training to work for up to four years in an underserviced area. Increased remuneration for working peripherally may not compensate for the inconvenience to the physician and his or her family.

Many IMGs experience a marked status shift; the medical resident who is from a low- or middle-income country may become more wealthy and comfortable than ever before, whereas physicians who were full professors from some countries in Eastern Europe who must repeat all of their training to obtain accreditation are often devastated initially. Regional differences in patients' acceptance of racialized groups or of those who speak with an unfamiliar accent can be significant, and many IMGs experience hostile and racist reactions from the patients they are expected to treat.

North Americans who complete medical school abroad are not exempt from added strain during their residency. Although they return to a culture they have known, it has continued to evolve in their absence; indeed, they often return to a different medical system (e.g., the Caribbean- or UK-trained resident who returns to American medicine). They may feel apologetic or inadequate for not having been accepted to a North American medical school or for having learned different or less technological protocols. Canadian-trained physicians who acquire residencies in the United States are often bewildered by non-universal medical care.

SUGGESTIONS FOR IMGS

- Apply to a residency program that has significant representation of, or a special entry program for, IMGs or refugees. Current physician shortages in Canada have led to an increased number of positions and gateways to practice. The AMA provides an excellent online IMG toolkit (ama-assn.org), and AIMG is a portal for international trainees in Canada.[64]
- Determine any contractual or practice-related restrictions before accepting a training placement. If necessary, consult a lawyer who can help you avoid being exploited.

- Form a support group with other IMGs to prepare for qualifying exams (for information on the ECFMG exams, see ecfmg.org). You can also meet others in your situation at exam preparation courses.
- Find out about community resources for newcomers. The ECFMG also has IMG consultants you can speak with as part of their Acculturation Program.
- Seek a mentor who is also an IMG (perhaps someone from your own country or culture), or someone informed on IMG issues whom you can consult from time to time for advice and support.
- As you adapt to a new culture, maintain close social ties with your family and ethnic community. Attend organized events with your family.
- Find out about harassment and racism policies at your school. Speak up if you encounter discrimination!
- Anticipate religious and cultural holidays that are important to you and ask for time off in advance.
- Make friends with your North American colleagues.
- Consider bringing a family member from your homeland for support or childcare during your first year.
- Guard against a tendency to be overcritical of yourself because what you know is different. Ask questions and be open, rather than apologetic, about protocol differences. Ask your senior resident for intermittent one-on-one attention if you are struggling in a particular area. Point out how you can enrich your program through your knowledge of other cultures and languages
- Contact the national and international medical ethnic groups and associations. Your housestaff organization may also have special committees and initiatives related to IMG training.
- Online resources for IMGs:
  - Accreditation Council for Graduate Medical Education (acgme.org/acgmeweb)
  - American College of Physicians Programs and Policies of Special Interest to IMGs (acponline.org/about_acp/international/graduates/practicing_in_us/programs.htm)
  - Canadian Information Center for International Credentials (cicic.ca)
  - Educational Commission for Foreign Medical Graduates (ecfmg.org)

- Electronic Residency Application Support for IMGs (ecfmg. org/eras)
- Federation of Medical Regulatory Authorities of Canada (fmrac.ca)
- Foundation for Advancement of International Medical Education (faimer.org)
- International Federation of Medical Students Association (ifmsa.org)

Religious Residents

Religiously observant or devout residents, whether Christian, Jewish, Muslim, Buddhist, Sikh, Hindu, followers of a Native or Indigenous traditional way, or others with strong spiritual convictions, may experience dilemmas of conscience about such matters as abortion, contraception, medical assistance in dying (MAID), non-marital unions, gender identity, the rights of sexual minorities, and when asked to carry out duties or confirm advice that they find immoral, unethical, or otherwise in conflict with their values. Nonetheless, you must respect your patients' choices and assist them in finding alternate/optimal care if you cannot provide the care they need.

Suggestions for Religious Residents

- Apply to a residency program with significant diversity representation or a religious affiliation that aligns with your own.
- Know your spiritual and cultural legacy and draw on it for strength. Talk to your spiritual leader/clergy about your life in residency.[66]
- Request religious holidays off well in advance and, if timely, explain the significance of the holiday to broaden your colleagues' world views. (For example, let folks know how fasting might affect you during Ramadan.)
- Consider finding a mentor with similar cultural or religious traditions so that you can share problem-solving issues.
- Speak with the hospital ethicist or chaplain about the best way to make your views known to, and understood by, colleagues and patients.

- Challenge generalizations and stereotyping when you encounter them clinically. Discuss overt or persistent discriminatory behaviors with your chief resident and program director so that your training program, hospital, or affiliated medical school can organize seminars on cultural safety, countering racism, and anti-oppression framework training.
- Consider forming a support group with other residents whose background or traditions are similar to yours.
- It's not your job to correct systemic neglect or ignorance. Residency programs should formally address issues of diversity, inclusion, and equity. All residents should aim to expand their world views and to reflect on unexamined assumptions, prejudices, and blind spots.
- Consider inviting speakers and holding seminars for the hospital at large on treating specific patient populations.
- Although the system may encourage "tokenism," affirm your individuality and level of skill and resist the temptation to blend in, overcompensate, over-accommodate, or prove something.
- Contact resource groups for information on conferences, grants, minority research opportunities, and services.
- All residents should recognize that there is value in finding or rediscovering a spiritual or faith-related focus when facing the stresses and challenges of residency, as it can be an important source of sustenance and growth.
- Check out the following online resources:

  - Annual Conference on Medicine and Religion (medicineandreligion.com)
  - Center for Spirituality and Health at the University of Florida (spiritualityandhealth.ufl.edu)
  - Center for Spirituality, Theology and Health at Duke University (spiritualityandhealth.duke.edu)
  - George Washington Institute for Spirituality and Health (gwish.org)
  - Robert Wood Johnson Foundation (rwjf.org)

Prayers on Healing

Here are some sample medically themed historical prayers on healing from different religious traditions.

The Prayer of Maimonides

Almighty God! With infinite wisdom has thou shaped the body of
man. Ten thousand times ten thousand organs has thou put within it
that move in harmony and without ceasing to keep in all its beauty
the whole – the body, the envelope of the immortal soul ...

To Man has thou given the wisdom to soothe his brother's suffering, to know his disorders, to extract what substances may heal, to
learn their powers, and prepare and use them suitably for every ill
... Inspire in me a love for my art and for thy creatures. Let no thirst
for profit or seeking for renown or admiration take away from my
calling ... Keep within me strength of body and of soul, ever ready,
with cheerfulness, to help and succor rich and poor, good and bad,
enemy as well as friend. In the sufferer let me see only the human
being ... If those should wish to improve and instruct me who are
wiser than I, let my soul gladly follow their guidance; for vast is the
scope of our art ...

In all things let me be content, in all but the great science of my
calling. Let the thought never arise that I have attained to enough
knowledge, but vouchsafe to me ever the strength, the leisure and
the eagerness to add to what I know. For art is great, and the mind
of man ever growing.

Almighty God! In thy mercy thou has chosen me to watch beside
life and death in thy creatures. I now go to the work of my calling.

In its high duties sustain me, so that it may bring benefit to mankind, for nothing, not even the least can flourish without thy help.[65]

Medicine and Illness

Honor the doctor for his services, for the Lord created him.

His skill comes from the Most High, and he is rewarded by kings.

The doctor's knowledge gives him high standing and wins him
the admiration of the great.

The Lord has created medicines from the earth, and a sensible
man will not disparage them. Was it not a tree that sweetened water
and so disclosed its properties?

The Lord has imparted knowledge to men, that by their use of his
marvels he may win praise; by using them the doctor relieves pain
and from them the pharmacist makes up his mixture.

There is no end to the works of the Lord, who spreads health
over the whole world.

My son, if you have an illness, do not neglect it, but pray to the Lord, and he will heal you.

Renounce your faults, amend your ways, and cleanse your heart from all sin.

Bring a savoury offering and bring flour for a token and pour oil on the sacrifice; be as generous as you can.

Then call in the doctor, for the Lord created him; do not let him leave you, for you need him.

There may come a time when your recovery is in their hands; then they too will pray to the Lord to give them success in relieving pain and finding a cure to save their patient's life.

When a man has sinned against his Maker, let him put himself in the doctor's hands.[67]

A Physician's Prayer

Dear Lord, give skill to my hand, clear vision to my mind, kindness and sympathy to my heart. Give me singleness of purpose, strength to lift at least a part of the burden of my suffering fellow mortals and a true realization of the privilege that is mine. Take from my heart all guile and worldliness that with the simple faith of a child I may rely on thee.[68]

Maimonides's Code for Physicians

O god, may the love of my art actuate me at all times; may neither avarice, nor miserliness, nor the thirst for glory or a great reputation engage my mind, for, enemies of truth and philanthropy, they could easily deceive me and make me forgetful of my lofty aim of doing good to thy children. Endow me with strength of heart and mind, so that both may be ready to serve the rich and the poor, the good and the wicked, friend and enemy, and that I may never see in the patient anything else but a fellow creature in pain.

If physicians more learned than I wish to counsel me, inspire me with confidence in and obedience toward the recognition of them, for the study of the science is great. It is not given to one alone to see all that others see. May I be moderate in everything except in the knowledge of this science; so far as it is concerned, may I be insatiable; grant me the strength and opportunity always to correct what I have acquired, always to extend its domain; for knowledge is boundless and the spirit of human kind can also extend infinitely, daily to enrich itself with new acquirements.[69]

LGBTQ2S+ Residents

The 2S refers to two-spirited members of the Indigenous communities in Canada. We use the word "queer" here as a sort of umbrella term. Planned Parenthood provides a helpful definition: "Queer is a word that describes sexual and gender identities other than straight and cisgender. Lesbian, gay, bisexual, and transgender people may all identify with the word queer. Queer is sometimes used to express that sexuality and gender can be complicated, change over time, and might not fit neatly into either/or identities, like male or female, gay or straight."[70]

Gay and lesbian residents, who make up an estimated 10 per cent of the resident population, not only face particular challenges in their daily lives but also must deal with a medical hierarchy that can at times be homo/transphobic, rigid, and intolerant. Gay men and women historically have been an invisible, rejected minority, and those in many residency programs still find it necessary to hide their sexual identity from colleagues. This results in social isolation, stigmatization, and missed peer support about shared issues, such as couple relationships.

There is now also an increased representation of trans and non-binary trainees who have to negotiate pronouns and stereotyping in a profession that has been slow to embrace all sexual minorities. One study showed that 78 per cent of trans and/or non-binary trainees censored their own speech or mannerisms to avoid unintended disclosure of their gender identity "at least half of the time," and 69 per cent heard derogatory comments about sexual minorities in their medical school or residency program.[71]

A queer resident's partner may experience increased isolation because of a reluctance on the resident's part to socialize with colleagues, which may produce added couple conflict. Historically, queer residents have lacked role models who were "out" about their sexuality and comfortable with their own professional and sexual identities, and therefore could not find a mentor. Fortunately, more and more attending physicians are out and modelling personal authenticity in their medical lives.

Queer residents can be victims of social or sexual harassment from superiors but may remain silent to protect their own identities. They may let homophobic/sexist/transphobic remarks by patients and colleagues go unchecked for fear of disclosing their identity and thereby attracting hostility or suspicion. Such situations result in much unresolved anger and moral distress, which are additional risk factors for burnout. Historically, some residents reported being refused entry into specific programs because of "perceived homosexuality" or "presumed" HIV-positive status.

Finally, many men and women only start to come to embrace their queer identity during the years they spend in residency. Regrettably, training demands can delay such important discoveries and personal growth.

The experience of trans and non-binary residents remains as yet under-documented in the medical literature but needs to be a part of this discussion over time.

SUGGESTIONS FOR QUEER RESIDENTS

• Contact the Gay and Lesbian Medical Association (glma.org) and the local gay press for notices of meetings of gay health-provider organizations in your city. These groups are welcoming to bisexual, non-binary, and transgendered members as well.

• Choose a residency program in a city with an active and political queer life. Such a city will also have a higher visible percentage of queer physicians who can help you in your career and serve as role models. Many cities have LGBTQ2S+ doctors' groups that host educational and social events. Many specialty associations have LGBTQ2S+ interest groups who meet at annual conferences, such as the Association of LGBTQ+ Psychiatrists (AGLP) that has close ties with the American Psychiatric Association (APA).

• As you get to know other residents and interns you will gradually perceive whom you can tell about your life. Do not shut yourself off from possible peer support and friendship for you and your partner.

• All residents (queer or their straight/cis-gendered allies) should challenge sexist, racist, homophobic, and transphobic remarks and not let them go unchecked. Respond firmly and calmly. Use the situation as an opportunity to educate and speak of the historical oppression of queer people in and outside of medicine. Then ask your program for formal teaching on the care of LGBTQ2S+ people, using anti-oppression framework principles.

• Resist any tendency to overcompensate because of being gay, lesbian, or trans. If you are having particular difficulties with reconciling your sexual and professional identities, seek help in the form of psychotherapy.

- Remember that you are not obliged to answer questions pertaining to sexual orientation or gender identity in residency applications or employment interviews. The choice is yours.
- Encourage your program to provide sensitive, appropriate training regarding the care of gay, lesbian, and transgender patients. For further reference to these and related issues, see the recent University of Toronto publication *Caring for LGBTQ2S People: A Clinical Guide.*[72]
- The Centers for Disease Control and Prevention (CDC) keeps an up-to-date list of all LGBT health-related organizations/ coalitions at cdc.gov/lgbthealth.
- The Harvey Cushing/John Hay Whitney Medical Library at Yale University is a guide "designed to assist students, researchers, and health professionals in finding health and other information related to lesbian, gay, bisexual, transgender, asexual, intersex, queer, and queer-questioning communities."[73]

Residents with a Disability, Chronic Illness, or Learning Challenge

Residents who are blind, use wheelchairs, are neurodiverse, have ADHD/learning disabilities, or have a chronic illness (such as diabetes, inflammatory arthritis, bowel disease, chronic pain, lupus, asthma, or a mental illness) experience increased stress as a result of their disability that may in turn be worsened by residency-related stress. Residents with a visible impairment may have to work harder to establish credibility with patients and to deal repeatedly with social awkwardness in patients and colleagues in a way that sometimes wears down a successful coping style. Colleagues, in particular, may try to be overly helpful or may be reluctant to acknowledge the disability. Precedents of residents with most disabilities (including blindness, quadriplegia, and learning difficulties) now exist, but program directors may still be worried about these residents' "efficacy and suitability" for the specialty. Two-thirds of trainees with disabilities do not seek support or information on resources available to them.[74]

The resident who becomes seriously ill during residency must contend with issues of loss, pain, and uncertainty in addition to the stresses of residency.

SUGGESTIONS FOR RESIDENTS WITH A
DISABILITY, CHRONIC ILLNESS, OR LEARNING
CHALLENGE

- Good support from family, other housestaff, and hospital support staff is essential. Calculate the help you need regarding such matters as navigation, elevator service, and special meals, and request it. Never ask someone junior to you to make decisions for you. Try to form particular ties with porters, orderlies, nurses and nurses' aides, mail carriers, and elevator operators, who will probably be glad to help.
- Discuss your disability or illness openly with your program director and chief resident so that he or she can help you develop strategies. Do not hide periods of illness from colleagues, as such stoicism may compromise your own and your patients' care.
- Maintain close links with your personal physician so that you can get quick follow-up, treatment, and letters for sick leave or change of duties if required.
- Some patients are comforted to learn that their physician is not omnipotent and shares the experience of illness. Avoid the tendency to overcompensate, to neglect your personal life, or to be a "super doctor" because of your disability, but remember that you may have something valuable to teach your housestaff team about the experience of being a patient.
- Find out about program resources and accommodations for learning difficulties and how to access them.
- All residents (not just those living with disabilities) should challenge ableist attitudes. Ask your program for lectures from disability scholars and for educational sessions where patients tell their own stories. (Education on the lived experience of disabled patients and practitioners is woefully absent in many North American medical schools.)
- Resident Doctors of Canada (residentdoctors.ca) details the accommodations offered by specific programs. For other online resources for disabled doctors see:
  - US Equal Employment Opportunity Commission (eeoc.gov)
  - Canadian Association of Physicians with Disabilities (capd.ca)
  - Society for Physicians with Disabilities (physicianswithdisabilities.org)

- Medical Students with Disability and Chronic Illness (msdci.org)
- Society of Healthcare Professionals with Disabilities (disabilitysociety.org)

Key Trends around Residency Stress

The first year of postgraduate training, especially the first two months on rotations in medicine, surgery, and intensive care units, are frequently reported to be particularly stressful. Studies of working-hour reforms suggest that first-year residents may have benefitted most from new restrictions.[75] However, senior residents are also reporting high levels of stress related to final examinations, higher expectations, and career planning. Keep in mind that stress-related symptoms are ubiquitous and intermittent, even when they do not become severe enough to lead to depression or drug abuse. As you'll see, resilience in the face of stress can be learned and maintained. Prolonged symptoms can, however, lead to professional burnout, which is characterized by emotional exhaustion, depersonalization, detachment, and a low sense of personal accomplishment and job satisfaction.

Burnout is defined as a deteriorating or unsuccessful response to repeated stress and is characterized by a negative attitude towards oneself, others, and work; emotional exhaustion; and feelings of despair. It leads to what Christina Maslach calls "erosion of the soul."[76] Other authors have referred to "training toxicity" as being the cause of such stress.[77] (For excellent reviews on burnout in medical residents, see Prins,[78] Niku,[79] McCray,[80] Low,[81] and Rodrigues.[82])

So, are you burnt out? Ask yourself the predictive questions from the Maslach Burnout Inventory (MBI) shown here. Keep in mind that when you take the test (post-call vs. while on holiday) will affect your score!

MODIFIED QUESTIONS FROM MASLACH BURNOUT INVENTORY[83]

Depersonalization

- I feel I treat some patients as if they were impersonal objects.
- I do not really care what happens to some patients.
- Patients blame me for some of their problems.

Emotional exhaustion

- I still feel tired when I wake up on workday mornings.

Personal accomplishment

- I can easily understand how my patients feel about things.
- I deal effectively with my patients' problems.
- I can easily create a relaxed atmosphere for my patients.
- I feel exhilarated after working closely with my patients.

Major Manifestations of Burnout[84]

Physiological

Fatigue and chronic exhaustion, recurrent upper respiratory tract infections, persistent viral infections, headaches, lack of concentration, somatic problems, muscular pain and tension, weight problems, gastrointestinal disorders, and injuries caused by high-risk behavior are all physiological manifestations of burnout.

Psychological and Emotional

Negative thoughts and feelings (despair, feelings of impotence, boredom, disillusionment, guilt, reduced self-esteem, irritability, social isolation) are major psychological and emotional manifestations of burnout.

Behavioral

Shutting down emotionally, absenteeism, unproductivity, hyperactivity, exaggerated response to stress, inappropriate comments, social withdrawal, and increased risk taking are behavioral manifestations of burnout. Some residents experience these symptoms only during a particularly difficult rotation. However, others experience full-blown burnout and what has been called "the house officer's stress syndrome," which is characterized by family problems, cynical attitudes, emotional lability and anger, personal conflict, and transient cognitive impairment. One study of internal medicine residents using the

Maslach Burnout Inventory showed that 76 per cent of respondents met the criteria for burnout.[85]

It's no surprise that the number of hours worked per week appears to be the best predictor of professional burnout and that this is a systemic problem, not a "weakness" in individual residents. Apart from somatic and emotional symptoms, high levels of chronic malaise in young physicians can produce a lasting change of attitude towards both the medical field and patients. Residency can be a time for learning coping patterns for an active, demanding medical career and for attaining new levels of compassion and resilience. However, as you've probably already noticed, some graduates emerge as insensitive, distant, cynical, and authoritarian physicians who make inappropriate comments and judgments about their patients. They become emotionally withdrawn and self-important, and their self-esteem becomes intrinsically linked to, or exclusively defined by, professional and financial performance to the neglect of satisfying personal relationships.

When several members of the health care team are experiencing burnout, an organizational impact is noted as well. The quality of services declines, creating a toxic climate of hostility, competition, and mistrust, and authority conflicts and impaired communications lead to decision making in isolation.

Individual Vulnerabilities

We all have our own personality traits, strengths, and quirks shaped by genetics and our early family lives. The literature on resident impairment allows some degree of prediction about who among us may be at risk in the face of high stress levels. An editorial in the *Annals of Internal Medicine* even posed the question, "Who is sicker, patients or residents?"[86] Residents who over-identify with patients and have passive-aggressive, avoidant, or dependent coping styles are predisposed to burnout. Those having difficulty expressing difficult emotions also struggle (i.e., those with an obsessive personality style). Hostile or aggressive Type A residents may alienate their colleagues. Those who lack support from colleagues, friends, and families exhibit more symptoms of somatic and psychological origin and are more detached and avoidant. Trainees who can't delegate responsibility or share teamwork also become more stressed.[87]

Most residents occasionally experience feelings of loss of control over their lives and even over decisions about patient care. Those who reported "an external locus of control" (where others make decisions for them) also have higher stress levels.

Certain psychological defense mechanisms that we all have to some degree can also lead to difficulties. These include denial and rationalization about failures and errors and limitations, depreciation (ironic or disrespectful humor), isolation of affect (emotional numbness or dissociation), and projection of negative feelings onto others. Many residents believe that they don't learn to communicate effectively with patients during their training, so burdened are they by technology, medical jargon, and the safe anonymity of group work and laboratory result rounding. Time pressures, fatigue, and maintaining self-confidence tend to be the focus of the most difficult or stressful aspects of residency training. Other sources of stress, apart from those listed earlier in table 1.2, include role ambiguity with expectations beyond one's level of expertise, ethical dilemmas, time-management struggles, lack of mentoring or role models, and conflicts in personal and professional relationships. Once again this points to weaknesses within larger systems and hierarchies, and not weaknesses in individual residents.

Read on for tips on coping with all of these.

Generational clashes with older physicians who doubt the dedication of a new breed of "balance-minded trainees" (especially in the context of recent work-hour regulations) are increasingly common. Many physicians in later phases of practice have often defined their lives by service, availability, and sacrifice, but may not have fully considered how medical culture has been shaped by patriarchal and privileged attitudes and significant power differentials. Recently certified/licensed physicians are more aware of the need to take good care of themselves in order to take care of patients and to sustain efficacy over time. Many are informed by social justice and anti-oppression principles, lobbying for safety and equity for all (including themselves).

These are different world views and need to be discussed openly and respectfully.

Developmental Issues

Most residents in North America are twenty-five to thirty years old. In the most frequently studied groups – psychiatry, internal medicine, and family medicine programs – those in their early twenties and late thirties seem to be more affected by the rigors of residency.[88] One study showed that women housestaff experienced more self-doubt and feelings of professional inadequacy,[89] and another pointed to lower scores of quality of life and higher rates of daytime fatigue.[90]

Trends in difficulties delegating duties for women have also been noted (see above). Family practice residents have worried most about making mistakes in treatment and diagnosis and residents in psychiatry were most concerned about chronically ill patients. On-call anxiety was more frequent among residents in family medicine, psychiatry, and pediatrics.[91] It's hard to have to prove yourself over and over on new rotations. The particular challenges experienced by specific resident groups, including women and international medical graduates, are discussed above.

If you're not careful, the professional stresses of residency may adversely affect or postpone personal development and key milestones because of a lack of time to reflect and explore creatively. Young physicians in their twenties and thirties customarily leave their families in hometowns, and experience changes in financial status. They date, form sexual relationships, marry or cohabit, and have children. Many physicians postpone having children despite falling fertility rates over time. Some residents divorce, become ill, or experience a loss in their families. They search for a balance between work and play and may develop interests in political and community causes.

What Residents Want[92]

A Canadian study based on surveying respondents from several provincial housestaff organizations led to a report called "Features of High Quality Residency Programs – A National Resident Perspective." The following components of an ideal program were identified:

- A collegial working environment free from intimidation and harassment
- Adequate transition to practice, with preparation including appropriate, graded responsibility over time
- An appropriate education to maintain a balance of life and service

- Mentorship from the program director and faculty supervisor
- A curriculum with diverse clinical and procedure exposures
- Timely assessments with face-to-face feedback
- A program director who is supportive of resident concerns

Residents training in the US point to similar factors.[93] The top four factors in choosing a program include the ability to promote a healthy work-life balance, the quality of the program director, the quality of other residents, and the perceived goodness of fit. The emergence of work-life balance was identified as a new factor in the selection process for the first time ever in 2019, an encouraging sign!

It is indeed hopeful that residents are increasingly able to identify what they need to thrive, and then be willing to request it from their program directors. They are also familiar with a growing literature emphasizing resident wellness and wholeness rather than the previous focus on risk and impairment. Some of the predictors of increased personal growth during residency include[94] setting a time for reflection; having a strong desire to develop personally as well as professionally; maintaining a strong sense of self; feeling committed to core personal values; and feeling supported in one's life. Furthermore, although some educators disagree, a number of studies have looked at and confirmed the health-related and professional benefits of reduced work hours in North American residency programs.[95]

Emerging evidence suggests that the development of the following skills is associated with improved personal health outcomes and professional sustainability:[96]

Personal awareness: being aware of values, beliefs, and unexamined assumptions and blind spots and their world view, and having a reflective practice.

Critical appraisal of the self, which includes introspection: being able to look at a specific situation, describe it, identify feelings about what happened, then look at what went well, what didn't go well, form conclusions, and make an action plan for change.

Emotional intelligence: the ability to perceive, understand, and manage emotions in one's self and others. A recent study showed that emotional intelligence can, in part, be taught and that EQ scores can actually[97] increase significantly over the course of training![98] You can check your EQ at www.queendom.com and www.greatergood.berkeley.edu/ei_quiz/ (search for the Baron-Cohen test).

Leadership: As you've observed, the contemporary doctor plays a complex role in the process of ensuring the community's health. Doctors are expected to be leaders in their communities and in their clinical setting, to be articulate, to advocate for their patients, to have a clear sense of their own values and beliefs, and to have the skills to attract and maintain relationships with others in a way that motivates action based on integrity. Recent systematic reviews continue to emphasize the value and importance of leadership and advocacy training, while also noting the most appropriate educational methods to do so are yet to be fully understood.

Well-being, resilience, and happiness: The formation of a sound professional and work identity as a physician cannot be achieved independently of other developmental concerns, although the latter are sometimes ignored. Young physicians must be able to find a balance between their own vulnerability and their role as non-omnipotent healers. You must recognize when to act and when to wait, observe, and listen. Residents can still feel helpless and exploited in the medical hierarchy, but must develop problem-solving skills, assertiveness, and expertise in order to allow feelings of commitment to develop with a regained sense of personal control. You must learn boundary maintenance, combining empathy with objectivity and avoiding both undue familiarity and aloofness with colleagues and patients. Residents can and should acquire these skills and insights during their residency training. The emerging healer must develop a sense of identity, balance, and well-being in the face of professional and developmental stressors.

The potential risks to both physical and emotional health may be significant, but so are the opportunities to learn resilience and coping skills that will last throughout your life and medical career.

 TIP

"I have benefited enormously from keeping a little log of my experiences. I think a lot of residents can benefit from keeping a diary. I am careful never to mention anyone by name, it is a private thing, it is never to be published, but it's nice to look back on who I was."

Figure 1.1 offers one model of successful versus unsuccessful coping. It's a useful exercise for you to define what well-being means to you as a doctor. The following list provides a set of characteristics[99] that includes the key elements of that state.

Figure 1.1 Stress and Coping Model for Physicians

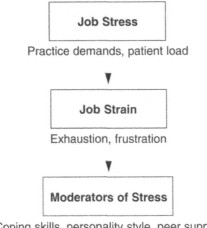

Source: May, H.H., & Revicki, D.A. (1985). Professional stress among family physicians. *J Fam Pract*, 20: 165–71.

Elements of Physician Well-Being[100]

- Quality care, including continuity of care
- Commitment to professional values and professional growth

- Shared responsibility with the patient for the patient's health and well-being
- Full expression of the physician as an autonomous person
- Maintenance of personal, physical, and mental health
- Balance of family, social, physical, mental, spiritual, creative, and financial domains
- Self-validation and personal satisfaction
- Recognition and acceptance of time and technological limitations, of change as a normal phenomenon, and of the profession's inherent problems and opportunities
- Collegiality, teamwork, and work group loyalty; a sense of belonging

Resilience for All

The flip side to burnout (whatever its causes) is definitely resilience. Resilient physicians have increased career satisfaction, higher personal life satisfaction, enhanced performance and efficacy, and an engagement with lifelong learning and skills.

Resilience can be defined as a process of adapting well and "bouncing back" in the face of stress, trauma, adversity, tragedy, or threat. Resilience does not mean that you never get stressed. It means being able to recover and recalibrate after difficult experiences and to learn from them.

Other factors associated with resilience include having caring and supportive relationships, being able to make realistic plans, and taking steps to carry them out. Having a positive view of oneself, being able to communicate and problem solve, and having the capacity to manage strong feelings and impulses are also key aspects. A common misconception is that some people have "grit" and others do not.

The American Psychological Association identifies the following ten ways to build resilience:

- Make connections
- Avoid seeing crises as insurmountable problems
- Accept change as a part of living

- Move towards realistic goals
- Take decisive actions
- Look for opportunities for self-discovery
- Nurture a positive view of yourself, including self-confidence
- Keep things in perspective, and don't blow them out of proportion
- Maintain a hopeful outlook
- Take care of yourself with proper diet, exercise, and sleep

(Adapted from www.apa.org)

For physicians, the following elements are also highly predictive of professional resilience:

- A sense of self and personal competence, as well as possessing personal beliefs and values that contribute to a sense of agency
- Attitudes and perspective that correlate with being self-aware, being reflective, and attuned, having core values and an optimistic philosophy of life and being altruistic
- Having a healthy temperament and a sense of humor; not taking things personally
- Acceptance of self and others, and being able to forgive self and others
- Feeling that one is making a difference in one's profession (purpose)
- An ability to learn from past challenges and stressful situations

Stanford University's WellMD & WellPhD Center is an incredibly active, innovative, and practical home to world-class research into physician wellness and resiliency. At www.wellmd.stanford.edu you can access self-assessment instruments, explore resiliency- and wellness-enhancing toolkits, watch videos and attend virtual workshops, learn more about their model of physician fulfillment, and learn more about how to create and nurture physician well-being programs at your site.

What about Happiness?

It is encouraging that nowadays we are not only speaking about physician well-being, but about what defines happiness for all human beings, including physicians. As mentioned above, we all start with genetic strengths and vulnerabilities, and our personalities are shaped by our early family experiences and socio-cultural experiences. It is also encouraging to see evidence emerge summarizing the value of living as healthy a lifestyle as possible, as well as embracing positive psychology approaches, to enhance resiliency and reduce burnout.[101] Predictors of quality of life in residency include satisfaction with the program, seniority (year 2 and 3), time for leisure, and less than thirty hours per week of caring for critically ill patients.[102]

Happier residents have reported improved relationships with patients and colleagues, improved patient care, and greater motivation ("zeal") for their work.[103] Martin Seligman[104] and others have looked at the science of happiness and what features determine it. Interestingly, they found that this has nothing to do with climate, wealth, or the number of years of education. (This may be important because some residents tell themselves that these things will make them happy.) It's all about the two Ps: having a sense of Purpose and Pleasure in your life. Here are actual predictors of happiness based on Seligman's research:

- Finding meaning in one's work
- Not dwelling on negative events, errors, or self-criticism (i.e., an optimistic outlook)
- Being part of a couple and having a strong social network, which includes family relationships
- Financial stability but not excessive wealth
- Good health
- Personal freedom and the opportunity to live by one's personal values

Other important ingredients identified by Seligman include developing a sense of day-to-day gratitude and seeking/offering forgiveness.

Many physicians, including residents, have enjoyed the free Science of Well-Being course offered by Dr. Laurie Santos at Yale University. Funded by the David F. Swenson Fund for Innovation in Teaching, it will help you identify common misconceptions about happiness, apply change science to your current life situation, and successfully incorporate a specific wellness activity in your life. You can access it by visiting www.coursera.org and then searching "Science of Well-Being."

The chapters that follow will provide concrete strategies aimed not only at coping, but at finding the potential for happiness in your complex role as an apprentice physician. This means paying close attention to your unique personal development, to mental and physical health, to relationships, and to developing an authentic sense of self with values you can live by. The overall residency training system has improved, but it's not perfect. You can learn to manage your stress and become the kind of healer (and human being) you want to be!

2

Preventive Medicine

Choosing a Humane Residency

In the past, graduating medical students, when choosing a residency program in North America, focused more on the program's reputed standards or prestige than on the quality of life they could expect during that four- to six-year period of their lives. They sometimes based their choices on hearsay or on information acquired by chance. In interviews they concentrated on practical questions such as the size of a program or the opportunities it offered for research. Because selection was highly competitive, students seldom introduced other, more humanistic concerns for fear of appearing demanding or not sufficiently dedicated. Nowadays, medical students are figuring lifestyle choices and balance into their choice of specialty, and they are receiving guidance in career choices. And it's about time!

Two trends in North America seem to have produced a change in the attitudes of candidates and residency directors towards such concerns. First, the growing number of women in medicine, who now constitute 50 per cent or more of most US and Canadian medical classes, has forced universities to consider part-time and shared residencies as well as parental leaves. Such modifications in response to women's demands have been achieved with great struggle; yet men now acknowledge that they also benefit from these new policies.[1]

Second, restrictions on the number of hours worked by residents in Canada (which was a pioneer in this regard), the United States, and the European Union have thankfully legitimized discussions of resident health, lifestyle, and well-being worldwide.

Residency training programs have thus become more sensitive to residents' growth and comfort than was the case even ten years ago. Overall, the choice of program has become more complicated because more factors now influence the selection of a specialty and training programs. Navigating the match is an art in and of itself!

Specialty Choice

Program Factors

Because of the considerable variation in the size, content, and administration of residency programs across the United States and Canada, medical graduates must exercise great care in their choice of program to try to ensure maximum learning and personal satisfaction.[2] This means gathering a large body of information about each center from a variety of sources before applying, because it is not possible to discover accurately all the features of a program in a single interview.

Data should be obtained from the program or hospital prospectus, medical school counsellors, and published specialty manuals such as the Fellowship and Residency Electronic Interactive Database (FREIDA), the National Resident Matching Program Handbook for Students (in Canada, see the Canadian Resident Matching Service, www.carms.ca). Local faculty members at the undergraduate and postgraduate levels and student members of specialty associations (who often link up on Facebook, Twitter, and via blogs) can also be sources of information.

Classmates gathering similar data can share facts and ideas. It is a good idea for you to make informal contact with junior and senior residents at each center being considered, or perhaps with graduates of one's own school, and to obtain a copy of the hospital, provincial, or state contract for residents. Observerships during clerkship are helpful. Doing an elective there during med school is also a good idea, but experiences may vary considerably from site to site. A day-long visit to the teaching hospital can help one assess working conditions and resident morale. A virtual or Zoom meeting with a resident in the program is another option. Applicants should ensure that they have gathered all pertinent information before accepting a residency position.

Here are key considerations you should take into account when selecting a specialty:[3]

- Spousal preference regarding lifestyle and location (though climate does not actually impact stress levels!)
- Lifestyle and workload
- Job and academic prospects
- Competitiveness and availability of programs
- Expected salary and medical school debt load
- Lawsuit potential
- Gender equity training
- Age preference (young vs. old patients)
- Length of training
- Balance between emphasis on patient contact and communication skills and on manual and technical skills
- Research potential, scientific interests
- Local licensing requirements ("portability" of the specialty)
- Personal issues (family or personal history of a particular illness or exposure to specific specialty care)
- Success and satisfaction levels in undergraduate rotations
- Positive exposure to resident or mentor role models
- Family factors (family member in the same specialty, partner's preferences)
- Intellectual preference and background
- Availability of subspecialty options
- Your own personality style
- Public and media perceptions of the specialty
- Market forces/job prospects – some surgical residents have struggled to find employment and have had to sub-specialize. Physician unemployment actually exists.

Personal Health Risk (Burnout, Infectious Diseases)

- Government manpower shortage policies (incentives and disincentives) affecting practice-setting options on graduation
- Autonomy versus team approach
- Debt load (sadly, many trainees in the United States still avoid family medicine, a career they would enjoy, because of financial

constraints. In contrast, family medicine is a popular choice in Canada.)

Picking a Specialty

Many medical schools now hire career counsellors to help students make decisions around specialization.

Consult specialty association websites that also have up-to-date resident-specific content. Here is one career counseling website that will help you decide which specialty fits your talents, personality, and learning style: Careers in Medicine, at www.careersinmedicine.aamc.org/.

Considerations in Choosing a Residency

Here are some factors to contemplate as you make your decision.

The Program

- Accreditation data and ratings
- Number of residents in each year of the program and the number expected to begin in the first year of the next session
- Compliance with work-hour restrictions
- Diversity, equity, inclusion, and cultural safety initiatives (including teaching on anti-oppression frameworks)
- Number of hospitals in the program
- Housestaff/resident and fellow association resources
- Benefits, including health services, stipends for conference attendance, and access to childcare
- Amount of time spent in each hospital
- Financial resources of the program
- Location of each hospital
- Amount, location, and flexibility in scheduling and content of elective time
- Amount of supervision, volume of activity, and length of shifts in emergency rotations
- Anticipated major changes in program policy or administration that might affect residents

- Availability of rural primary-care rotations and clinical exposure
- Area housing/schools
- Cost of living in the specific urban center
- Potential for advancement (postgraduate opportunities: MA and PhD programs, fellowships, chief residency, and staff positions)
- Availability of job-sharing options
- Success rate of residents in fellowship or Board exams
- Availability of support groups and residency well-being resources (see chapter 4)
- Resident satisfaction/input to program design
- Disability accommodations
- Availability of intimidation and harassment policies
- Genuine approach to decolonization and Truth/Reconciliation efforts with Indigenous Nations
- Appreciation for the lived experience of racialized and other minority residents
- Availability of concurrent graduate degree training (i.e., ethics/humanity, etc.) and combined residency (i.e., med-peds, peds-psych, FM-ER)
- Gut feeling (don't discount this!)

The Institution

- "Unionized or nonunionized"; availability of resident representation or collective bargaining (Some programs don't like the word "union," so look for availability of contracts/collective agreements. These should be available online or you can request a copy of the postgraduate medicine syllabus for that training site.)
- Type (specialized, military, veterans, private, county, provincial, or state)
- Availability of resources and innovative techniques
- Number of beds and admissions per year
- Research and teaching possibilities
- IMG-friendly, friendly to cultural, racialized, religious, and sexual/gender minorities
- Popularity of the hospital among housestaff
- Commitment to teaching versus service/"scut"
- Involvement of HMOs or managed care and how that affects exposure to a broad clinical base and continuity of care

- Patient type (geographical area served, socioeconomic and ethnic status, variety in age, and proportion of acute vs. chronic problems, recognition of the role of social determinants in health care, commitment to social justice)
- Commitment to resident well-being (Which well-being resources are in place?)
- Community versus hospital-based

Attending Staff

- Background of the service chief, department head, chief resident, and attending staff (Bios can be found online.)
- Availability and approachability of the residency training director
- Interest and availability of staff for teaching, consulting, supervising, and mentoring
- Exposure to well-known clinicians in the field
- Emphasis on innovation
- Supportive attitudes to team members

Duties

- Time spent on service versus teaching
- Expected ward patient load and possibility of service re-deployment during health care crises (like natural disasters, pandemics)
- Organization of rotations: emergency, elective, chronic, clinic, and inpatient
- Frequency of night calls, number of residents on call, and extent of cross-coverage of wards
- Scheduling of rounds (mornings, weekends, etc.)
- Expectations regarding follow-up on patients treated on wards or in emergency department
- "Scut" level and availability of support staff: nurses, physicians' assistants and extenders, paramedics, blood and intravenous drip teams, messengers, porters, librarians, secretarial staff, and medical records staff
- Record of compliance with legislated limits to number of hours worked and contract protections
- Types of electronic medical and health records employed
- Expectations and guidelines around the use of virtual care (video or telephone)

The Human Factor[4]

Learning and training considerations should always be balanced against those that affect your desired quality of life. Residents pay rent, manage debts, go on holiday, have social commitments, seek out a life partner, and perhaps raise a family. Therefore, you'll need financial information on salary level, frequency of payment (weekly or biweekly), and possibly options for moonlighting. Benefits such as life, health, disability, and malpractice insurance should be provided or made available at reasonable rates through the hospital housestaff union or local medical association. Find out what you can from senior residents in the program.

You may want to know about policies and practices on parental leave, accommodations for disabilities, job sharing, part-time residency, and compassionate and sick leave. Again, much of this information should be available online. Are wellness resources available (e.g., mentoring, tutoring, fitness facilities, career coaching, personal counseling)? The size of the program will determine the level of familiarity and intimacy among staff, residents, and patients. Some trainees may view residency as a time to explore new approaches, freedoms and lifestyles in a new city; others may decide to settle where they have completed medical school so as to build a reputation and career there.

Applicants also need to learn about the availability, cost, and safety of housing, and about its proximity to the hospital. They may want to know whether schools, daycare, and shopping facilities are nearby. A support system of family and friends provides protection against stress during residency, and its presence or absence may affect the decision to relocate. Climate and cultural events or athletic facilities may also be important considerations. Access to religious and community or cultural resources may be a key factor for you.

Some residents believe that raising such matters during an interview may jeopardize their chances of acceptance because they may introduce personal information – about marital status, sexual orientation, plans to have children, health, and so on – that may not be supplied otherwise. It may be wise to obtain information about these issues elsewhere, but a program that penalizes an applicant for raising such issues, or that has no provision for such benefits or resources, may not be the one for you.

This personal and professional information must be sorted out if applicants are to choose a program where they will learn happily.

Family members, medical school counsellors or mentors, friends, and significant others should all be recruited to help weigh the elements involved. For a wonderful resource on coping as a couple and family, written by a medical spouse, see "Surviving the Medical Marriage Residency" by Kristen Math (www.kristenmath.com). There are also numerous blogs and online communities (both local and national) that discuss the impact of residency on couple and family life.

The Interview

This is your chance to determine if a program is right for you. Dress professionally and comfortably and pay attention to grooming. Arm yourself with as much information as possible about a program before your interview. You can then be attentive to important details that will help you make your final decision. Was the program helpful and flexible in making arrangements to meet you? Were interviewers punctual? Did they refer to your CV and ask pertinent questions related to it? Did they put you at ease? (One resident in psychiatry reported some years back that an interviewer – believe it or not – asked him to leave the room and return as his mother!) Know and note the names and titles or positions of all interviewers in smaller programs and consider sending them a follow-up thank-you note. There may also be pre- and post-interview social events where you can mingle and get the "vibe" of the institution. Be courteous to all support staff you contact around the interviews because it's the right thing to do, and they may be asked their opinion of you. Certain topics and questions should not be raised by interviewers in Canada and the United States because they are inappropriate on human rights grounds. You should nevertheless prepare for them because they invariably arise. Rest assured that interviewers will also check out your social media presence/posts as a part of their due diligence. And have a good look to see if you see potential supervisors and mentors who have a shared lived experience as your own. While you may be called upon to be a trailblazer in your own right, it can be wonderful to have access to leaders who understand and appreciate the opportunities and challenges of your own life path.

The Interview

I'd been to enough interviews already that I was almost ready to sleepwalk through the questions I expected: "Why do you want to pursue this specialty? What attracts you to our program?" I knew my interviewers and was sure about how they'd interact with me. I was paired with a good cop and a bad cop: a friendly resident I'd worked with before, and the head of the program, a thin, severe woman who never wasted her time on a smile. At least, that was what I thought until they opened their mouths. And then the questions started.

"So," said the resident, looking wounded, "most of your personal statement is about how much you love another specialty. Are you actually interested in our program?"

It took almost a minute for me to think the unthinkable thought: I really had submitted the wrong personal statement to the program. Every answer I gave turned into an apology. No, I tried to say, I really did love their program. I really wanted to be in it. But the damage was done. In their eyes, it seemed, any attempts to repair the damage meant that I was sloppy at best and a liar at worst.

There was a second interview an hour later, with another interviewer I'd also worked with. In between, I scrambled to find a computer and print off the personal statement I'd meant to send. The second interviewer was another staff physician I'd worked with. I figured I might as well start by addressing my mistake.

"I submitted the wrong personal statement," I said. "Here's the one I actually meant to submit."

His usual broad smile burst into a laugh. "Don't worry about it," he said. "These things happen. I know you want this specialty. Let's talk about your research experience and what we can offer."

Inappropriate Interview Questions

Here are some examples of inappropriate interview questions:

- How old are you?
- What is your marital status?
- What is your sexual orientation? Gender identity?
- What is your nationality, secondary citizenship, or cultural background?

- Do you have plans for marriage or pregnancy?
- Outline your medical and psychiatric history.
- What is your Hepatitis/HIV sero-status?
- Have you had drug/alcohol problems?
- What is your ethnic, racial, religious, and family background?
- Will you select the program if you are ranked highly? (This violates match agreements, though you may wish to volunteer this information. Don't rely on verbal promises.)
- Where else have you interviewed?

Asking "May I know why you ask that?" in response to such questions suggests to the interviewer that certain details are private and gives you time to compose a suitable response.

Some provocative questions are reasonable and appropriate. You should not only expect them but also rehearse your replies, because they will give an interviewer an accurate sense of your character and career goals. Be sure to appear interested, motivated, and enthusiastic.

EXPECTED INTERVIEW QUESTIONS

Here are some examples of questions that you should expect during an interview:

- Tell me about yourself. What makes you unique?
- What makes a good doctor in your view?
- What are your weaknesses and strengths?
- What are your long-term plans?
- Is there anything about you that might prevent you from successfully completing your residency in "x" number of years?
- What is your most important achievement to date?
- Why have you selected "x" as a specialty? Why not "y"?
- What is the most significant error you have made in your clinical work so far? How did you manage it?
- Tell me about a time that you advocated for a patient.
- How has a recent public health crisis (like the COVID-19 pandemic) affected your view of your work as a doctor?
- What attracted you to this program?

- What are your interests outside of medicine?
- Have you any questions about our program?
- Tell me about an interesting/memorable patient.
- What would you change in our health care system?
- Have you any plans to do research or teach?
- What does it mean to be professional?
- How are you at teamwork?
- Where do you plan to be ten years from now?
- What do you want out of life?
- Tell me about a significant medical error you witnessed and how you dealt with it.
- Tell me about "x" (a recent news event or recent medical breakthrough).
- What have you been reading outside of medicine lately?
- How can disciplines like ours contribute to the good work of Truth and Reconciliation for Native or Indigenous populations?
- How do you weave principles of social determinants of health into the care you offer at the bedside?

Residency interviews go both ways. It's fair for you to make certain inquiries as well. The following are some questions you should ask faculty:

- What makes this program unique?
- Why did you train here and stay on?
- What are the strengths, innovations, and weaknesses of the program?
- What is resident morale like? How family-friendly is the program?
- Are any major changes pending?
- Where do most of your graduates go/work?

You might also pose questions for residents at the program[5]

- What's call like?
- What do you like/dislike about the program? What is the quality of teaching and supervision?
- What made you choose this program? Are you glad you did?
- What resources/well-being/social programs are in place for residents?

Preparing a Curriculum Vitae

A professional-looking CV can move you up to the top of the interview pile. Here are some suggestions for preparing one.

- Type the following clearly on quality, white, 8½ x 11 inch paper, allowing for excellent scan quality.
- DATE IT, check for typos, and send a clean, typed or scanned copy!
- Have someone else read it before you send to capture things you might have missed.

Sample Curriculum Vitae Outline

Personal Information

- Full name
- Citizenship
- Languages (optional)
- Home address, telephone number, email address
- Professional address, telephone number, email address
- Present academic rank and position (if applicable)

Education

- Name of institution, degree(s), and date(s)
- College or university
- Medical school
- Residency
- Fellowship
- Other

 TIPS FOR VIRTUAL/VIDEO INTERVIEWS

In a post-COVID-19 world, more and more interviews are being scheduled virtually. This saves travel costs and time.

Here are some tips for presenting well virtually:

- Practice, record, and review mock interviews with another learner or faculty member.
- Check out your posture, gestures, and speech tone, speed, and quality in the videos.
- Turn off your cell phone and any other potential notification alerts!
- Familiarize yourself with the video platform being used (including potential glitches).
- Choose a quiet location at a table or desk.
- Choose appropriate lighting and backdrop (i.e., not a messy bedroom!).
- Dress and behave professionally as if you were meeting in person.
- Place the interviewer's image on screen under your camera to maximize eye contact.
- Use a professional headset to ensure you can be heard with ease.

Certification (i.e., LMCC, USMLE)

- Certificate number

Board Certification (if applicable)

- List month and year of successful completion

Medical Licensure (if applicable)

- Indicate province/state and license number only

Honors and Awards (including scholarships)

- List chronologically, beginning with earliest appointment

Military or Volunteer Service (if applicable)

- List branch of service, rank, place, and dates

Academic Appointments and Positions

For example:

- Academic research, clinical appointments; list chronologically, beginning with earliest appointment
- Teaching:
    - List dates and names of courses taught, time spent as leader of rounds, seminars presented, student advisor roles filled, etc.
    - Institutional, departmental, and divisional administrative responsibilities, committees
    - Medical school
    - Graduate school
    - Continuing education
    - Other institutions
    - Other relevant past employment

Journals

- List membership on editorial boards, positions as scientific reviewer for medical journals, etc.
- List chronologically, beginning with earliest appointment

Memberships and Other Activities

- List all, including years active
- List chronologically, beginning with earliest appointment
- If still active, list date as follows: 2011–

Professional and Society Memberships

- List dates, offices held, and committee responsibilities
- List chronologically, beginning with earliest appointment

Invited Visiting Professorships

- List dates, places, and professorship title
- List chronologically, beginning with earliest appointment

Presentations at National Meetings

- List dates, meeting names, places, and topics
- List chronologically, beginning with earliest presentation

Presentations at International Meetings

- List dates, meeting names, places, and topics
- List chronologically, beginning with earliest presentation

Intramural or In-House Presentations

- Presentations at the physician's hospital or institutions; presentations, Mortality and Moribundity Conferences, or journal club meeting at Grand Rounds; or formal presentations to medical students
- List chronologically, beginning with earliest presentation

Research Grants

- Grant number and title, time period
- List chronologically, beginning with earliest award

Hobbies/Interests/Civic Activities

- List both medically and non-medically related activities

Publications – Journals

- Published articles: list chronologically, beginning with earliest publication
- Use "In Press" for those articles accepted but not yet printed
- Use "Submitted" for those submitted but not yet accepted or rejected
- Use "In Preparation" for those written but not submitted

Publications – Abstracts, Editorials, Book Chapters

- After the title, identify in parentheses whether the work is an abstract, an editorial, or a book chapter; put all abstracts in a separate grouping
- List chronologically, beginning with earliest publication

References (contact information for at least three)

- Colleagues, professors, mentors, former students

The following should NOT appear on your CV

- Date of birth
- Sex/gender
- Family information
- Social Insurance, Social Security, or passport numbers
- Health insurance number
- Education or awards prior to university unless relevant
- Details that you would not be willing to discuss openly in an interview.

Before Signing On: What to Look for in Residency Contracts[6]

The American Medical Association has published a document called "Understanding Employment Contracts." Resident Doctors of Canada and the Committee of Interns and Residents (CIR) in the United States can also be contacted for contractual questions, although Canadian contracts tend to be standard and uniform.

Among the essential points to look for in a written agreement are the following:

- Specified salary year by year (which should be the same for all residents at your level)
- Work hours (including maximum call and days off)
- Available leave (including bereavement, illness, personal/family, educational – with duration specified)
- No limitations on off-duty involvements (i.e., you're free to moonlight)
- Holiday time details
- Contract termination procedures and appeal possibilities (related to quitting, transferring, or being fired)
- Transfer provisions (should your program close or amalgamate)
- Other benefits (living quarters, uniforms and laundry, meals, staff health services, pagers/cell phones, lockers, library facilities)
- Policies related to sexual harassment, diversity/equity/inclusion, racism/discrimination, disciplinary protocols, and grievances
- Flexibility regarding changing programs

Navigating the Match: Tips and Strategies

Check out these links for tips on succeeding in the match process and getting the placement you want.

- American Academy of Family Physicians, Strolling through the Match, www.aafp.org
- Association of American Medical Colleges, Roadmap to Residency: From Application to the Match and Beyond, www.members.aamc.org
- CARMS: The Canadian Resident Matching Service, www.carms.ca
- Electronic Residency Application Service, www.aamc.org/services /eras/
- National Residency Matching Program, Data and Reports, www .nrmp.org

3

Physician Heal Thyself

The Vending Machine

Call nights as a medical student were always hectic. At first, it seemed like there was never a moment to sit down or even take a washroom break, and I went at least one whole night without one. But as I spent more time in the hospital at night, I came to recognize a rhythm that allowed for a quiet break around 3 a.m. every night.

There was a vending machine near one of the inpatient wards. I took to visiting at least once each call shift. I'd buy a bag of sour cream and onion chips and finish the whole thing on one of the nearby couches, half-listening to the reassuring snores and unsettling gasps of my patients down the hall. For a few minutes each night, I had a small sanctuary from the chaos.

When I became a senior resident, I started to bring all sorts of snacks to the room where my team reviewed our consults in an attempt to recreate that sanctuary, but this time bringing my interns and med students into it. What I brought reflected the stock of the hospital's drug store, which varied seasonally: iced tea in August; for some reason, popcorn in December. And always a couple big bags of chips!

Taking Care of Your Body

Residents sometimes seem to forget, as they become used to ignoring physical cues including hunger, fatigue, and bathroom breaks, that they themselves have bodies! This chapter offers some suggestions for keeping healthy physically during your years of training. Readers are also directed to a wonderful and practical resource: the American Medical Association's Healthier Life Steps™ program at the AMA[1] (available at www.ama-assn.org), which is designed to help physicians support their patients, and physicians support themselves and each other, to make healthy lifestyle choices over time. Topics are focused, providing strategies to enhance motivation, when to get regular check-ups and screening based on your age, health risk factors, and according to periodic medical exam guidelines, and links to excellent resources on nutrition, fitness, and mental health.

Sleep

TIP

Historically, a lack of sleep has represented the most significant stress to physicians in training, who commonly worked thirty-six-hour shifts as frequently as every second to every fourth day.

"I find it very beneficial to take a nap as soon as possible on call, e.g. if it's 5 p.m. and there are no pages, I can lie down until they come. This allows me to start refreshed, whenever."

While on duty, they averaged 2.7 hours of sleep. Studies of shift workers abound,[2,3,4,5] and, increasingly, more have examined residents.[6,7,8,9] They have shown a variety of negative effects of reduced sleep and increased fatigue, including the following: selective attention, processing speed, working memory, mathematical ability, accuracy in electrocardiogram reading, anger or irritability, impaired concentration, depersonalization, and fine motor skills. One older study noted post-call car accidents in 35 per cent of a sample of medical interns who were followed up for one month.[10] Since the last edition of this book, additional research[11] demonstrates residents who work extended-duration work shifts have an increased risk of potentially life-threatening driving accidents.

Other professions have acknowledged categorically the risks attendant on sleep deprivation. Nurses, air pilots, air traffic and other transportation controllers and operators, army recruits, and nuclear inspectors and attendants all have regulated hours for reasons of individual and corporate safety. It is acknowledged by sleep experts that at least five hours of sleep are required for a worker to maintain cognitive and motor skills.[12] Medicine has been slow to acknowledge this risk to trainees and patients, in part because of the cost of replacement services and in part

Table 3.1. More resources on sleep and safety

- Resident Duty Hours: Enhancing Sleep, Supervision and Safety. National Academies Press, Washington, 2009
- Sleep Deprivation Module, AMA GME Competency Education Program, https://edhub.ama-assn.org/gcep. This study identifies a number of concrete strategies residents can engage to improve their sleep habits, including strategic napping, asking for a break, taking time out to eat and hydrate, asking for help, napping in-house before driving home, seeking help and counseling if needed.
- Fatigue management tips, includinjg an overview of the sleep, alertness, and fatigue education in residency (SAFER) program, can be found at the Loma Linda University resident resource database at www.lluh.org/health -professionals/gme/resources-residents-fellows/fatigue-management.
- McGill University's THRIVE program also has a focused resource on sleep in residency: www.mcgill.ca/thewelloffice/files/thewelloffice/thrive_summer _2018.pdf.

---

because of a traditional stoicism that equates forgoing sleep with dedication and opportunities for learning. However, in July 2003 the Accreditation Council for Graduate Medical Education (ACGME) implemented work-hour limitations, including a maximum of eighty hours work per week. Not surprisingly, some attending physicians have celebrated these changes. Others have pointed to negative impacts on learning and patient care, particularly in surgery.[13] Older studies had already demonstrated better cost and work efficiency when residents are less fatigued. Newer research has confirmed that residents with modified working schedules are likely to make fewer medication errors, increase their productivity, and discharge patients faster. They also report enhanced career satisfaction and lower levels of exhaustion.[14,15] However, other studies have flagged that there may have been unintentional impacts of restrictions on duty hours,[16] particularly among surgical residents.[17]

Frequently changing or disrupted sleep schedules and sleep deprivation alter natural circadian rhythms and cause gastrointestinal complaints (e.g., indigestion, constipation, and dyspepsia), loss of appetite, mood swings, forgetfulness, chronic fatigue, and irritability. One study showed that up to 25 per cent of all beeper pages were unimportant or unnecessary and actually interrupted patient care.[18] People with diabetes, epilepsy, depression, and respiratory disorders are at higher medical risk when they are deprived of sleep because of disrupted physiological cycles and altered efficacy or absorption of medications that are designed to coincide with these rhythms.

Nodding Off

I couldn't believe it. I actually fell asleep in a patient's therapy session. I'd had a string of bad calls and just never seemed to catch up with my sleep. You probably know the feeling – your head is nodding, your eyes are closing and no amount of tongue biting, knee pinching, shifting positions or deep breathing is going to preserve wakefulness. The head bobs downward and that's that.

The patient was a man with schizophrenia, about fifty.

I'll never forget my embarrassment or his kindness.

"Doc – you look exhausted. Make sure you take care of yourself."

Top 10 Cognitive and Neurobehavioral Effects of Fatigue[19,20,21]

- Alertness and vigilance become unstable; lapses of attention increase.
- Cognitive slowing occurs; time pressure increases errors.
- Working memory declines.
- Tasks may begin well, but performance deteriorates with increasing rapidity.
- Perseveration on ineffective solutions increases.
- Neglect of activities judged to be nonessential (loss of situational awareness) grows.
- Involuntary microsleep attacks occur.
- Increased compensatory efforts required to remain effective.
- Risks of critical errors and accidents increase.
- Cognitive deficits can be masked by stimulation.

Although improved work hours have been in place in Canada for many years and have been adopted by programs in the United States, you can still enhance your sleep by applying a few strategies. Planning and conducting rounds before retiring, including giving clear instructions to nursing staff about pending laboratory results or vital-sign changes, can prevent unnecessary calls. If you are a senior resident and take calls from home, go to bed early so you get some rest before the pages come in. Ideally, for in-house call, you should have your own room key and ready access to a telephone and bathroom with shower, and you should have the option to stay overnight in the room if late working hours make it inconvenient or unsafe for you to return home. In addition, it is not unreasonable to ask the head nurse or nursing supervisor to screen nursing requests before you are paged. Splitting the night with a colleague (midnight to 4 a.m., 4 a.m. to 8 a.m.) can ensure four hours of sleep without frequent interruption. Dedicated call-room facilities (i.e., not cloakrooms) should be quiet, cleanly maintained, close to wards, and unshared (i.e., one person to a room). When possible, you should be paired with another resident to permit task splitting (e.g., emergency admission vs. ward work), and you should be allowed to leave the next day after signing off patient care post-call, as specified in your contract. Insist on a proper handover, such as that advocated by organizations such as the Royal College of Physicians and Surgeons of Canada.[22]

TIPS FOR FIRST AND SUBSEQUENT CALL NIGHTS

- Pay close attention at evening sign-out rounds to particular problems with patients. Prioritize the sickest or most unstable patients. Make a to-do list. Clarify management instructions from your senior resident.
- Clarify with your senior how to proceed during call if you have questions and how to reach her to discuss cases. Clarify your role with the medical student as well. Do not hesitate to ask for teaching or help – that is why you are there.
- Make sure your beeper works and/or your phone is charged. Respond to pages and texts quickly. Have a charger handy and an extra battery in your bag.
- Learn your hospital's electronic medical record (EMR) system and review steps for order entry.
- Prevent rather than treat. When you see a patient on a ward, ask if there are other concerns or problems while you're there. Make a list of results you need to check.
- When you are called to assess someone, see the patient, and write a timed and dated note on every patient (as legal documentation and medical update). Leave clear instructions with the nurse about when to call you again. If the nurse calls to inform you of something, discuss whether the patient needs to be seen.
- Carry good pocket manuals or smartphone apps for differential diagnosis content and treatment guidelines (see below).

- Organize your time strategically. Deal with all problems and review all laboratory and X-ray results service by service or floor by floor. Keep a detailed list. Assessing the patient and writing/entering orders in the emergency department will save you travel time and additional work, because most tests and blood sampling can be done there.
- Although you have back-up and may not even be the first to see patients, discipline yourself to conduct thorough physical exams, differential diagnoses, work-ups, and treatment plans to avoid the temptation, especially when tired, to readily accept someone else's management. After residency you will not have this opportunity to test yourself under supervision.
- Rehearse particular emergency management plans in your mind on the way to assess the patient. This will reduce anxiety and increase efficiency. The book *On-Call Principles and Protocols* is an excellent resource that takes you step by step through key on-call problems and their management.[23]
- Be open to asking for help from your team and your supervisors.
- Determine handover time the next morning and your role in the process (e.g., presentation of new admissions).
- Look after yourself the next day, including hydrating and eating. If you're sleep deprived, be really honest with yourself before driving. A ride-share, bus, or taxi ride might be much better than risking an accident.
- Seek out state-of-the-art smart phone apps and online resources by subject. (Some are free. Others charge fees. Your medical library and resident colleagues may be able to recommend useful electronic content free of charge.)

Tips for Regular Sleep[24]

You won't have control over how busy your shifts are, but there are some things you can do to protect your sleeping patterns:

- Sleep when you can. Follow your body's cues.

 TIP

"It should be made clear to on-call residents and nursing staff what tasks must be handled overnight and which can wait until morning. For example, it should be made clear that most paperwork can wait until morning, etc. Night call should focus on patient care."

- Prioritize household tasks and check your emails and texts later, after you get some sleep.
- Leave work at work. You've signed off and signed over care.

 TIP

"Many hospitals offer residents discounts on apps – ask what is available!"

- Aim for a consistent post-call sleeping pattern or ritual.
- Take a twenty-minute wind-down period or warm bath before going to bed.
- Reduce the frequency of large meals and intake of greasy foods before retiring but eat enough to prevent your waking hungry.
- Reduce or eliminate alcohol, caffeine, and other substances before retiring. Be cautious about regular use of over-the-counter sleep products, including melatonin, or using cannabis/CBD products.
- Increase exercise, but not immediately before bedtime.
- Use the bed for sleep only; if you cannot sleep, do something else out of bed and delay your usual bedtime by one or two hours.
- Close the blinds.
- Use ear plugs, unplug the phone, and make sure the temperature and noise levels of your sleeping quarters are comfortable.
- Shut off your phone/laptop. The light emitted by these devices disturbs sleep patterns/melatonin release, and the alerts can easily rouse you from sleep.

Diet

A recent study of residents and medical students showed that both groups failed to achieve recommended daily servings of fruits and vegetables. Stress and lack of sleep may suppress your appetite or lead to increased consumption of junk food or caffeine. Time pressure and the poor quality or variety of hospital cafeteria food often make residents decide to skip meals entirely. The hypothalamic response to prolonged stress – such as occurs in residency – results in increased turnover of protein, carbohydrates, and fats and, if severe, may deplete vitamin and mineral reserves. This is itself a physiological stress factor. A lack of exposure to sunlight can lead to vitamin D deficiency.[25] Although nutrition guidelines have traditionally recommended a specific daily intake from each of the four food groups (dairy, meat and other protein, breads and cereals, and fruits and vegetables), several modifications can be useful. Monitor your fluid intake to avoid dehydration.

Small frequent meals fit more easily than large ones into crowded schedules, produce less postprandial fatigue, and may lessen stress-induced dyspepsia or nausea, a common complaint of residents. Eating foods with a high fiber content will prevent changes in bowel habits, whereas a high level of fluid intake will prevent dehydration. Healthy snacks from the hospital cafeteria and vending machines should replace chocolate, pastries, and caffeinated beverages. Sweet snacks give only short-lived energy boosts, followed by rapid swings in blood sugar levels with a resultant crash or let-down fatigue. Caffeine may be tempting if you are tired, but it may produce increased anxiety, tremor, and irritability!

Many healthy foods can be requested of the hospital and stocked in the interns' lounge or in lockers so they are available when meals are missed (see below). Vitamin supplementation remains a controversial issue because there is no definitive proof that increased emotional stress depletes nutritional stores. A "B-C-E-D vitamin/mineral" complex may, however, be useful in the face of irregular eating habits and skipped meals. Certainly, a woman with a tendency towards anemia will have impaired energy levels if she does not receive an iron supplement.

Fuel-Efficient Snacks

If you have to eat on the run, here are some fuel-efficient snacks:

- Fruit (apples and pears)
- Low-fat yogurt, cottage cheese, skim milk, hummus (high in protein, may boost energy)
- Whole wheat/multi-grain bagels, bread, and toast (with peanut butter)
- Dried fruit (e.g., raisins)
- Graham crackers and whole-wheat ginger snaps
- Carrots and celery
- Pretzels
- Nuts
- Cheese slices
- Protein shakes

Eating Strategies

Keep regular track of your weight and nutritional status in a way that works well for you. It may be helpful to reflect on the fairly new literature that shows that residents are at risk of developing problematic eating (e.g., not following nutritional guidelines, skipping breakfast, being chronically dehydrated) for reasons that are often external (i.e., lack of breaks, heavy workload, lack of access to healthy food choices, lack of role models). Further, learning to monitor your own nutritional habits and skills is more likely to predispose you to helping your patients adapt similar healthy approaches.

Here are some helpful eating strategies:

- Make sure you hydrate properly (6–8 glasses of water/day) and keep a bottle with you on duty that can be easily refilled. If you find yourself thirsty all the time, you are likely dehydrated.
- Eat small meals frequently, and don't skip meals.
- Have only light meals before sleep.
- Eat a diet composed of 55 per cent carbohydrates, less than 30 per cent fat, and 15 per cent protein.
- Recognize the value in buying vegetables that are already prepared for eating (i.e., precut, prewashed).
- There is no shame in using grocery delivery services, meal preparation services, or joining a community meal-preparation service – whatever helps you meet your nutritional needs.
- Consider vitamin supplementation.
- Decrease your intake of caffeine, tobacco, alcohol, fatty foods, and simple carbohydrates.
- Increase your intake of complex carbohydrates.
- Avoid fad dieting.
- Pack healthy, high-protein snacks for on-call periods.
- Prep a week's worth of healthy meals at a time.
- Role-model healthy nutritional behaviors for others where possible, particularly for medical students, by taking nutrition breaks, making hydration stops, and showing them where they can store or purchase healthy food.
- McGill University has a toolkit on nutrition for residents that can be accessed at www.mcgill.ca/thewelloffice/files /thewelloffice/thrive_fall_2018.pdf. Hategan, Saperson, Harms, and Waters (2020)[26] have written an excellent book focused on both humanism and resilience in residency training with specific chapters on nutrition and activity that is worth checking out.

Being Mindful about Substances

Stress, sleep cycle disruption, and demands of work can all have major impacts on sleep, nutrition, and physical health. It is not uncommon for residents to consider using recreational substances (e.g., tobacco, cannabis, alcohol) or over-the-counter substances (e.g., melatonin, appetite suppressants, sleep aids, wakefulness aids). Some may also consider substance with higher risk profiles, such as illicit drugs or those that require a prescription. No judgment here, but we encourage you to learn all you can about how substance use can impact your health and well-being. Drug use, and resources for finding help, are discussed in chapter 6 ("The Impaired Colleague").

Other Stress Busters

Here are some tips for time management.[27]

1. Read emails or touch paperwork only once. This will help you declutter and prevent you from postponing tasks, answering queries, or losing information.
2. Make task lists every day. Indicate their priority – i.e., what's urgent, what can wait, what imminent deadlines exist.
3. Keep your paper or virtual calendar up to date regarding social and professional engagements. Use the "month at a glance" feature to scope an overview and to review deadlines and other important dates.
4. Develop useful routines: make a point of completing notes after every patient visit, dictating summaries the day of discharge, picking a regular time to review lab results and check your mail.
5. Use unexpected gifts of time in ways that best serve you – perhaps crush a few items on your to-do list, or take a few moments to be mindful. Those spare minutes add up.
6. Maximize rounding efficiency:
   - Start and end on time.
   - Set goals.
   - Review/track down lab results prior to rounds.
   - Be ready to introduce your patient and present your case succinctly and respectfully.

The Royal College of Physicians and Surgeons of Canada has published a guide on time management specific to the needs of residents and practicing physicians that may be of interest and value.[28]

Exercise

Regular exercise seems almost impossible to schedule for most interns and residents because of fatigue and time pressure. It takes some inventiveness to incorporate exercise into a busy routine. Even though you may be physically active while on duty, some rotations or disciplines may be more sedentary than others. This can create a risk to both physical and mental health, and the risk can be additive over time. Physical activity is the main way to reduce this risk and brings with it natural ways of improving your cognitive capacity and mood, reducing stress, and influencing your practice of counseling your patients to be active as well.

Aerobic exercise, for periods of twenty to thirty minutes, up to 150 minutes per week, is an ideal solution to emotional stress because it enhances relaxation through endorphin release, decreases depressive symptoms, increases energy levels, improves sleep, dampens the fight-or-flight response, and improves the physiological response to emotional and physical challenge. Many residents walk, ride, or run to work and climb stairs at work rather than take the elevator. Others enjoy virtual reality devices (e.g., oculus), stationary bicycles/rowing machines, or augmented/hybrid devices that can access online training and content and are increasingly popular. If you're moving to a new community, consider a condo or apartment with a pool or gym to facilitate easy access during busy weeks. Some residents also find that their university or hospital has gyms and pools that are available at no or low cost. For fun, you can also count your steps at work each day!

Besides regular exercise, various simple techniques of relaxation can significantly reduce physical tension, anxiety, and fatigue.[29] You may also want to learn more about yoga, meditation, and mindfulness stress reduction. Some hospitals even offer free classes for staff. One study showed that offering access to a no-fee hospital-based fitness center to surgical residents improved their productivity and quality of work.

Simple Relaxation Exercises

Abdominal Breathing

Most people under stress take frequent, quick, shallow breaths using only their diaphragms. To change this pattern, use the abdomen and take deeper breaths, by letting your belly fall out. Breaking inspiration into sniffs to the count of four and then exhaling to the count of four soon induces relaxation. Each breathing cycle takes eight seconds; the appearance of sighing signals that the exercise is working.

Shoulder Shrugs

Shrugging your shoulders reduces tension in the upper body, which is usually affected during periods of stress. Inhale while pulling your shoulders up towards your head; rotate your shoulders so that your shoulder blades come together, and exhale while letting your shoulders fall back down. Three to five repetitions in a sitting or standing position usually result in quick relief.

Head Rolls

Relieve neck tension by exhaling while letting your chin fall towards your chest. Breathe in while rotating your head to the right and to the back, and then exhale while rotating your head to the left and forward to your chest. Repeat three to five cycles in a sitting or standing position.

Progressive Muscular Relaxation

This is a useful technique that can also be taught to patients who feel under stress. Alternately tense and relax each muscle group in sequence from your toes up to your buttocks; extend or puff out your abdomen and chest; finally, progressively tense and relax your fingers, arms, shoulders, and facial muscles. Do this exercise while you are lying down in a quiet place, inhaling during the muscular tension phase of a few seconds and exhaling during a few seconds of letting the muscles go limp. Five minutes should be sufficient for this total-body relaxation exercise.

Remaining Mindful[30]

Mindfulness involves bringing one's complete attention to the present experience, moment by moment. This allows you to observe mental and bodily experiences more clearly and without judgment, and to put them in perspective.

- Check your breathing throughout the day. Take ten full, deep breaths.
- Watch your posture whenever you move from standing to sitting, lying down or walking. What is your body telling you?
- Check in with your five senses – what are you seeing, hearing, tasting, touching, smelling?
- Listen to others without interruption or judgment. When it's your turn, make your point calmly, with your body relaxed.
- Check your muscle tone during the day. Are your muscles stiff, sore, tight, relaxed? Stretch out the tension.
- Whenever possible, eat slowly. Taste. Chew. Enjoy. Pay attention!
- Make a point of paying attention to daily, even routine, activities (instead of doing them on automatic pilot). Observe yourself brushing your teeth, washing the dishes, tying your shoelaces. Be present. Be here, now!
- Observe your thoughts and feelings in a given moment – whether irritated, amused, overwhelmed, happy. Name the feeling for yourself. Take a breath and don't judge what you're feeling. At the same time, don't act on it or speak out without reflecting.

Protecting Your Physical Health

- Get a family physician and make a point of checking in for an annual physical and health review. Like other safety-sensitive occupations, medical professionals have unique risks to their health that warrant regular check-ups. You can link these to other self-care activities such as your annual flu shot, or other health promotion/screening activities. Your university, state, or provincial physician health program may have special programs to help you access primary care.

- Meet with an immunization professional to collect and unify all of your vaccination records into one booklet, and then tuck it away in a secure physical and/or online location for future use. You may discover that some vaccinations are obligatory for your program (i.e., COVID-19, measles, mumps, rubella), while others may be required for electives outside of your program or country. You also may be asked to complete screening tests for various infections, such as blood-borne pathogens or tuberculosis, as per your regulatory body, hospital, or university protocols. You may be also surprised to discover you're due for a tetanus booster, too.
- Women of child-bearing age should have a rubella hemagglutination inhibition test to determine their immune status.
- If you are living with a health condition that influences your immune system, you may also wish to consider specific vaccination protocols that may reduce your risk of illness.
- Before you travel to a new country, carefully review any additional vaccinations that may be appropriate to consider (i.e., Japanese encephalitis, yellow fever, m-pox, rabies) or treatments to consider (e.g., anti-malarial medications). This is also an opportunity to discuss any treatments you may need to take with you such as those for altitude sickness or travellers' diarrhea.
- Prevent lower-back injuries by avoiding excessive leaning over a patient; raise the bed, not the patient. Pay attention to posture when you are sitting or standing for prolonged periods. Obtain help when lifting patients or equipment. Get close to the patient or object and lift with your legs. Ask an orderly to show you how.
- Avoid radiation exposure by standing at least 18 meters from portable X-ray equipment. Ask for a portable radiation meter if you are working in an area of high exposure (e.g., radiology).
- Request adequate training for the handling of toxic substances (e.g., anti-neoplastic agents) and information on local "right to know" laws about exposure to toxic materials.
- Ensure your N-95 mask fitting is up to date and in keeping with your workplace protocols.

- Review your institution's pandemic or disaster protocols.
- If you are sexually active, consider having frank and open discussions with your physician about infection prevention strategies, including PrEP and regular screening tests.
- Do not drive a car or ride your bicycle if drowsy!

Protecting Yourself from Workplace Violence[31,32,33,34]

Trainees often forget that distressed patients may lose control and lash out physically. You can learn to recognize these signs of imminent danger:

By Patient History

- Past history of violence or criminal involvement
- History of threats of violence (may be flagged on registration system)
- Poor social functioning (e.g., conflict with authority, job/school conflicts)
- History of trauma, such as childhood maltreatment or exposure to war
- Mental health diagnoses that reflect a risk of affective dysregulation, impulsivity, or aggressions (e.g., substance use, personality, neurocognitive, psychotic)

By Diagnosis

- Substance-use disorders
- Acute mania or psychosis (including command hallucinations)
- Neurocognitive disorders or delirium
- Seizures (temporal lobe, partial or complex)

By Behavior

- Loud, threatening speech
- Tense, clenched posture
- Agitation or restlessness
- Racist, sexist, homophobic remarks
- Pacing, easy to startle
- Rapid breathing
- Violent gestures (pounding the table, pointing)

Strategies to Ensure Safety

- Know your hospital's safety policy and determine what rights you have as an employee.
- Familiarize yourself with security measures already in place (video cameras, alarm buzzers; weapon and firearm checks by security; hospital emergency code protocols).
- Review hospital procedures for physical restraint.
- Warn others of high-risk behaviors if you witness them. Don't allow a situation to escalate.
- Watch how you dress. Accessories, ties, pens, pins, necklaces, chains, and scissors are all potential weapons. Long hair can be pulled.
- Be courteous and non-provocative regardless of the patient's behavior. Do not lecture, condescend, or express annoyance. Kindness and compassion can have a powerful impact on risk reduction.
- Make sure the examining area is well lit and clutter-free (e.g., with no throwable objects).
- Never stand between the patient and the door, and when sitting make sure you have the closest access to the exit or door.
- If you feel you are in danger, do not continue the exam or interview. Leave at once and caution security.
- When in doubt about a patient, call a support staff member or request the presence of a third party.
- Do not stare at, point at, or touch an angry patient.
- If a patient is agitated, carefully consider with your team the potential need for physical restraint during your examination, especially if drawing blood. Avoid needle-stick injuries!
- Make sure your call room door is locked.
- Be cautious when leaving hospital grounds at night. If in doubt, take a taxi or request that a security guard accompany you to your car.
- The American Academy of Family Physicians produced a toolkit in 2021 on preventing violence in health care, covering a diversity of topics such as workplace violence, intimate partner violence, harassment and bullying, and crisis-prevention. You can find it at www .aafp.org/dam/AAFP/documents/practice_management/admin _staffing/AAFP-Preventing-Violence-In-Health-Care-Toolkit.pdf.
- Suggestions for handling disruptive colleagues can be found in chapter 6.

AVOIDING VIRAL AND BACTERIAL INFECTIONS

- The COVID-19 pandemic has made us all aware of the value of knowing and deploying layers of protection, including use of PPE, social distancing, handwashing, and vaccination. Follow stringently all isolation and hand-washing precautions for both your safety and that of your patients. Keep your hands away from your eyes and face to reduce the incidence of viral infections. Use antibacterial hand gel throughout the day.
- Reduce your risk of needle-stick injuries by never recapping needles; never manipulate used scalpel blades without an instrument; never leave used needles around (e.g., on beds); dispose of all sharp objects in an appropriate container that is not full; and seek help for blood-related procedures when a patient is agitated. Should you sustain a needle-stick injury, let the wound bleed, wash it with soap and water, disinfect it with alcohol, and then immediately call the staff health unit for follow-up procedures. Protocols for post-HIV exposure (i.e., drug therapy) now exist and you should request treatment if indicated.
- Make sure that all equipment you use is adequately maintained, disinfected, and sterilized.
- Use precautions against human immunodeficiency virus infection.[35] Follow the universal blood and body-fluid precautions and recommendations concerning handling of body fluids and procedures for using gloves and washing hands listed below. The risk of occupational HIV transmission varies by type of exposure and is considered an uncommon event. The CDC updates their advice on a regular basis, currently located at www.cdc.gov/hiv/workplace/healthcareworkers.html.

Universal Blood and Body-Fluid Precautions

The COVID-19 pandemic more than drove home the need for rigorous infection control protocols to protect both physician and patient health. Most hospital have online videos to walk you through the use of PPE.

The use of gloves, followed by handwashing, is recommended for procedures that involve contact with the following body fluids (visit www.cdc.gov for updates):

- Blood
- Blood-contaminated fluids
- Sperm
- Cerebrospinal fluid
- Pleural fluid
- Pericardial fluid
- Peritoneal fluid
- Synovial fluid
- Amniotic fluid

Body fluids for which gloves are not recommended (if not contaminated by blood), but handwashing is recommended, are as follows:

- Saliva
- Stools, diarrhea
- Vomitus
- Tears
- Nasal secretions
- Oral secretions

Procedures for which gloves followed by handwashing are recommended include the following:

- Intubation
- Bronchoscopy
- Dental procedures
- Wound irrigation
- Phlebotomy
- Finger and/or heel stick
- Vascular catheter placement
- Tracheotomy suctioning
- Rinsing of used instruments
- Lumbar puncture
- Amniocentesis
- Puncture of other cavities

Masks and eye barrier protection should be used whenever splattering is likely. Diaper changing is usually done without gloves but followed immediately by handwashing.

ILLNESS DURING TRAINING

Residents and interns are not immune from health problems, although they like to believe that they are. The following suggestions are made to residents who become ill during training.

- If you're sick, don't come to work. This includes obvious physical health issue (i.e., infectious respiratory disease) and may also extend to some mental health issues (i.e., moderate to severe depression). Be as kind and honorable to yourself as you would be to your patients, and let your doctor provide you with the same degree of excellent care you offer every day. Besides, it is appropriate to role-model appropriate self care, particularly when there can be a risk of error, transmission, or injury to patients and colleagues. COVID-19 protocols shifted several times during the pandemic. It is always best to carefully consider the recommendations and follow the up-to-date orders of the relevant public health authorities during new or emerging public health crises.
- Do not use denial to avoid receiving the medical attention you need.
- Maintain a good link with your treating physician, who can see or refer you, or admit you to hospital quickly.
- Do not self-treat and do not play "doctor games" with your physician about knowledge and control issues. Find someone competent and caring, and let yourself be cared for; relinquish the need for total control. Further, self-treatment may be a violation of the professional legislation or standards of your jurisdiction and can have a significant impact on your license, career path, and level of stress.
- Do not expect special treatment or automatic professional courtesy. An inflated sense of entitlement may complicate your relationship with your caregivers.
- Take the time you need to get better. Let your physician manage any administrative pressures from your superiors that may hinder your recovery. Most contracts allow for sick leave, so you will not be penalized for absence from work.
- Never self-prescribe medications or order investigations – see the classic article by G.E. Vaillant: "Physician cherish thyself: The hazards of self-prescribing."[36]
- Living with chronic health conditions, such as HIV, long COVID, recurrent mental health conditions, diabetes, epilepsy, cardiac or GI disease, is not at all uncommon in resident

cohorts. If you face any difficulties with reasonable accommodation or, worse, harassment or discrimination, reach out to
your advocacy organizations for support. Most training programs have become very skilled, and collaborative, in ensuring
residents living with health conditions have every reasonable
possibility to enjoy a long and successful career.

Why Do We Wait So Long to Obtain Help?

It's both paradoxical and ironic that physicians who advocate healthy
lifestyles to their patients often neglect their own health and ignore
early warning signs of significant physical or mental illness. Doctors are
forced to embrace a level of stoicism and perfectionism in their training
and often come to ignore their own physical cues. They may believe
that their white coat somehow magically protects from them from serious illness and use denial around symptoms they would investigate
and treat actively in a patient.

Doctors are often pressed for time, may have significant educational
debts, and are afraid of taking time off work or being placed (or forced)
onto disability. Many residents and fellows do not have their own family doctor, and this can delay obtaining appropriate care and specialty
referrals.

When it comes to issues of burnout or mental illness, doctors are
understandably reluctant to be treated by colleagues they know within
their hospital network as they fear confidentiality may be breached and
they may be stigmatized. Their families may have made sacrifices to
educate them or to permit the building of a practice and the physician
may fear losing status and idealization from family members.

Furthermore, many physicians fear that their health concerns will be
reported to licensing bodies,
thus damaging their careers
and earning potential. Promoting the role of physician PHP's
health programs and residency
well-being programs is a good
way to reduce stigma and to
encourage good self-care.

 TIP

" I know now that if anyone in medicine asks me for help that I should act
right away. Chances are they've been
sitting on it for some time."

Staying Whole:
Maximizing Supports and Finding Balance

Chapter 3 suggested ways of safeguarding physical health by improving your eating, sleeping, exercise habits, resilience, and stress-busting. This chapter discusses two important strategies for protecting your mental health: establishing adequate support systems and maximizing a sense of personal control and balance.

Relationships with family and friends are discussed in chapters 5 and 6, since most residents tend to go to these individuals when experiencing difficulty during training. Other types of support that you might not have considered are available from the following people, groups, and organizations.

Maximizing Support at Work

Family Physician

Surprisingly, many residents and physicians do not have their own physicians, preferring to treat themselves or somehow expecting preferential care from colleagues, often with problematic results. (As mentioned in the last chapter, this may in fact result from our own fears about being a patient.) One study of internal medicine residents in a US school revealed that 37 per cent had no primary care physician and 12 per cent acted as their own doctor![1] Plan early. Before beginning your training, find a family physician who will treat you as a patient but can adapt to your erratic schedule. He or she can be an invaluable referral source for quick initial assessment and treatment, sick notes, stress management, and support. Your program may keep a list of local doctors willing to see residents.

Chief Resident

The chief resident should be your advocate, open to feedback about your rotations, and a mediator between residents and staff. He or she can initiate you into the conditions and customs in a new hospital or ward setting, arrange coverage when you are absent, ease necessary contacts with superiors, and field your call requests for the night duty roster.

 TIP

"The chain of command and people who can provide backup should always be clear. For example, a junior resident should know what senior residents and members of other services (e.g. ICU, anesthesia) are available to help as needed, how to contact staff, etc."

Senior Resident or Fellow

Local politics aside, this person can be a source of teaching, support, conflict resolution, and service orientation, and can help you organize your work. Do not hesitate to ask this person questions.

Residency Program Directors and the Postgraduate Medical Education (PGME) Office

Many residents unfortunately do not get to know their residency program director at either the hospital or the university program level. This important ally can provide information about rotations, electives, evaluations, exams, training options, and requirements. She can handle grievances about rotation abuses, requests for absences, or program changes, and can make recommendations about staff conflicts or learning difficulties. Schedule at least two appointments a year with the program director for feedback and to discuss your progress and career plans. As well, the PGME office can provide resources and usually has an online or print orientation guide with key information on politics and procedures, including codes of conduct, intimidation and harassment protocols, and details on the accommodation of special physical

or learning needs. Some schools even have a resident advocacy committee to help address concerns.[2]

The postgraduate medical education office can provide information
on training requirements and program resources and may also be able
to link you with a residency advocate or ombudsman.

Hospital Housestaff Association or Resident Representative

This person should address such issues as duties, call frequency,
adequacy of supervision, staff relations, leaves of absence, benefits,
legal protection, and potential political action. All Canadian teaching
institutions have a representative of the provincial hospital housestaff
association in addition to a residency program delegate. Your hospital may have residency representatives to the hospital or program
administration.

Religious Representatives

Scheduling a visit or having lunch with the hospital chaplain, priest,
imam, rabbi, Indigenous Elder, or other religious representative can
help you to explore existential questions and clarify dilemmas that arise
during the dark nights of the soul that many residents experience. Visits
from them can also help some patients; ask your patients if they would
like a visit arranged.

Diversity/Equity/Inclusion Officer

Most hospitals now have expert consultants who can give training
workshops and consult on policy failures or adverse and discriminatory clinical and educational encounters.

Indigenous Learner Supports

Increasingly, universities and hospitals are providing culturally safe
supports to Indigenous learners, and also helping settlers on their journey towards realizing the aims of the Truth and Reconciliation Commission. These specialized services can also be a rich resource to learners as they enhance the quality of the care they provide to First Nations,

Métis, Inuit, American Indian, and other Indigenous patients, families, and communities.

Case Manager

This person (on the ward or off-site) can be a vital resource for discharge planning and linking your patient to community resources. Residents struggle with helplessness and moral distress around their patients' poverty levels of personal safety or housing situations. The case manager can help you in your role as advocate.

Hospital Bioethics Consultant

Residents may feel ill at ease following certain recommendations of a senior person or experience moral conflicts in treating patients. These circumstances create great moral distress. Most teaching hospitals and universities have an ethics consultant who can be asked about such cases and be invited to give formal or informal seminars on key topics.

Hospital Lawyer or Risk Manager

This person can answer questions about consent, confidentiality, incompetence, and termination of treatment and end of life decisions, either personally or in requested lectures. Contact with this person is especially important in the United States, where the high risk of malpractice suits lends particular cogency to arguments for reducing residents' hours and improving working conditions. In Canada, contact the CMPA first.

Hospital Employee Assistance Programs or the Provincial/ State Medical Association Hotline or Local Physician Well-Being Committee

The people from these services can tell you in confidence how to find help for yourself or your colleagues should someone increasingly resort to drugs or alcohol or to other maladaptive behavior in response to stress. One excellent example is Ontario's PARO Helpline at 1–866-HelpDoc (435–7362). These individuals can also refer you, when necessary, to the state or provincial physician health program (PHP) and to occupational health, career counseling, professional coaching, and human resources in your hospital. The mandate and breadth of offering of PHPs continues to expand with an emphasis on wellness, career enhancement and satisfaction, and building resilience rather than managing impairment.

Other Hospital Professionals

A hospital is a complex organization of professionals and nonprofessionals working together daily. You can have satisfying, friendly exchanges with any of them. If you can avoid taking a physician-in-charge stance, it is possible to develop relations of collaboration, camaraderie, and even friendship with paging operators, security guards, kitchen and cleaning staff, secretaries, orderlies, and X-ray and laboratory technologists, as well as with nurses, pharmacists, social workers, dietitians, and occupational and physical therapists. Take the time to learn their names and build a sense of community. Most residency programs emphasize and evaluate teamwork, collaboration, and respectful inter-professional exchange.

Mentor

Young professionals in any discipline need at least one mentor (a superior who is guide, tutor, and even friend) to help form their identity. Although some residency programs assign tutors, you may wish, or be obliged, to find a mentor yourself. In the latter case, ask an inspiring lecturer or attending physician for a meeting or ask the residency program director for a list of people with similar clinical and research interests. Mentors are usually but not necessarily older people and may be of the same gender as you. This last characteristic may be an important factor in the process of identification and life modelling that takes place in such a relationship. Many residents prefer same-sex mentors.

Finding a mentor or career coach may be the single most important step you take in obtaining professional support during residency. He or she can encourage you when you feel overwhelmed by your duties, buffer disillusionment, and help you with your career decisions.

A Good Mentor

A good mentor is someone who

- Is experienced, enthusiastic, sparks your interest, and can skillfully guide your reading and learning

- Provides a role model with respect to manner, professional identity, ethics concerns, and lifestyle, and sees medicine as a vocation, not just a job
- Maintains clear boundaries and directs you for added support and consultation where needed
- Is patient, nonjudgmental, and non-evaluative (is NOT grading you for your work)
- Has artistic, research, advocacy and/or clinical interests similar to yours
- Is flexible with time, does not compete with you, and is not threatened by your enthusiasm or intelligence
- Is well connected to resource networks and key workers in your field
- Will help you choose a subspecialty or fellowship and develop leadership skills
- Is willing to write letters of reference

Remember that we all need and can provide mentorship over the span of a medical career, so nurture those relationships over time!

Psychotherapists, Counsellors, Coaches, and Peer Counsellors

Many residents, particularly those in psychiatry programs, begin a psychotherapeutic exploration during residency, often as a result of crisis (career uncertainty, substance abuse, depression, or decreasing performance) and sometimes because they believe such work will make them happier people and better physicians. Your family physician, residency program director, hospital or provincial or state physician well-being committee, physician hotline, or you yourself, privately, can usually arrange a referral. Some residency programs include funded counseling networks or access to hospital employee assistance programs (EAPs). Don't let fear or stigma stand in the way of getting help.

Select a therapist carefully; as one of our colleagues in Montreal observed, "You don't get to pick your parents, so you'd better be extra careful finding a therapist." Interview prospective therapists about philosophy and length of treatment, an active versus a silent approach, availability of a professional rate, and flexibility of hours, all the while assessing personal fit or compatibility (Is this someone I can talk to?). Decide whether you want here-and-now support or a perceptive examination of past conflicts, and whether you want to do short-term work or to keep the therapy open-ended. Make a contract with the therapist who sets goals, expectations, and basic ground rules (rates, attendance, holidays, cancellations, etc.).

The logistics of attending therapy sessions during residency are complex but not impossible to manage. Virtual appointments are now more common and save travel time. If your residency program director has provided the referral, he or she may help you to be seen quickly and can be quoted during rotations as supporting therapy work. The referral source and therapist will keep your work confidential, but you will still have to explain absences to your senior or chief resident. Explain only as much as you want to, but at the least indicate that your work should not suffer from regular one- to two-hour absences each week. Having a therapist in the same hospital or nearby is an obvious advantage. Remember to keep any receipts for income tax purposes and to discuss with your therapist whether treatment will restrict medical and disability insurance access later on.

The Residency Wellness Office at your university or within your program may provide direct access to certified career coaches or keep a list of reliable career consultants. They can help residents identify professional goals, develop leadership skills, and plan both short- and long-term career strategies. Coaches help you identify strengths, potential, transferable skills and abilities, goals, dreams, risk tolerance, and perceived obstacles.

As a general rule, coaches work with a functional situation in the present, which can be explored and moved forwards, and not with past issues, which require counseling or psychotherapy (thorough examination and resolution) before progress can be made.

Most of your friends in other professions (like the law, accounting, finance, tech) set out five-year career plans. Doctors are finally catching on to the idea that they should do the same, and a skilled coach can ask the right questions needed to set priorities and make changes.

Peer Support: One-on-One and Group Peer Counseling

Here are five facts about peer support:

- Most people want to connect with someone who understands them. That understanding often comes from similar experiences and can be reassuring when someone is stressed or uncertain. Peer support

is rooted in the belief that everyone can recover from trauma, mental health or addiction issues, mistakes, burnout, depression, and other concerns.
- Peer support starts with an authentic human connection. Peer supporters share their own stories of similar experiences and how they got through them. They walk beside someone – not directing but listening to and validating their feelings. They maintain healthy boundaries.
- While peer support complements clinical approaches, it is not clinical. Peer supporters do not provide diagnoses, recommend specific treatments or give other medical advice. They help colleagues discover and build on what works for them.
- Peer support improves outcomes. People who use peer support show improved coping and self-management skills, have stronger social networks and tend to be less isolated. Their symptoms are reduced, they use substances at a lower rate, they require shorter and fewer hospitalizations, and they have less need for intensive services.
- Peer support is growing and formalizing. More services are employing peer workers as a part of interdisciplinary care teams, and peer-led services continue to grow.

Adapted from the Canadian Mental Health Association Wellness Hub, here are five things to know about peer support.[3]

The goals of peer support are to

- Help people discover and build on coping strategies that work for them
- Promote a broader sense of community and a positive, supportive training and practice culture
- Help people overcome challenges and manage wellness
- Complement clinical approaches

One-on-One Peer Support

You may want to develop peer counseling skills during residency, when you can obtain faculty coaching or supervision.

Here are some tips on how to provide informal one-on-one peer support:

- Be available. Suggest a time and space to meet, listen, and talk if needed.
- Provide the person with a safe zone to express their thoughts.
- Listen actively, openly, and non-judgmentally, and encourage discussion.
- Be kind, empathetic, and understanding, and share your experience so the person doesn't feel alone.
- Speak from the heart and share insight and knowledge gained through your experience.
- Encourage the person to seek help even if they feel fine.
- Stimulate conversation by asking, "I've noticed X or Y in you. How can I help?"

Source: Adapted from the CMA Physician Wellness Hub.[4]

Resident Peer Support Groups

Some very worthwhile friendships form during internship and residency because of the intensity of the shared experience, the similar goals, and the countless hours that residents spend together. Many residents unfortunately miss the opportunity of giving and receiving informal peer support because they are competitive or believe they have to appear all-knowing and omnipotent. They are reluctant to discuss anxiety, sickness, self-doubt, experiences of racism or other forms of discrimination, or feelings of failure and loss after a patient's death. Build a community, and not just with residents in your own residency program. Link up with colleagues from other clinical disciplines as well. Allow yourself to let off steam, because it will help open exchange and normalize the many feelings that get stirred up in all residents during training. Ask for help when you need it, cover for each other, do favours, and talk through intense shared experiences together (like the death of a patient). Build in play time (like a movie night or a softball game). All these activities are rewarding and protective. When you are a senior, look out for those you supervise, recognize their anxiety, and ask them to talk about such key experiences as the first night of call. Be a role model by showing that residents should talk about such things. Always set up a formal orientation or "boot camp" for new interns or new residents on your service.

The literature on resident stress and impairment has established the usefulness of a variety of formal group experience for residents, including exercise programs.[5,6] Women's groups, spouses' groups, couples' groups, trainee-staff retreats, first-year orientation weeks or months, medical society memberships, process or Balint-type groups, and peer/process support groups have all been used with success in teaching centers across North America. They may be optional or an established part of the program, time-limited or open, led by a behavioral scientist or self-run, and held weekly, monthly, virtually or in-person, or semi-annually. Interns in particular benefit from such groups because they help to manage the stress of the first postgraduate year, which for most is the most stressful.

Recent innovations in resident support include "boot camps" and welcoming retreats with content and hands-on experience (simulation) for handling emergencies, worst-case scenarios and particularly stressful situations,[7] transition to residency workshops and simulations for graduating med students,[8,9] communication and stress-management training,[10] Neighbourhood Watch initiatives, and formalized lectures on issues like personal development, coping with stress, and maintaining balance.[11]

Nowadays, residents also keep in touch by blogging, texting, and contributing (in a professional manner) to trainee websites (both intranet and Internet), forming virtual support communities.[12]

Resident Support Structure – What's Ideal?

The Accreditation Council for Graduate Medical Education (ACGME) now requires that support services be available to all residents. A literature review in *Academic Medicine*[13] highlights the stressors cited previously in chapter 1, but also mentions the dilemmas faced by international medical graduates (IMGs), residents who are matched to programs they don't want, pregnant and minority residents, and those with learning difficulties. The following are the ingredients of an ideal assistance service:

- Confidentiality
- Support from program staff
- Short-term counseling or stress management for trainees and their family members
- An objective, confidential third-party referral service

- Ongoing follow-up for severely stressed residents
- Social activities and retreats
- Support groups for residents and family members
- Stress management seminars
- Childcare and financial resources

The various residency program print or online syllabuses and information networks now list and describe the support programs available at every hospital or university setting. See chapter 2 for information on choosing a healthy residency program. All of this information should figure highly in the choice of a program. Our hope is that Canadian and US residents will share successful strategies about what works nationally so that local programs don't have to re-invent the wheel each time.

But the System Needs to Change – A Call for Institutional Leadership

Residents often complain that they can work on their well-being with individual steps and strategies, but national, state or provincial, and local hospital and residency programs need to acknowledge the prevalence of physician burnout caused systemically and then implement institutional change through dedicated leadership. Explore options for learning leadership skills in your program, university environment, or medical association for when you have more power and can effect system-wide change.

Here are some organizational strategies for doing so:

1. Acknowledge and assess the burnout problem. (Burnout has multiple definitions and that affects statistics on prevalence. Use one consistent description.)
2. Harness the power of leadership.
3. Develop and implement targeted interventions.
4. Cultivate a sense of community at work.
5. Use rewards and incentives wisely.
6. Name and align institutional values.
7. Promote a culture of flexibility and emphasize work-life integration.
8. Provide resources to promote resilience and self-care.

9. Remind institutions that burnout leads to medical errors and lawsuits.
10. Evaluate outcomes and track benchmarks. Facilitate and fund metrics of success.[14]

Housestaff Representation

Meanwhile, while you're a resident, political support and influence are necessary to change the many stressful conditions still prevalent in the residency experience. All Canadian residents are employed by provincial agencies and represented by provincial housestaff associations, which provide uniform contracts. The Canadian Association of Interns and Residents, now called Resident Doctors of Canada/RDC (www.residentdoctors.ca) has been serving as the umbrella organization for all provincial housestaff associations, excluding the Fédération des Médecins Résidents du Québec (FMRQ), since 1970. Residency groups from across the world have consulted CAIR because of its pioneering approaches to protecting the well-being of residents. The RDC executive committee consists of provincially elected members who meet three times a year in different Canadian cities and sit on several of the major medical bodies, including the Canadian Medical Association (CMA), the Canadian Medical Protective Association (CMPA), the Royal College of Physicians and Surgeons of Canada (RCPSC), the College of Family Physicians of Canada, and various government and accreditation committees (e.g., on national manpower). RDC publishes news and events online and issues other communications, which residents can request, and the association has a useful library on its website. They have a vital social media presence. RDC has also been active in sharing its expertise with its USA counterparts, as they have been at the forefront with respect to addressing residents' rights and working conditions.

The Canadian Medical Association website (www.cma.ca) has an excellent Resource for Residents section with a Wellness Hub and interesting content on topical issues like climate change.

The situation in the United States historically has been quite different. Residents were generally hired and paid by their specific hospital center, and not all hospitals have had official housestaff associations with collective agreements. The Committee of Interns and Residents

(CIR – www.cirseiu.org) is the oldest and largest housestaff organization in the United States, with chapters across the country, and has an affiliation with the Service Employees' International Union (SEIU), which is the single largest American union of health employees. The CIR's services include consultation and advice on contract negotiations, union formation, and policies regarding call duties, licensing, funding, debt repayment, and other housestaff issues (e.g., quality of training and quality of life for patients and residents). The CIR publishes a newspaper, *CIR Vitals,* available online, which monitors these concerns and carries information packets on affirmative action, IMG rights, legislative issues, public sector health care, contract negotiation, parenting issues, setting up a housestaff organization, limiting hours, improving safety and quality control, and issues like the impact of the COVID-19 pandemic or other public health crises on residency training.

Historically, other examples of more local unions or resident representation could be found at the University of Michigan and the University of Colorado, as well as specific county hospitals (like Cook County Hospital in Chicago). Other schools and hospitals have housestaff associations that organize collectively on behalf of residents, but don't bargain and are not recognized under the National Labor Relations Act, as unions are. (The term "union" can actually be a dirty word for many medical educators and administrators because they feel any call for strikes or labor action would be "unethical" and not "physician-like".)

The American Medical Association plays a significant role in the lives of residents in the United States. Its Resident and Fellow Section (RFS) is the largest organization of medical residents in the United States and contributes directly to the AMA policy-making process. Its journal (*JAMA*) publishes content that highlights key developments affecting young physicians in terms of legislation, debt repayment, practice formation, and training. The AMA also offers expert speakers to help residents explore their representational options (for information consult the AMA website, www.ama-assn.org).

Other organizations of interest to interns and residents in the United States include the following:

- American Medical Student Association (AMSA – www.amsa.org), which describes itself as "the largest and oldest independent

association representing physicians-in-training, including pre-
medical students, medical students, interns and residents. Founded
in 1950 to provide an opportunity for medical students to participate in organized medicine, AMSA began as the Student American
Medical Association under the auspices of the American Medical
Association (AMA). In 1967, AMSA formally ended its affiliation
with the AMA and has since remained an independent organization. Governed by a student Board of Trustees, much of the association's energy today is focused on reforming the medical education
system, improving work conditions and developing physician
leadership for the 21st century. AMSA has nearly 30,000 members in
168 chapters." AMSA also publishes and posts the *New Physician*, a
magazine on training issues and members' work with CIR.[15]

- The Accreditation Council for Graduate Medical Education
  (ACGME – www.acgme.org) is the only accrediting body for the
  more than 6,000 residency training programs in the United States.
  Representatives from the AMA, the American Board of Medical
  Specialties, the American Hospital Association, and the Association of American Medical Colleges (AAMC), along with resident
  representatives and representatives from the public sector and the
  federal government, make up this body. The ACGME insists that
  every residency program have a grievance policy overseen by the
  hospital graduate medical education committee. It also investigates
  complaints about programs. They have wonderful web resources on
  multiple topics for residents.
- The AAMC (www.aamc.org) has an Organization of Resident
  Representatives who discuss issues pertinent to resident well-being.
  Their Student and Resident website section walks learners through
  every step of becoming a doctor and practicing specialist.

Visit the websites of all the organizations listed above as they contain
helpful, up-to-date information on well-being, learning, finances, and
contractual issues, and provide hundreds of useful links of interest to
residents. Your own national specialty association is likely to have a
section for residents and fellows as well.

Setting Up Your Own Support Group

- An up-to-date practical guide to creating both one-on-one and
  group peer support programs can be found at www.cma.ca
  /physician-wellness-hub/content/facilitating-peer-support.

- Establish resident interest in attending a group and determine feasible frequency.
- Decide if there can be a virtual format for residents offsite.
- Offer healthy food at in-person gatherings (if allowed by current infection control guidelines!).
- Approach the program director for expertise, suggestions, and funding if a mental health professional is to lead the group. The director's support is necessary, particularly if residents are to be freed from their duties to attend.
- Decide whether the group is to be self-led or led by a non-evaluating faculty member or mental health professional. Keep in mind that most residents prefer to meet on their own and lead or chair their own meetings.
- Plan logistics carefully. Aim for weekly or biweekly meetings lasting forty-five to sixty minutes, possibly over lunch, and attended by seven to ten people. Arrange coverage for those attending and provide food.
- Consider holding a resident retreat away from the hospital once or twice a year.
- Prepare and publicize a list of resources for emergency health care should members need outside help.
- Remember your goals: the group provides support, not psychotherapy. It will help members to air their feelings ("gripe sessions"), normalize stresses, and solve problems. Topics can be chosen in advance or pressing concerns can guide the format of each meeting. The amount of self-revelation will vary, but the focus should be on shared problem-solving regarding residency stresses and on physician–patient and physician–staff relations. Members should speak for themselves, not for each other.
- Prepare a list of ten to twelve difficult situations or scenarios that residents are likely to face in training (e.g., verbal abuse, arranging organ donation, facing a clinical error. MAID [Medical Assistance in Dying] is a frequently asked for session in Canada).
- A good group leader will encourage but not teach or guide content and will defuse conflict and comment on process only if it impedes members' giving mutual support. (The leader may be more active, interpreting underlying conflicts, if the group is an experiential or process one.)
- You can learn how to sharpen your facilitation skills at www.sessionlab.com, accessing Leadership Training through your program, the CMA or AMA or through meeting with your mentor or career coach.

- Speakers can be invited and films shown. Topics for discussion can include burnout, fatigue, the "difficult patient," resident competence versus fear of error and failure, the dying patient, bearing bad news, handling staff conflict, ethical dilemmas, the impaired resident, stress-management techniques, enhancing inclusion for all (patients and learners), career and financial planning, balancing family life, and a review of local, provincial or state, and national resources.
- To improve accessibility and attendance, offer virtual access with moderated discussion. Consider recording the session and banking videos to share and discuss later. See the list at the end of chapter 8 for films, videos, and literature that will prompt discussion on physician identity.
- Provide links to online support and/or social media, including Facebook, for residents and their spouses. Swap strategies with colleagues in Canada and the United States.

Family medicine faculty at the Oakland University William Beaumont School of Medicine created and assessed an innovative, popular lunchtime curriculum on Meaning in Medicine. Here is their list of topics, which you may want to use or adapt in your own setting:

A Sample Lunchtime Curriculum

Discussion Topics for PGY 1 and 2
- Reflecting upon patients' perceptions of health care providers
- Stereotyping in patient care
- Finding renewal
- Being present in what you do
- Dealing with patient death
- Recognizing changes in empathy along the way
- Reflecting upon what advice would have been helpful as a PGY 1 in July
- Developing skills (courage) to be imperfect
- Learning how to reach out and be connected
- Focusing on importance of teamwork and collaboration during and after residency
- Establishing goals for wellness – both personally and professionally

- Avoiding/dealing with burnout
- Focusing on mindfulness for providers and patients
- Creating strategies for improving teamwork and morale
- Utilizing personal strengths to cope and to improve professional and personal life

Discussion Topics for PGY 2 and 3

- Managing difficult patients
- Ethical issues of patient care
- Educational goals
- Time management and office efficiency
- Work–life balance
- Leadership considerations in future practice
- Postgraduate plans and career transition
- Managing technology (this can include the EMR/EHR)
- Board preparation
- Patient anecdotes
- Improvements in residency training
- Emotional responses to bad outcomes
- Lifestyle considerations in future practice

Maximizing a Personal Sense of Control[16]

Tait Shanafelt has written powerful and moving pieces on finding meaning, balance, and personal satisfaction in medicine.[17] He encourages physicians to identify their personal and professional values to see how these mesh or conflict over time. He has compiled the following list of questions to help identify your values:

Personal Values

1. What is my greatest priority in life? Have I been living my life in a way that demonstrates this?
2. Where am I most irreplaceable? At home? At the hospital? Elsewhere?

3. Do I have adequate balance between my personal and professional lives?
4. Am I asking more of my spouse and children than I should?
5. What kind of a legacy do I want to leave my children?
6. What person or activity have I been neglecting?
7. If I could relive the past year, what would I spend more time
doing? What would I spend less time doing? What changes do I
need to make to help this happen this year?
8. Why did I choose my profession? What do I like most about my job?
9. What would I like my life to be like in 10 years?
10. What do I fear?

Shanafelt encourages doctors to reflect on their answers and to rank
important priorities, noting areas of conflict or incompatibility. He
suggests that physicians identify the areas of their work that are the
most meaningful and satisfying to them (teaching, research, patient
care, palliative care, etc.) and to let those insights guide career plans.
Similarly, acknowledging areas of weakness may lead to extra training, shared learning, improvement of skills, and reduced stress.
Finally, individual wellness strategies should be prioritized throughout a medical career, as described throughout this book. These
include nurturing relationships, exploring spirituality, developing
non-medical hobbies, travelling, ensuring adequate sleep, exercise,
nutrition, medical care, and protecting time for reflection and personal reassessment.

Identifying Personal Strengths

Now that you've identified your personal values, consider your
strengths as a unique human being.

Instead of being a perpetual perfectionist and over-identifying with
your flaws and weaknesses, take a moment to consider what makes
you a resilient and unique human being? What are your core or signa-
ture strengths? How would others describe you? As wise? Humanistic?
Fair? Kind? Level-headed? Transcendent?

To help define and identify these strengths, the VIA Institute on
Character offers a free online survey using twenty-four identifiers.

Go to www.viacharacter.org/resources/activities. Find out how you score and what attributes you would like to further explore and develop. How can you use your top five strengths to cope with daily challenges on the wards? How can you deepen these strengths? Are there any personal attributes not listed that you value?

VIA Institute Personal Strengths are as follows:

Appreciation of beauty
Bravery
Creativity
Curiosity
Fairness
Forgiveness
Gratitude
Honesty
Hope
Humility
Judgment
Honesty
Kindness
Leadership
Love
Love of Learning
Perseverance
Perspective
Prudence
Self-regulation
Social intelligence
Spirituality
Teamwork
Zest

Practical Tips for Keeping Control and Balance at Work

Be creative in getting the most out of your training and free time. Allow yourself to think (and feel) "outside the box," as optimal learning requires use of both sides of the brain.

Table 4.1. How do I make decisions?

If we were to add one attribute to the above list, it would be the ability to think nimbly and critically. Jerome Groopman has written brilliantly about this in his bestselling book called *How Doctors Think*. He keeps the patient perspective at the forefront of his analysis.

Clearly, a lot of factors go into making a clinical decision in a given moment. Increasingly, AI (Artificial Intelligence) will be harnessed to facilitate this process rapidly, based on all available evidence.

Given the incidence of medical errors in most hospital settings, medical educators now invite trainees to explicitly weigh the following elements in choosing a specific intervention, investigation, or course of treatment. Knowing more about how you think and problem-solve will deepen your capacity to reflect while keeping yourself accountable and improving patient care and reducing medical error:

1. RATIONALITY. Is the decision logical, evidence-based, and does it follow the laws of bio-medicine?
2. CRITICAL THINKING. This is the ability to analyze and question facts in order to form a judgment. It demands clarity, precision, logic, and accuracy.
3. COGNITIVE AND AFFECTIVE BIASES. Residents need to develop the ability to identify and modulate their implicit biases (i.e., personal judgments, assumptions, preferences, biases, blind spots, and external pressures on decision-making, such as like the wish to impress or placate an attending physician).
4. META-COGNITION. This is the ability to think about one's own thinking process.
5. REFLECTION. This is the ability to step back and consider thoughts and feelings in the moment so as to evaluate past outcomes in light of current, "here and now" demands. This can include mindfulness and personal awareness of self in a given moment.
6. COMMUNICATION. Clarity of communication with a team member, patient, or the patient's family or representative impacts decision-making throughout care. Responses to queries need to be timely.
7. INVESTIGATIONS. Ordering and interpreting appropriate tests and investigations can lead to timely, appropriate action, but decision-making can be sidelined by unnecessary testing and incidental findings. You should be clear on your reasoning and timing for any test you order.
8. PATIENT PREFERENCES. These must always be taken into consideration. No decision about a patient's care should impinge on their autonomy or be made without their informed consent.

Source: Croskerry, P. (2017). A model for clinical decision making in medicine. *Med Sci Educ* 27, 9–13.

- Try to plan your rotation schedule, aiming to alternate between difficult and easy, in-and out-patient rotations. If feasible, submit your requests to your residency director well in advance.
- Request a transparent call and holiday request system that all residents can access and verify. Take all your holidays – they don't carry over into the next year!
- Find out the names and rotation schedules of good senior residents and attending physicians, and try to arrange to work on their services.
- Obtain a list of hospital statutory holidays and request some long weekends that are important to you well in advance. If a day that is important to you and your cultural background is not identified in the list, seek permission to swap another holiday.
- Plan and schedule holiday time well in advance; it provides an important respite and should be used strategically.
- Choose hospital assignments that require fewer call or home call commitments. If possible, live close to the hospital, thereby saving travel time and increasing sleep time.
- Keep track of all night calls, particularly weekend or statutory holiday calls, so that you can request compensation for extras if appropriate. Inform your residency director or housestaff representative of contractual abuses.
- Remember the seasonal nature of rotations and plan accordingly (e.g., the pediatric outpatient department is flat in the summer, and surgery is slow during the winter holidays, such as at Christmas).
- Maximize elective time by arranging interesting locations and subject matter. Do not be afraid to request something or somewhere original, and document all arrangements by letter or email.
- Pamper yourself when you are stressed (e.g., take an Uber, order out, hire a cleaner, buy yourself flowers, video-call a friend).
- Control your own learning. Ask questions and request increased teaching, supervision, or lectures. Ask for one-on-one instruction if you need it.
- Be aware of all the benefits available to you through the hospital and university: library and sports facilities, legal and financial advisers, leaves of absence. Use allotted conference times to learn, explore new locations, and make valuable contacts. Professional, specialty, or society meetings are often inspiring.

- Sometimes crossing each day off on a calendar is a satisfying symbol of getting through. Buy a one-year print calendar to record holidays and rotation or set one up online. Note pay days, special occasions, and deadlines (e.g., references for jobs and exam applications).
- Plan your time every day, listing priorities and scut work and eliminating unnecessary tasks. Order consultations, tests, and support staff services (e.g., electrocardiograms and intravenous drips) early in the day when they are available. Save yourself travel time by developing a system for doing all work (e.g., X-rays) floor by floor or department by department. Make lists when you feel you are losing control and note pros and cons and options.
- Consider keeping a journal, or jot down milestones or key events (like first delivery, first solo resuscitation) on your calendar for a personal record of your journey through residency.
- Make a list with your colleagues of "time drainers" on your service (disorganized sign-outs, lack of access to computers, EMR documentation glitches, delays contacting insurance companies) and problem-solve together to find and prioritize solutions. Make a list of your own "time wasters" and find solutions for each.
- Learn more about your hospital's EMR/EHR. Ask for training with a tech representative. Find out which MACROS will save you time. Ask other residents and staff for time-saving strategies. (For some specialties, the ratio of time spent "clicking" or documenting to actual patient care can be as high as 5 to 1!)
- Remember that you are entitled to sick days, which can be taken when you are feeling particularly under stress. Do not be irresponsible to resident colleagues or expect them to do your work, but consider taking a mental health day, which will allow you to return rested and more effective. Find out if you are required to work back those days. Offer to cover for a stressed-out colleague if you feel up to it.
- Some programs tolerate leaves of absence lasting from twenty days to three months without penalty at the discretion of the residency program director. Find out to whom your leave will be reported (i.e., licensing bodies). Keep this option in mind if you are becoming unwell and discuss it with the director.
- Take rotation evaluations seriously and do not sign one that you disagree with. Request clarification or rewording rather than

waiting for surprises; request regular feedback if you are not getting it during rotations.

TIP

"I recommend batching tasks, if possible, for example, reviewing all outstanding bloodwork and imaging at 10 p.m. if possible and deferring any non-urgent checks until, for example, 6 a.m."

- Periodically ask for access to your personnel file to verify its content and accuracy.
- Obtain a copy of your hospital or work contract and read it carefully. Know what is expected of you and what protection you can expect.
- Remember to keep your options open. Learn the local requirements for a general license so that you can take outside work. Find out the varying provincial and state requirements for internship and residency, and keep copies of all correspondence should these requirements change.
- If you are disappointed or overwhelmed, you can attempt to change programs or hospital bases as other positions become vacant (check the specialty journals), sometimes even in mid-year.
- Work on your assertiveness skills and conflict resolution techniques (see table 4.2 below).
- Don't complain and don't blame. Get political. Advocate for yourself and others. Consider running for a position in your hospital, national, provincial, or state housestaff association, or as chief resident, faculty representative, regional representative to your specialty association, regional AMA resident physician representative in the United States, or representative to the university or to the university's committee on residency training.
- Find out about PHPs and physician well-being groups in your area. Talk to the hospital program director about setting up resident–staff feedback (or gripe sessions), a resident support group, or a resident one-on-one peer review system in which residents participate in evaluating each other's progress and in selecting new candidates of the residency program. If you are a US trainee and there is no "union" or negotiation mechanism at your hospital, talk about starting one.
- Complete all professor and rotation evaluations. This is not a hopeless gesture but an important source of feedback for program

change. If your program doesn't have them, develop the forms yourself. Be fair, honest, and don't complete them on a day when you're fed up!

Personal Strategies for Maintaining Balance and Resilience[18]

Check in with yourself on a regular basis. Are you happy? Thriving? Fulfilled? Well supported?

- As Shanafelt suggests, list your goals: professional, personal, romantic, family, financial, spiritual, physical, and so on. Decide to what degree you have attained some of them and what now prevents you from attaining others. Pay attention to your creative side and to how music, literature, and film relax you and enrich your interactions with and understanding of patients. (A medical humanities bibliography is provided at the end of chapter 8.)
- Consider keeping a journal or writing narratives about your ward experiences as ways to promote self-reflection. This will be a real-time record of your apprenticeship as a physician. It can be free-floating (free associations), written in point form or prose or poetry, full of doodles and drawings (if you're more visual), or more structured, based on writing prompts or reflections on specific experiences and encounters. Include expressions of gratitude in what you write.
- Practice self-compassion. Mindfully accept moments of suffering or disappointment, treat yourself with kindness and care, and remind yourself that imperfection is a universal human experience. Accept mistakes as a part of growth by learning from them. Check out www.centerformsc.org for tips and strategies for being kinder to yourself. This is a way of being that can be learned and deepened over time with practice.
- Tackle your inner critic head-on. Challenge harsh judgment, negative thinking, and cognitive errors. You cannot control everything (though you would like to). Identify one satisfying event or exchange every day. Remember: you know more today than you did yesterday. Try to live day to day because you cannot delay gratification indefinitely. Give yourself the kind of advice and reassurance

you would give a friend or loved one. Don't keep an extra-severe or double standard when it comes to your own struggles.

- When stressed we all make cognitive errors, like "personalizing" situations that aren't personal, "mindreading" (assuming that people think the worst of us), or "catastrophizing" (imagining the very worst-case scenario).

Other cognitive distortions identified in the cognitive behavioral therapy field listed include the following:

- All-or-nothing thinking: I'm totally incompetent or totally competent – there's nothing in between.
- Over-generalizing: I'm always making mistakes.
- Discounting the positive: It's a fluke that this situation turned out okay.
- Jumping to conclusions: If X is true, Y has to be.

 TIP

"I think it is important to make a point of taking breaks on call. Even on a busy service, taking a few minutes to go to the washroom, close my eyes, breathe, play with my phone for a few minutes, makes me feel a lot better when I get back to work ten minutes later."

- Fortune telling: I know this is going to happen in the future and I'm helpless to change it.
- Emotional reasoning: I feel this way so it must be true.

Pay attention to negative or distorted thoughts, name them when they come up, and look at the real-time evidence to disprove them. Then neutralize them with self-compassion!

- Learn to reframe stressful situations in a positive way.
- Remember past successes, slow down, and take stock of the situation. Think of the present challenge and what you can learn. Focus on the task or connection with the patient – not the outcome.
- Decide what you can and can't control but rehearse for the worst so you can prepare for when a patient crashes.
- Remember that we all make mistakes and deserve a second chance. Assert yourself appropriately and professionally. Name what you're feeling and take a deep breath.

- Practice STOP:
  - S-top what you're doing,
  - T-ake a deep breath,
  - O-bserve what you're thinking, feeling, how you're relating to others and what your body is telling you and
  - P-roceed to make a change that will ground you in the moment without judgment.
- Set your smart watch to prompt you to do a mindfulness check three times per day. (One resident suggested checking in with yourself every time you wash your hands – which is many times a day!) Check out free mindfulness and stress-reduction apps like www .uclahealth.org/ucla-mindful-app.
- Identify and develop your personal coping skills. Chatting with others, humor, naps, hobbies, exercise, and leisure time help reduce stress. Determine which activities are most effective for you and build them into your schedule, even if it means sometimes saying no at home and at work.
- Identify one interest or activity that grounds you outside of medicine and make time for it at least once every week. Go to nature and immerse yourself in BLUE (being near water) or GREEN (visiting parks or forests).
- Try to have one meaningful conversation per day at home and at work.
- Draw a self-esteem pie chart and indicate what portions currently represent work, love (relationships), play (hobbies, creativity), and meaning making or spirituality. Not all the slices have to be the same size. Post the diagram on your fridge next to what you would like your pie to look like if it were more balanced. Update it each year or even after every rotation.

- Keep your home a safe refuge. Make it as comfortable and beautiful as you can. Don't live in boxes!
- Take a break from social media – you don't need your mind to be more cluttered or distracted. Be here now!
- How can you improve GRIT? Grit has been defined as unwavering determination or "perseverance and passion for long-term goals and continued fortitude in the face of hardship" and is

being distinguished from resilience ("the ability to recover from a setback") by some medical educators. For working definitions, see The Short Grit Scale.[19]

Table 4.2. What are the five tips for assertive communication?

Here are five ways to communicate assertively:
- Allow yourself to feel anger or disappointment. Pay attention to thoughts, feelings, and the signals your body is sending you. THEN TAKE A BREATH. DON'T RESPOND IMPULSIVELY. MENTALLY REHEARSE WHAT YOU'D LIKE TO EXPRESS or ASK FOR.
- Make clear, assertive requests. BE SPECIFIC. START WITH SMALL TARGETS and GAINS.
- Validate the other person's feelings. ACKNOWLEDGE THEIR POINT OF VIEW AND WHERE THE DISCONNECT IN EXPECTATIONS MAY HAVE HAPPENED.
- Be a good listener. DON'T INTERRUPT. DEMONSTRATE THE WISH TO LEARN MORE.
- Be collaborative. WORK ON "WE" SOLUTIONS AND EMPHASIZE WORKING TOGETHER MOVOING FORWARD.

Table 4.3. Are you flourishing or just surviving?

Physician health experts are moving away from models of impairment and are now asking what physician happiness and flourishing might look like. How do you score on the following? If you are not flourishing, what are you able to change in the here and now? In the short term? In the long term?

Flourishing Questions

Domain 1: Happiness and Life Satisfaction	1. Overall, how satisfied are you with life as a whole these days? ___ 0=Not Satisfied at All, 10=Completely Satisfied 2. In general, how happy or unhappy do you usually feel? ___ 0=Extremely Unhappy, 10=Extremely Happy
Domain 2: Mental and Physical Health	3. In general, how would you rate your physical health? ___ 0=Poor, 10=Excellent 4. How would you rate your overall mental health?___ 0=Poor, 10=Excellent

Domain 3: Meaning and Purpose	5. Overall, to what extent do you feel the things you do in your life are worthwhile? ___ 0=Not at All Worthwhile, 10=Completely Worthwhile 6. I understand my purpose in life. ___ 0=Strongly Disagree, 10=Strongly Agree
Domain 4: Character and Virtue	7. I always act to promote good in all circumstances, even in difficult and challenging situations. ___ 0=Not True of Me, 10=Completely True of Me 8. I am always able to give up some happiness now for greater happiness later. ___ 0=Not True of Me, 10=Completely True of Me
Domain 5: Close Social Relationships	9. I am content with my friendships and relationships. ___ 0=Strongly Disagree, 10=Strongly Agree 10. My relationships are as satisfying as I would want them to be. ___ 0=Strongly Disagree, 10=Strongly Agree
Domain 6: Financial and Material Stability	11. How often do you worry about being able to meet normal monthly living expenses? ___ 0=Worry All of the Time, 10=Do Not Ever Worry 12. How often do you worry about safety, food, or housing? ___ 0=Worry All of the Time, 10=Do Not Ever Worry

On the promotion of human flourishing by Tyler J. VanderWeele is licensed under a Creative Commons Attribution-NonCommercial 4.0 International License. Creative Commons License /accessed 2022:

Based on a work at http://www.pnas.org/content/114/31/8148. Permissions beyond the scope of this license may be available at http://www.pnas.org/content/114/31/8148.

For further information on the psychometric properties of the Flourishing measures, see: Węziak-Białowolska, D., McNeely, E., and VanderWeele, T.J. (2019). Human flourishing in cross cultural settings: Evidence from the US, China, Sri Lanka, Cambodia and Mexico. *Frontiers in Psychology*, 10 (Article 1269): 1–13; Węziak-Białowolska, D., McNeely, E., and VanderWeele, T.J. (2019). Flourish index and secure flourish index – validation in workplace settings. *Cogent Psychology*, 6 (1598926): 1–10.

5

Protecting and Deepening
Personal Relationships

The people who thrive during residency are those who maintain friendships and family relationships and build new relationships as they go. As mentioned earlier, having a loving partner and supportive community are necessary ingredients of happiness for all human beings, but will also protect you from some of the effects of work stress. On the flip side, the busy schedule during residency may make it difficult for you to spend time with those you love. Here are some tips and strategies for doing so.

Couple Life

The stresses of training that tax residents particularly affect their couple life. Residents' lack of time, exhaustion, absence, and general unavailability (both physically and mentally) often produce conflict at home. Because most residents' partners also work outside the home,[1] the scheduling of quality time and household duties is complex. Historically, wives of physicians have scored high on interpersonal sensitivity, depression, and hostility scales.[2] Husbands of physicians may feel threatened by their wives' success, level of responsibility, or income and decision-making power, based on outdate notions of masculinity. In his book *Doctors' Marriages: A Look at the Problems and Their Solutions*,[3] Myers points out that the key stressors for the married resident often depend on the developmental level of the couple (e.g., newly married vs. settled, childless vs. with children).

Large educational debts, the increasingly uncertain future of some specialties, and moonlighting for extra cash at the expense of free time also make money a significant issue for couples.

October 1st
by Mairi Leining[4]

You ask about my day –
I should have taken a Polaroid;
lime curtains, black sheets,
yellow man, your age,
rusted nails on restless fingers,
pregnant belly with twisted purple veins,
afraid to ask for directions.
Said he drank to escape the loneliness.
That down escalator, no basement floor.
I hold his hand, breathe through my mouth,
Discuss the facts from yesterday's spill;
a new liver, perhaps.
You ask about my day –
I tell you it was fine;
my side of the bed grows farther.

Moving to another city adds pressures to relationships. Residents find that getting started in their training program can give a stimulating and structured focus to relocating. Their partners, however, may feel ambivalent about the move and burdened by the logistics. They can feel isolated and lonely for friends and family in the new city. They can sometimes feel like their career or personal aspirations come second. This can be especially true for the spouses of international medical graduates. Social life gradually diminishes because there is little time to see other couples or family members. The common-law, gay, other-race, or recently immigrated partner of a medical resident may feel particularly stigmatized in a conservative medical social milieu or general community. Some couples are geographically separated by the match and try to maintain long-distance relationships, which involve their own stressors.[5]

The resident's personality may change so much during training (e.g., with a tendency towards irritability, hypersensitivity, or reduced self-confidence or over-confidence) that the partner may feel abandoned. Residents concerned about their career choice or competence may become more preoccupied and withdrawn, and they may shut out their partners because of feelings of shame and failed responsibility. The high levels of resident exhaustion can cause changes in the quality or frequency of a couple's sexual life, which the partner may perceive as rejection. Partners may also believe that their concerns are dwarfed by those of physicians who are diligently saving lives and who have grown accustomed to adopting a direct and authoritative stance. Some residents even develop a psychiatric illness (see chapter 1), which may precipitate or aggravate conflict or estrangement in the relationship.

Decisions that are usually shared, such as the timing of having children and settling versus moving, become more complicated for both partners, particularly for women physicians, who experience "role strain" (the wish to be super-physicians, mothers, wives, and daughters all at once). Household tasks and raising children often constitute the most frequent sources of resident couple conflict. Unfortunately, medical colleagues may not acknowledge the value of male residents' trying to reduce the risks of conflict by participating in these tasks. One recent study showed how stressed resident spouses were as compared to faculty spouses.[6]

Surviving Residency, a wonderful book written by Kristen Math, a medical spouse, has tips on moving, finding housing and schools for your children, and organizing finances.[7]

Avoiding Trouble in Couple Life[8,9]

Here are some tips and considerations to help you avoid trouble in couple life:

- Make sure your spouse always "ties for first place" alongside your career aspirations. He or she should never feel taken for granted or that they come second.
- Express gratitude for your relationship and the help and support you receive. (Repeatedly.)
- Remember that your partner is not medically trained and may need frequent explanations about expectations, scientific terms, causes of stress, procedures, and duties; however, avoid constant shop talk.
- Write out a schedule of shifts and rotations or online call schedules with probable hours so your partner knows what to expect. Make a

list of household tasks with your partner and discuss how to share them, taking into account each other's workloads.
- Plan quality time alone together in advance, rather than hoping it will happen. Go out on a date at least once a week!
- Read books/articles on what constitutes a healthy couple relationship; discuss and implement some of the tips.
- Consider going on a couple's retreat or marriage enrichment weekend to gain new insights on the state of your relationship.
- Leave the job at the hospital. Avoid constant calls or texts to the hospital, online double-checking, or worrying about things you might have forgotten.
- Clarify and divide roles and chores, but try to be flexible and generous.
- If you're both doctors and don't have children, try to book the same on-calls.
- Your residency program may have social groups (virtual or in-person) for medical spouses.
- Acknowledge when you are tired, angry, or sad, and state the source of the feeling (the job, home, or elsewhere). Try not to take out your day's frustrations on your mate.
- Set aside a regular time to talk about your priorities and long-term goals as a couple, emphasizing things to look forward to. What are your shared values and what brings meaning and substance to your couple life?
- A sense of humor goes a long way when the going gets tough.
- Call, text or video-chat home at least once a shift.
- Do things to increase closeness: have dinner together at the hospital on a call night, telephone each other, leave notes, arrange surprises, buy gifts, make playful gestures.
- Develop shared hobbies and activities: sports, gardening, home improvement, family visits, and so forth. Spend more time together in nature.
- Maximize support from family, friends, social events, and residency resources.
- Schedule time for sex – because of fatigue levels, if you don't, it might not happen![10]
- Communication, compromise, and joint decision-making are predictors for a happy "medical marriage."

Signs of Trouble in Couple Life

When there is trouble in couple life, try to recognize it early. Here are some of the signs:

- Increased quarrelling, particularly over "picky" issues; excessive criticizing or expressions of contempt and disrespect
- Sarcasm and passive-aggressive behaviors
- One or both of you numbing yourself with alcohol, food, drugs, or social media and compulsive use of your phone
- Decreased relating (talking, sex, leisure, play, or vacation time); shutting down emotionally; not sharing thoughts and feelings
- Avoidance behaviors (like over-booking your personal schedule)
- Sexual infidelity or porn addiction
- Fear of having nothing left in common; feeling bored or lonely
- Symptoms of anxiety, depression, or substance abuse in either or both partners
- Increased unresolved anger or anger exhibited passively or violently

TIP

"It may be good to spend a half-hour extra at the hospital tidying stuff up or doing non-clinical work (e.g., research) so that one can be fully devoted to home life at the end of the day.

I encourage my interns and students going home for the holidays to ask their family members and loved ones who are not in medicine what those people want in a doctor, and to reflect on whether that's what my trainees want to be; and to reflect on why or why not."

Dealing with Conflict

Couple life involves conflicts, not only in couples in which one or both are medical residents. The following are some ways of dealing with conflict:

- Label problems in a non-accusatory way.
- Use "we" rather than "you" in discussions.
- Read up on effective assertiveness strategies summarized in the previous chapter.

- Separate internal (couple) issues from external ones (e.g., residency time pressures).
- Listen openly and avoid a defensive stance or attitude.
- Acknowledge that problems may be situational or temporary, but do not pretend they will simply disappear.
- Try to develop mutual support and support from family, friends, and other couples.
- Protect or add time for talking, play, sex, and vacations.
- Investigate options such as residency support groups, marriage retreats, and counseling through your religious community, resident services, wellness office, or the hospital department of psychiatry or psychology.
- If you are looking for a couples' counsellor, ask your residency wellness office or family doctor for a referral.

Models of conflict management at work are described in the next chapter. You'll see that many of those principles can apply to personal relationships as well.

Keeping in Touch with Your Non-medical Friends and Family

Social media (despite some of their professional drawbacks described later) in some ways make it easier to let people know you're thinking of them to chat or make plans for when you are free. You can text, email, Zoom, or Skype when you have a free moment with your smartphone or laptop. Be sure to ask family members and friends how they're doing, as they may be inclined to focus on you and on what they know of residency stress. Let your parents, grandparents, siblings, nieces and nephews, and godchildren know that you love them, and that you haven't changed (or are not letting yourself change) when it comes to them. Don't lose touch with old friends. They knew you before you entered and were changed by the big medical machine.

Should You Medically Treat a Friend or Family Member?[11]

It's not unusual for family members to ask for medical advice or treatment. You should always feel free to firmly say NO, to remind them you're still learning and re-direct them to appropriate care. To avoid potential complications and the boundary blurring inherent in caring for family and friends, here are key questions to ask yourself before medically treating a friend or family member.

- Does my relative's presenting problem fall into my area of expertise? Am I trained and equipped to deal with the problem?
- Am I equipped to deal with a relative's personal or sexual history in an objective way?
- Could I deliver bad news or a poor prognosis honestly if required?
- Am I objective enough not to defensively over-treat, or not to use denial regarding the severity of the problem and undertreat?
- If I help a particular family member medically, what effect will this have on family conflicts, patterns, or dynamics?
- Will my friend or family member do as I suggest (comply with treatment) or take advice less seriously because of the personal connection?
- Will I, through anxiety or a sense of entitlement, interfere with care once my friend or family member is referred to a colleague?
- Am I willing to be held accountable ethically, financially, and medico-legally if my care is judged substandard, incomplete, or inadequate?

Generally, with the exception of absolute emergencies, it is preferable to refer a family member to a colleague, a walk-in clinic or to the ER. Refer to the state or provincial associations and regulators for specific guidelines. They usually discourage or even forbid treating and prescribing for family and close friends.

Parenting

This section is addressed principally to all residents and may be of particular use for female residents; however, their partners and other supportive colleagues who share the responsibilities of parenting should learn to appreciate the importance of the issues and the suggestions they present. Happily, male residents (including gay dads) are increasingly making use of paternity leave as well.

- Let go of perfection! As the famous child psychoanalyst D.W. Winnicott said to parents, you just have to be "good enough."

- During parental leave, keep up to date by reading journals or exploring online resources in your specialty, and consider the rewards of returning to work you do well; do not view your return to residency as the enemy.
- Investigate childcare options (daycare, in-home babysitting, or live-in help).
- Given irregular work schedules and the frequency of childhood illnesses, remember the need for backup; daycare centers tend to have fixed drop-off and pick-up times. When hiring at-home help, interview applicants with your partner and check all references. Look for someone with a flexible attitude towards duties (including cooking and light housekeeping), availability, and hours; procedures on rotations and rounds will make the timing of your arrival home unpredictable. Before you finish your parental leave, arrange to observe how candidates interact with your child. Do not scrimp or rush when hiring a caregiver with whom your child will form a significant bond. You must be satisfied that the relationship will be a good one.
- Remember that a portion of childcare costs may be tax creditable; keep receipts.
- Because residency hours tend to be inflexible, flexibility at home is important. Discuss and agree with your partner on how to share the parenting responsibilities, and try to arrange elective rotations with flexible hours for your return after parental leave.
- Ask your attending physician to finish rounds at a reasonable hour and arrange coverage with another resident for emergencies.
- For family emergencies, recruit other support for your role as a parent among friends, neighbours, family, and in-laws by asking them to help and to visit your child regularly.
- Ask colleagues with children for other strategies.
- Be available on your cellphone for calls or texts so that your caregiver can reach you in emergencies (you will feel more comfortable knowing that you are available), and call home, text, or video-chat every day to say hi to older children.
- Establish regular rituals with your children to ensure you spend quality time with them; when you come home tired at the end of the day, for example, try a five-minute cuddle session. Set a time that follows your own rest period for playing or reading stories.
- Make your off-call time inviolate for your family; plan holiday time in advance, even if you stay home, so that the whole family has something to look forward to.

- Try to do your reading and studying at work because it will be next to impossible to do it at home.
- Make sure your financial paperwork is up to date: disability coverage, health insurance, emergency funds, a budget, life insurance, and your will.
- Stay off your devices and ask your kids to do the same. You can never recover lost family time.
- Avoid a tendency to reproach yourself for not being the ideal parent-physician. You and your family will survive the rigors of residency!

The Single Resident

Medical residents who are single and live alone may be at increased emotional risk because of a lack of support mechanisms; they may become increasingly isolated socially because they have little time or energy to meet new people or to date. They may also be reluctant to acknowledge feelings of loneliness to themselves or others because such feelings are not part of their self-concept as competent professionals. Most of their initial social contacts come from the hospital because they are often in a new city, and their schedule tends to keep them from exploring. For some residents, this is not a happy prospect.

Coping Mechanisms for Single Residents

- Remember your need for support from family and friends throughout residency and avoid the tendency to withdraw socially when fatigued or to deny feelings of loneliness.
- Attend hospital social events, especially at the beginning of residency. You have to start socializing sometime, and you will meet other, non-hospital-affiliated people at these occasions.
- Make it a rule not to talk shop with medical friends at social occasions. Cultivate non-medical friends through sports, hobbies, volunteering, or religious groups.
- If you live alone, check your texts, emails, social media, and other notifications regularly so that you don't miss invitations.
- Order groceries, meal kits, and take-out (as a treat) for delivery with your preferred app,
- Use social media judiciously to date, make friends, and build a community. Remember that posts and pictures are there forever!

(See guidelines in the last chapter.) Do not share explicit photos or comments if you are online dating. Prospective employers will be checking your social media presence (and gaffes).
- Consider joining a health club, a religious group, your building's tenants' association, or special-interest or political groups, realizing, however, that you may have to miss some meetings.
- Make yourself go out socially, even if you're tired.
- Consider living with a compatible medical or non-medical room-mate. Establish clear rules about quiet time (post-call), sharing chores, and so on.
- Schedule vacations with friends well in advance so that you have something to look forward to.
- Request your call nights well in advance so that you can plan your social life (e.g., special concerts and long weekends away).
- Maintain links with family members, even if they live in another city, through visits, frequent video and telephone calls, texting, and email.

Should You Date a Patient?[12]

In today's medico-legal environment, socializing with patients may be ill-advised because of accusations of boundary violations. Most educators and licensing bodies now believe that the answer should always be a firm no.

Here are some previously suggested guidelines from the literature regarding romantic or sexual involvement with a patient. Check with your local medical professional association or licensing body for up-to-date local recommendations.

- Sexual relationships between patients in active (current) treatment and doctors must be avoided.
- A few jurisdictions specify that a period of time (usually one year) should lapse between the date of the last medical follow-up with the patient and the onset of the romantic or sexual contact. However, many regulatory bodies set a standard that sexual or romantic relationships between patients and physicians should never occur. The potential for patient harm is extremely high, and the risk to your own health and ability to practice medicine is equally high. Check your local licensing and registration body or college on current provincial and state regulations.

- Where treatment has involved psychoanalysis, psychotherapy, or extensive counseling, sexual or romantic involvement with the patient should be avoided completely (and is prohibited by many professional associations).
- Special caution should be exercised before a physician starts dating a former patient if the professional context with the patient resulted in the patient's emotional dependency on the doctor or created any other vulnerability that may have impaired the patient's judgment or ability to make free decisions.

Should You Date a Colleague?

As a resident, so much of your time (and life) will revolve around the hospital. It is thus not unusual that residents date other MDs, nurses, or other health care professionals.

Here are some guidelines:

1. Check your hospital and program guidelines around harassment policies, especially if there is a power differential based on your professional roles, rank, or seniority.
2. While at work, professionalism and patient care have to come first. Ask yourself if starting a romantic relationship in the workplace can negatively impact your day-to-day work or capacity to be part of a team.
3. What is the worst-case break-up scenario you can imagine, and how can you avoid it?
4. Be prepared to compartmentalize, that is, separate work matters from romantic ones. Professional differences and conflicts should be separated from your dating relationship. Keep work at work.
5. Respect each other's roles and schedules within the hospital hierarchy.
6. Respect your partner's right to privacy, even if the relationship doesn't work out. Don't gossip about or badmouth an ex. Stalking or vengeful behaviors of any kind will lead to dismissal.
7. Bear in mind that many universities, hospitals, and regulatory bodies have set explicit standards that physicians should never date a learner they are supervising, or dating should only occur once the supervisory period has come to a full conclusion and there is no potential for a power-over dynamic. Be aware of the professional expectations to which you are accountable.

6

Keeping Professional Relationships Healthy

You'll be spending more time with fellow residents, supervisors, and other health professionals than anybody else for the next few years. If you're lucky, you'll be part of a functional, caring team. Your team may start that way and then deteriorate or be dysfunctional from the get-go. As you experience different rotations, you will likely see a range of teams who have their own unique blend of strengths and growth opportunities. These experiences will offer you a chance to study leadership and followership in action and help shape your own leadership style as you transition into practice. This chapter will focus on a number of themes to consider as you lead yourself, develop your own approach to collaborating and communicating with other professional learners and practitioners, and manage unique challenges and conflicts in your workplace.

Impaired team relations usually go undetected by supervisors and are usually not addressed by residents themselves. Sadly, this is associated with increased rates of stress and burnout among team members, and some studies conclude that more than 70 per cent of medical errors are attributed to dysfunctional team environments.[1] For many years, residency curricula focused mainly on the mastery of medical knowledge and practice, neglecting to help professionals develop their talents of collaboration, communication, and leadership. Thankfully, this has changed dramatically in recent decades, with these elements being recognized as critical competencies in both training and continuing professional development. Further, many programs have developed residents as leaders programs, with many residents taking advanced training in management and leadership including additional certifications (i.e.., Certified Physician Executive) and degrees (Master of Arts in Leadership). In North America, both the United States and Canada have national organizations dedicated to the pedagogy, study, and ongoing quality improvement of physician-leaders, such as the American Association for Physician Leadership (physicianleaders.org) and the Canadian Society for Physician Leaders (physicianleaders.ca).

As you consider the themes in this chapter, we'd encourage you to build a habit of evaluating your new teams for potential sources of dysfunction. Patrick Lencioni, a global expert in team functioning, has identified five common dysfunctions of teams: absence of trust, fear of conflict, lack of commitment, avoidance of accountability, and inattention to results.[2] Increasingly, medicine is addressing some of the underlying contributors to these challenges by promoting psychological safety, encouraging vulnerability, teaching effective conflict management skills, enhancing the ability to give and receive feedback, and letting go of the individual ego to allow for the development of a patient-focused, team-driven approach to high quality care.

Perhaps one of the easiest ways to minimize conflict is to spell out roles, duties, and expectations at the start of a rotation (see tables 6.1 and 6.2).

Signs of Trouble among Residents[3,4]

 TIP

Where there is trouble among residents, there is also likely to be

- Increased sarcasm; snarky or petty comments
- Increased petty disagreements over esoteric points
- Formation of factions and bullying or scapegoating
- Increased sick leave, lateness, and longer rounds
- Decreased morale and increased anger, depression, and fatigue in team members
- Decreased attendance and helpfulness in teaching and coverage

"I think it is important to get to know about the other members on a team ASAP. For example, their life before and outside of medicine; their aspirations within medicine; their strengths and weaknesses as they identify them; and what they think about other members of the team (to identify problem spots earlier)."

Table 6.1. Know your roles

Year	Responsibilities	Key Role
Intern(e)*	Initial patient evaluation Routine patient care decisions Organize patients' care	Apprentice Junior teacher
Junior resident	Supervise interns and students Approve diagnosis and management Demonstrate ability other personnel to work with other personnel	Team supervisor Teaching role expected Troubleshooter for minor conflicts Key person for attending physician
Senior resident	Competent team supervision Able to handle complex patients	Senior advisor for junior residents Conflict resolution of more significant issues Competent team teacher
Attending Physician	Assures team can handle essential concepts of medicine Stimulates reading on core materials Reviews charts and orders for completeness	Teacher Mentor Handle major conflicts Supports new graduates in their tradition to practice Leads transformative change

Source: Adapted from Alguire, P., Whelan, G., & Rajput, V. (2009). *The International Medical Graduate's Guide to US Medicine & Residency Training*. ACP Press, Philadelphia.

*"Intern" is a term used in the US, but no longer in Canada.

Table 6.2. Know your responsibilities

Your Responsibilities

1. Admit new patients.
2. Visit and examine all patients on your team each morning.
3. Attend work rounds.
4. Present your case, update chart notes.
5. Teach medical students.
6. Communicate with other care-team members.
7. Order appropriate labs and imaging studies.
8. Order appropriate and early consultations.
9. Attend follow-up and sign-out rounds.
10. Plan discharge and dictate discharge note.
11. Arrange discharge meds.
12. Educate patient regarding discharge instructions and arrange follow-up.

Source: Adapted from Alguire, P., Whelan, G., & Rajput, V. (2009). *The International Medical Graduate's Guide to US Medicine & Residency Training*. ACP Press, Philadelphia.

- Power struggles (e.g., changing others' orders)
- Unfinished work (a risk to patients)
- Emergence or amplification of patterns of challenging behavior – dependency, entitlement, manipulation, passive aggressiveness, impairment

Dealing with Team Troubles

When there is trouble among residents, deal with it using the following strategies:

- Define the problem (e.g., external stress or interpersonal tension).
- Arrange an initial team meeting to share perspectives and be open about the impact of troubles on the health of individuals and the quality of the team's deliverables.
- Keep the discussion "team-" or "we-oriented" rather than accusing people. Talk about behaviors, not personalities.
- If the initial meeting is unsuccessful, recruit the attending physician, senior resident, or a hospital mediator to intervene.
- Lots of models are available to help you develop your skills in sharing and managing team troubles, such as Crucial Conversations for Accountability (www.cruciallearning.com) that have been adapted for health care teams.

PREVENTING CONFLICT

Best of all, however, is trying to prevent conflict in the first place. Both the American[5] and Canadian Medical Associations[6] are focused on creating a culture of wellness in residency and practice, and academic medicine is increasingly studying ways to build a learning environment that promotes resilience and enhances positive leadership outcomes.[7] Here are some tips for preventing conflict among residents:

- Define roles in each new team (see table 6.1).
- Lean into kindness, compassion, and calmness.
- Start with an assumption that people are doing their best.
- Be open to admitting you cannot see all sides to a situation and are open to learning more.
- Focus on being relational rather than transactional.

- Show respect by others by being non-judgmental, listening, minimizing assumptions, and being open and clear with your intent.
- Catch each other doing something right, and thank each other.
- Schedule in time to connect, even if it is a quick lunch or something more structured like a mid-rotation review session.
- Communicate more with your words, eye contact, and tone of voice and less with texts and emails.
- Bring your gift of humor where appropriate.
- Consider arranging occasional dinners or social meetings outside the hospital.
- Commit to developing your leadership skills every day.
- Participate fully in wellness activities when they are offered by bringing your genuine self.
- Role model humanity, healthy boundaries, and professionalism – you won't always get it right and then you can role model self-compassion!

How to Be an Emotionally Intelligent Team Member

Business leaders remind us how to exhibit high EQ on the job:

- Be able to identify and name your feelings.
- Stay curious about coworkers.
- Embrace change.
- Identify your own values, strengths, and weaknesses.
- Don't take things personally or get offended easily!
- Try to read people fairly, but shorten, avoid, and neutralize toxic encounters.
- Don't be a perfectionist and forgive others for their mistakes. Let go of grudges.
- Be assertive – learn how to say no or how to ask for what you need to succeed.
- Be grateful for what you have and be generous with others.
- Challenge negative self-talk when it occurs. Stick with the evidence about how you're really doing. (See above for examples of cognitive errors and distortions that we all make.)

Source: www.entrepreneur.com

Scholars like Dr. Brené Brown have uncovered a lot of evidence supporting the importance of boundaries and vulnerability in leadership. We'd encourage you to watch Dr. Brown's TED Talk, "The power of vulnerability" at www.youtube.com/watch?v=X4Qm9cGRub0. And we absolutely recommend her books, including *Dare to Lead*, *The Power of Vulnerability*, and *Atlas of the Heart* (www.brenebrown.com). Her academic work has had a profound impact on leadership science and how individuals can contribute to transformative change.

Often conflict between residents on different teams or services occurs because of unclear requests or expectations, turf wars, or patient dumping, when one team wants to transfer care. Here are some suggestions for effective consulting and liaison.

Avoiding Turf Wars: 10 Commandments for Effective Consultation[8]

These tips are adapted from a classic paper from the 1980s, but the rules definitely hold up today.

1. Determine the real consultation question – call the consultee when necessary. (Nowadays, you might text that person.)
2. Establish urgency – emergent, urgent, or routine.
3. Look for yourself – closely examine the patient, review old data, and collect new information. Summarize lab and key test data for yourself.
4. Be as brief as appropriate – there is no need to repeat in full detail the data already recorded in the chart. Provide a primary and differential diagnosis.
5. Be specific, brief, and goal-oriented regarding treatment recommendations.
6. Provide a prognosis and contingency plans – anticipate potential problems. Offer a decision tree for problem solving.
7. Honor thy turf – don't take over the patient's care unless requested to do so. Increasingly, specialists and family doctors are sharing care in an ongoing fashion, and this model has proven both efficient and effective.
8. Teach with tact – give references and communicate important information courteously and personally.
9. Provide direct personal contact – introduce yourself to the team members when you arrive on the ward and tell them how to get

in touch with you, especially if recommendations are crucial or potentially controversial.

10. Follow up – provide suggestions for follow-up in the hospital and make suggestions for arranging outpatient care.

The Impaired Colleague

Dealing with a colleague who is impaired poses a serious medical and ethical dilemma for physicians who feel torn between protecting a friend or colleague and protecting the patients that person serves. Further, you may be learning and practicing in a jurisdiction where you are mandated by law to report your suspicion of impairment to a regulatory body, a task that can trigger strong conflictual emotions for all parties.

First, how do you distinguish between stress and impairment? Signs of impairment, addiction, or burnout that exceed the intermittent symptoms of fatigue include the following:

- Unexplained lateness and absence
- Unexplained over-presence in the workplace
- Carelessness, indifference, apathy, and increased mistakes in patient care
- Overt signs of mental health struggles – panic symptoms, tearfulness, irritability, withdrawal, inferences of hopelessness, memory or attentional issues
- Increased preoccupation with marital or professional conflicts
- Decreased efficiency (unfinished work, sometimes despite longer hours)
- Physical deterioration: changes in weight, appearance, or hygiene
- Patient complaints about a physician's attitudes or demeanour

Signs of substance use include the following:

- Personality changes: increased anxiety, mood swings, disinhibition or impulsivity, decreased efficiency, reliability, or decisiveness
- Increased absenteeism
- Increased reports of drug loss, wastage, or spoilage on your ward

- Visible intoxication on the job; alcohol on the breath
- Individual insists on working alone
- Individual insists on wearing long sleeves (to hide needle tracks) or disappears frequently (e.g., to the washroom)
- Inappropriate affect, behavior, comments

You will encounter colleagues living with serious substance use or mental health issues at various times during your career. Your program ought to have a specific training program to help you develop comfort and skill in negotiating the sensitive discussions that you may need to have and complex medico-legal obligations that you may have to face. If not, reach out to your state or provincial physician health program and ask them to provide an in-service session for your residency group. In the interim, there are several ways of handling impaired colleagues.

If they pose *no immediate risk* to themselves or to patients:

- State your positive intent, humility, and concern in a gentle, private, and non-accusatory fashion: "I have a lot of respect for you and your skills as a resident. I'd like to share some observations that I'm having a hard time understanding and would really appreciate your hearing me out and sharing your thoughts. Is that ok?" A non-coercive approach, with the possibility of punishment or coercion in the background, has been shown to be most successful.[9]
- State your personal observations and those of others, so that denial can be reduced.
- Ask for the individual's view of the problem. Gently explore areas of difference, citing the facts you are bringing to the discussion.
- If it is clear that there may be a health issue at play, give the individual information on how to contact residents' professional associations that provide confidential help and ask her to tell you later what she has done. It can be kind and helpful to sit with them while they make a call to a physician health program, and even more so to help them attend their first appointment.
- Explain to the individual that if you do not receive any feedback, or if the problem worsens, you will be obliged to discuss the matter confidentially with your residency director or your regulatory agency (if mandatory in your jurisdiction). In fact, you ought to consider your program director an ally and a resource to help you with

this conversation before you have it.

- Point out that obtaining help does not have to result in suspension, loss of income, or expensive treatment, but that avoidance or delay might.

If they pose *an immediate risk to themselves*: accompany them to the emergency department or call the psychiatrist on duty in your hospital. Do not leave them alone. Consider calling your provincial or state residents' association hotline where available. Check to see if you are obligated to make a report to your licensing body.

If they pose *an immediate risk to patients* (e.g., are intoxicated before a delivery or a shift in the operating room or emergency department): confront them discreetly with their current inability to perform. Offer to cover for them or to find coverage through the chief resident. If they refuse, call your attending physician immediately and inform your residency director. Patient safety is your priority. Once again, check to see if you are obligated to make a report to your licensing body.

Fortunately, physician health programs have developed in most states and provinces in North America, and many hospitals and universities have developed their own services to support their residents and faculty members. You will likely have learned of your local services during your orientation; however, if not, be sure to reach out on your own. There are also conferences such as the AMA-BMA-CMA International Conference on Physician Health, the Federation of State Physician Health Programs, and Physician Health workshops and conferences held frequently around North America and the world. These efforts have been of great value in removing the stigma associated with help-seeking behaviors among members of our profession.[10]

Residents as Teachers: Working with Students

All physicians remember particularly good or bad residents in their training whose actions and characteristics strongly influenced their choice of specialties. Being role models and teachers for students adds a further stress to residents' professional lives. (See chapter 8 for specific teaching strategies and resources.) Often, no one has taught them how to teach, so they must learn by doing and

 TIP

"Senior residents should ask patients: 'Who is the person most responsible for your care? What do you think about them?' I take notes and feed this back to my trainees and attendings."

from observing good and bad examples. Interviews conducted with residents indicate that a good resident teacher

- Provided orientation when we arrived
- Is accessible physically ("answers pages quickly") and emotionally ("doesn't make you feel stupid")
- Is connected and involved
- Has a good sense of humor and a capacity for making learning fun ("not overly anxious or compulsive")
- Is efficient ("keeps rounds short") and punctual
- Is practical ("simplifies things," "avoids esoteric emphasis")
- Frequently gives positive feedback and patiently points out errors in patient care
- Stands up to the attending physician when necessary ("makes own decisions")
- Appears caring and conscientious and has good relations with patients and nurses
- Is fair (e.g., about call duty)
- Is available for one-on-one teaching
- Knows how to handle team or interdisciplinary conflicts
- Does not foster excessive competition
- Is open to feedback
- Delegates responsibility appropriately
- Demonstrates appropriate use of investigations and consultation
- Carries his own share of the workload
- Remembers what it was like to be a student or junior
- Creates a relaxed environment
- Is willing to teach hands-on procedures and assign level-appropriate tasks (Read the classic papers by J.C. Edwards and R.L. Marier, "Clinical teaching for medical residents: roles,"[11] and E.H. Morrison's "Yesterday a learner, today a teacher too."[12])

Research has also generated tips, such as the "five-step micro skills" model of clinical teaching:[13]

1. Get a commitment or "buy-in" – assess the learning needs, encourage the learner to own their learning, create a safe learning environment, prepare for teaching in advance, and have a teaching script for key learning sessions.
2. Probe for supporting evidence – apply Bloom's taxonomy of learning domains (a user-friendly way of understanding how we learn and what learning strategies best suit us for different situations) and start with "what" questions long before "why" and "how" questions.
3. Teach general rules – focused learning points, emphasizing the exact points to be taken away from the learning space.
4. Reinforce what is done right – catch people doing something right, especially when they are applying new learning from a teaching session.
5. Correct mistakes – build psychological safety and provide constructive feedback, being mindful of the value to praising in public and criticism in private.

Remember to take your role as teacher seriously. Queen's University in Canada has produced guidelines for ethical teaching, excerpted below, which will help you reflect on your role as a teacher and may help launch discussion among residents and attending staff.[14] Further, many medical organizations in the United States, such as the Association of American Medical Colleges, and the Society of Teachers of Family Medicine, have online programs to help residents develop their skills as teachers. If your program doesn't have a specific program focused on this competency, consider reaching out to one of the national programs to enhance your skills.

If you identify that a student is struggling, it is best to identify them early and strategize discreetly with your attending staff and educational consultants if available at your hospital.[15]

Guide to the Ethical Behavior of Clinical Teachers

The following are principles of ethical behavior for all clinical teachers, including those who may not be engaged directly in clinical practice.

1. Consider first the well-being of the patient.
2. Honor your profession and its traditions.
3. Recognize your limitations and the special skills of others in the prevention and treatment of disease.
4. Protect the patient's secrets (confidences).
5. Teach and be taught.
6. Remember that integrity and professional ability should be your best advertisement.
7. Be responsible in setting a value on your services.

Table 6.3. **An example of regulatory approaches to professional responsibilities in medical education: the College of Physicians and Surgeons of Ontario's policy on professional responsibility in medical education.[16] Selected elements include the following:**

- MRPs (Most Responsible Persons) and/or supervisors must provide appropriate supervision to postgraduate trainees.
- Postgraduate trainees must only take on clinical responsibility in a graduated manner, proportionate with their abilities, although never completely independent of appropriate supervision.
- MRPs and/or supervisors must ensure that they are identified and available to assist medical students and/or postgraduate trainees when they are not directly supervising them (i.e., in the same room) or if unavailable, they must ensure that an appropriate alternative supervisor is available and has agreed to provide supervision.
- In situations where medical students or postgraduate trainees are involved in patient care solely for their own education (e.g., observation, examinations unrelated to the provision of patient care, etc.), physicians responsible for providing that care must ensure consent to medical student or postgraduate trainee participation is obtained, either by obtaining consent themselves or, where appropriate, by another member of the health care team (including the medical student or postgraduate trainee involved).
- MRPs and supervisors must demonstrate a model of compassionate and ethical care while educating and training medical students and postgraduate trainees.
- MRPs, supervisors, and postgraduate trainees must not engage in disruptive behavior that interferes with or is likely to interfere with quality health care delivery or quality medical education (e.g., the use of inappropriate words, actions, or inactions that interfere with a physician's ability to function well with others).
- Physicians (including MRPs, supervisors, and postgraduate trainees) involved in medical education and/or training must not engage in violence, harassment (including intimidation) or discrimination (e.g., racism, transphobia, sexism) against medical students and/or postgraduate trainees.
- MRPs and supervisors must not enter into a sexual relationship with a medical student and/or postgraduate trainee while responsible for mentoring, teaching, supervising or evaluating the medical student and/or postgraduate trainee; or enter into a relationship with a medical student and/or postgraduate trainee that could present a risk of bias, coercion, or actual or perceived conflict of interest, while responsible for mentoring, teaching, supervising or evaluating the medical student and/or postgraduate trainee.

The Hotseat
by Richard M. Berlin[17]

I swear by Apollo the physician, and Aesculapius, and Hygeia and
Panacea, and all the gods and goddesses ... to reckon him who
taught me this Art equally clear to me as my parents ...

- From the Hippocratic Oath
0700 and thirty resident collapse
like shipwreck survivors.
after 24 sleepless hours
of children renounced by Hygeia,
our eyes are drowned in shadow.
A few nod before he enters
ruddy-faced and rested,
White coat starched and spotless:
Dr. Harry, Chief of the Mecca,
diagnostic wizard, the power
Who can crush careers with a word.
He slaps a chest film on the light box
and hooks a bleary intern:
Tell me, doctor,
What is the shape of this child's ears?
Fifteen seconds, thirty, a minute of silence,
sweat weeps from the intern's forehead
Harry scorches him with questions
and solves the riddle like Aesculpaius,
even kneads the intern's shoulders
as if soothing a bruise.
We curse him all day, stay awake
all night to earn his love,
and when we descend to Radiology
with our own tame students, we slap
a film on the light box and raise
their first beads of sweat.

Being a Team Player

Good relationships with nursing and other staff including physicians'
assistants, midwives, ward clerks, pharmacists, social workers, OTs/

PTs and emergency medical technicians can make or break a residency experience, given a resident's high daily level of contact with them. The resident who feels threatened by competent nurses or physicians' assistants, and who feels superior or is sexist in interactions with others will be labeled early in training and will find it difficult to achieve the level of teamwork and camaraderie needed in the modern treating context.

To facilitate a good working relationship with nursing and other professional staff, do the following:

- Introduce yourself to all the team members on your service when you begin to work there. If you find it congenial, give them permission to use your first name. Remember their names as well.
- Treat regulated and non-regulated health professionals with the same degree of respect. Everyone on the team, such as nurses, respiratory technicians, social workers, switchboard operators, housekeeping and janitorial staff, psychologists, health records staff, ward clerks, and so on. You're all part of the same team and ought to treat each other with dignity, respect, and collegiality.
- Be curious and seek their opinions; take their suggestions seriously. They may know the patient in very different ways than you do.
- Respect ward protocol and routines about orders, scheduling tests, and so on.
- Admit errors, including your own, and point out errors made by others in a private, non-accusatory, non-humiliating way. Always make it about improving patient care and safety, not individual egos.
- Do not show off or pull rank. Remember, you are working with fellow professionals.
- Do not bluff if you do not know something. Say that you will find out.
- Use appropriate humor. Avoid gendered or flirtatious remarks and behavior.
- Try to develop a rapport with the head nurse, who may be a source of teaching and resource information and support.
- Be courteous and polite; say please and thank you.
- Keep disputes patient-oriented; do not let them become personal.
- Request inter-professional education seminars to enhance shared learning and teamwork. Try to find out more about what your colleagues believe and actually do in their work lives.

- Communicate clearly.
- Provide information that is adequate and timely.
- Review notes from other team members before expressing your opinion.
- Document your communication with colleagues from other disciplines.
- The Canadian Medical Protective Association has an excellent open-source resource on team communication that is worth checking out.[18]

Beyond a discussion of "collegial relationships," there is an increasing emphasis on interprofessional education, which encompasses optimal communication, collaboration and conflict management among multiple health care professions and within teams. A detailed schematic framework for such learning is provided at www.ipe.utoronto.ca.

What Is Interprofessional Education?

The World Health Organization in 2010 defined interprofessional education as follows: "Interprofessional education occurs when students from two or more professions learn about, from, and with each other to enable effective collaboration and improve health outcomes." Traditionally, medical students and residents have received teaching from their own discipline/profession, in order to master a specific body of shared medical knowledge, skills, and modes of conduct. Nowadays, almost all clinical settings involve teamwork among several professions. Students from various professions now learn together as a team. This allows for members to understand the core principles and concepts of each clinical discipline and to be familiar with the language and mindsets of those disciplines (source: www.ipe.utoronto.ca).

Successful teamwork involves finding out what our colleagues believe, value, and do in their approach to patient care. A resident with good interprofessional skills can communicate clearly, effectively, and fairly, advocate for both patients and colleagues, recognize conflict and power differentials, and analyze personal values and professional beliefs (and entitlements) in an ongoing fashion.

The following question can be helpful in understanding and improving team and group interactions during case conferences, team interventions, seminars, and over the duration of specific rotations.

1. What professions are represented in this group?

2. How were different perspectives, communication styles, and approaches represented in this rotation or educational seminar?

 TIP

"I have found it very effective to meet with attendings before I work with them to get a sense of their styles, how they perceive their roles and the role of my team, and to make my own goals for the rotation clear."

3. How does your professional training and/ or professional lens inform your views and responses?

4. What similarities or differences have you observed among the different professions you have collaborated with? How do these relate to your own profession's values and roles in patient and client care?

5. How does the content in this discussion, case conference, or seminar reflect (or downplay) teamwork?

6. How can the different skill sets discussed be brought together to enhance the team response to patient care?

7. What have you learned and how well will this form your future work with colleagues of different disciplines?

8. Was the communication appropriate and equitable with respect to the information being exchanged by those present?

9. How well did your group members listen to each other?

10. How did you and others encourage collaboration as the group responded to new learning experiences? Who got left out?

Attending Physicians and Staff

Residents are in a unique and sometimes awkward position because they are hospital employees, student apprentices, and responsible physicians all at the same time. The attending physician is both a type of boss who does not pay or hire residents and a teacher who evaluates residents' performance and has considerable power over their future. Overall, clinical skills, personality, and teaching ability are what residents identify as factors in selecting a staff physician as a role model. Medical educators stress that five types of issues affect the relationship between supervisor and trainee: (1) compatibility of goals, (2) communication and feedback, (3) power and rivalry, (4) support and collegiality, and (5) level of expertise of both parties.[19] As residents' hours have become regulated, some staff doctors have grown resentful, assuming that young doctors aren't as dedicated or

TIP

"As a general rule, I think criticism should be private and praise should be public, and team members should NEVER be criticized in front of a patient."

are just in it for the lifestyle. Thus, an intergenerational clash of expectations can emerge. Attending physicians vary in their approaches, just as senior residents do; some have an interest in teaching and interacting with their learners, whereas others are remote or absent, and merely bill for residents' services. The concept of "medical student abuse" (either emotional or physical and sexual) applies equally to residents, who are particularly vulnerable because they need good evaluations to finish their training.

Signs of Trouble in the Resident–Attending Physician Relationship

The following are signs that there is trouble in the relationship between the medical resident and the attending physician:

Behaviors by Supervisors and Attending Physicians

- Sarcasm, harsh or hurtful criticism, verbal abuse, scapegoating (the target is usually a resident, who may complain covertly)
- Lack of positive feedback
- Racist, sexist, homophobic or transphobic, or other negative personal remarks directed at a resident
- Physical abuse (e.g., scalpel throwing, sexual advances)
- Decreased availability of the attending physician (late or absent for supervision, teaching, or rounds)
- The silent treatment, where a resident is ignored or bypassed in communications

Behaviors by Residents

- Covering up attending physician's mistakes or unethical behavior

- Increased resident anxiety in the context of supervision by the attending physician
- Perception of the attending physician as incompetent, impaired, or unjust
- Feeling that evaluations are unfair
- Ceasing to care about work ("decathecting") because of an inability to please the attending physician

The following are signs of unprofessionalism in colleagues, as identified by the American Board of Internal Medicine (www.abim.org):

- Unmet professional responsibility
- Needs continual reminders about fulfilling responsibilities to patients and to other health care professionals
- Cannot be relied on to complete tasks
- Misrepresents or falsifies actions or information; for example, regarding patients, laboratory tests, research data
- Lack of effort towards self-improvement and adaptability
- Is resistant or defensive in accepting criticism
- Remains unaware of own inadequacies
- Resists considering or making changes
- Does not accept responsibility for errors or failure
- Is overly critical or verbally abusive during times of stress
- Demonstrates arrogance
- Diminished relationships with patients and families
- Lacks empathy and is often insensitive to patients' needs, feelings, and wishes or to those of the family
- Lacks rapport with patients and families
- Displays inadequate commitment to honoring the wishes and wants of the patient
- Diminished relationships with health care professionals
- Demonstrates inability to function within a health care team
- Lacks sensitivity to the needs, feelings, and wishes of the health care team

In fact, disruptive physician behavior has become an increasingly studied phenomena[20] with specific assessment and intervention programs being developed across North America.

DEALING WITH UNPROFESSIONAL OR DISRUPTIVE BEHAVIOR BY RESIDENTS OR FACULTY

- Try to express your concerns privately.
- If you need to discuss your concerns with others, confide carefully and selectively to avoid gossip.
- Do not expose confidential issues in rounds or in front of colleagues.
- If you are acutely upset, excuse yourself briefly. Retain your composure, dignity, and professionalism. Do not retaliate and thereby lose your credibility.
- Document incidents, noting witnesses if necessary.
- Do not sign an evaluation that you think is unfair. If you disagree with it, appeal the evaluation according to established procedures.
- If you are injured or sexually harassed, check your contract and report the incident to the residency program director and consider legal action.
- If these measures do not resolve the problem, consult the residency program director about mediation or change of service or hospital.
- If there is still no resolution, contact the following (according to the increasing severity of the problem): the university department head or director of postgraduate education; the university harassment officer; the resident union lawyer; or the resident representative committees at the Royal College of Physicians and Surgeons of Canada, or the American Medical Association in the United States.
- Model professional behavior yourself when introducing the issue.
- Know the policies at your school, program, and institution.
- Gather evidence and data.
- Know when you're in over your head – contact your resident association for advice.
- Contact your state or provincial resident or postgraduate officer, who will have guidelines on dealing with workplace intimidation, harassment, and abuse.

Humanism and Patient-Centered Care: How to Be a Mindful, Caring Doctor

A critique of post-modern medicine has been that evidence-based medicine favours population health, universal trends, and commonalities, rather than the uniqueness of a patient's experience of illness and the perceptions of his or her family members. This can lead to a physician-centered, hospital-centered, and disease-centered approach to illness and does not assist the patient with making meaning of their experiences with suffering.

Optimal Patient Care

The Institute of Medicine published *Crossing the Quality Chasm: A New Health System for the 21st Century*,[21] with the goal of framing the emerging discussions on quality health care. Care should encompass the following aims and features:

1. Safe – care should be as safe for patients and health care facilities as in their homes.
2. Effective – the science and evidence behind health care should be applied and service standards maintained in the delivery of care.
3. Efficient – caring service should be cost-effective, and waste of equipment, supplies, ideas, and energy should be removed from the system.
4. Timely – patient should experience no waits or delays in receiving care and service
5. Equitable – unequal treatment should be of the past. Disparity in care should be eradicated regardless of gender, ethnicity, race, geographic location, and socio-economic status.
6. Patient-centered – the system of care should evolve around the patient, respect patient preferences, and put the patient in control.

Patient-centered care can be achieved by

1. Exploring the patient's reason for visit, their concerns, and need for supportive information

2. Providing an integrated understanding of the patient's world, understanding that there is a whole person with emotional needs and life issues, changes, and losses
3. Finding common ground of what the problem is and mutually agreeing on management
4. Enhancing prevention and health promotion and the continuing relationship between the patient, the doctor, and the patient's family and supports.

Source: www.nam.edu

In keeping with the goals of patient-centered care, "medical humanism" can be defined as the fostering of relationships with patients that are empathic and compassionate, and include behaviors and attitudes that are sensitive to the person's values, autonomy, dignity, and cultural and ethnic backgrounds. The medical humanism movement seeks to understand the patient as a complete person with individual values, goals, and preferences with respect to clinical care and definitions of wellness.

The Arnold P. Gold Foundation (www.gold-foundation.org/resources) funds and promotes initiatives for improving patient care, and states that "Humanism in healthcare is characterized by a respectful and compassionate relationship between physicians, as well as all other members of the healthcare team, and their patients." It reflects attitudes and behaviors that are sensitive to the values in the cultural and ethnic backgrounds of others. The humanistic health care professional demonstrates the following attributes as summarized by the acronym IECARES, as found on the Foundation's website:

- Integrity – the congruence between expressed values and behavior
- Excellence and clinical expertise
- Compassion – the awareness and acknowledgment of the suffering of another
- Altruism – the capacity to put the needs and interests of another before your own
- Respect – the regard for the autonomy and values of another person
- Empathy – the ability to place oneself in another situation, i.e., doctor as patient
- Service – the sharing of one's time and resources with those in need, giving beyond what is required[22]

Although the relationship with the patient has always been central to medicine, it may be the most neglected area of learning in residency training. Nowadays most residents estimate that they spend only 20 per cent of their time actually interacting with real patients. During training, personal discomfort, fatigue, time pressures, and team conflicts often erode this relationship to the point where residents become numb to the emotional needs of patients. This increased emotional buffering or distancing from patients and their suffering is the least adaptive and most damaging strategy used by residents to decrease personal levels of stress. It is a form of denial that precludes a unique possibility for supervised learning and for exploration of painful issues in care. Although technical medical care may be provided, no holistic healing takes place.

The growing emphasis on profit-driven, managed, and high-tech care may prevent residents from developing primary care, real-world skills, from being exposed to a wide range of socioeconomic and health-related problems, and from providing continuity of care.

Physicians who stop caring have low career satisfaction levels, more lawsuits, and difficulty establishing practices. What is more insidious and disturbing is that when empathy disappears from work it also disappears from life at home with one's partner, children, and friends.

Some patients are indeed difficult, argumentative, demanding, or angry. Others are so ill or upsetting to our wish to cure that we avoid them. Some reawaken our conflicts with parents and siblings and leave us bewildered at our response. Others simply happen to be number 32 of 70 in a busy emergency shift. Yet residents who do not learn to maintain empathy in the face of such stress compromise their present and future ability to truly heal their patients.

Aim to learn as much as you can about patient and family-centered care, the key concepts for which are dignity and respect, information sharing, participation, and collaboration in shared decision-making.[23] You can find an excellent resource at the Institute for Family-Centered Care (www.ipfcc.org).

Green Dress

I wore my green dress because it was still a beautiful July day, and if she had opened the blinds, she too would have seen the sun outside.

I was completely lost in the light blue of my office, reading in "Madness and Civilization" about the ship that sailed along the shore carrying all the "insane," when my pager went off. It was the first week of residency and C-L service was still quite slow.

I nervously pressed the hand-sanitizer on the wall outside her door so many times that large amount of gooey liquid filled my palm and dripped on my shoes. The sharp smell made me sneeze and my hands were now so greasy that I almost dropped my black clipboard with pages of instructions about doing a psychiatric interview. I held it close to my chest like a holy book as I stepped into the room.

"You must be Jean! I'm from Psychiatry," I said enthusiastically, still rubbing my hands. The blinds were shut, and it took my eyes a few seconds to adjust to the darkness. Jean was lying under the white sheets with her eyes closed. She did not move.

"Your team has asked us to see you. They have concerns about you refusing treatment, and I'd like to ask you a few questions, if that's okay?"

She opened one eye and inspected me up and down, but then looked away without a word. Her hair was purple and cut really short. I noticed a plastic bag on the chair that once held her belongings but now was torn, and her clothes were falling out.

"I want to start by asking you about yourself," I continued quite unsure about how to proceed.

Five minutes later, Jean was walking down the hallway in hospital booties dragging her IV-pole, with two nurses and me running after her. The second hospital gown she wore to cover the crack of the first one, flapped behind her like broken sails. She was swearing loudly at the walls but suddenly stopped and turned towards the nurses.

"And by the way," she shouted pointing at me, "tell Dr. Wilson that I don't need to see the damn psychiatrist, especially not the green lady from the beach!"

And she steered towards the elevators.

The following are signs of trouble in a resident's relationship with their patients:

- Lack of emotional response to tragedy; rote functioning without affect

- Increased anger towards patients manifested by rudeness, infantilization, and racist, sexist, ageist, or other disparaging or attempted humorous remarks
- Identification of patients by body part, disease, or room number. Trivializing their chosen identity
- Tendency to blame patients for illnesses or for physician-patient stalemates
- Rushed or perfunctory interviews; failure to obtain personal and social histories of patients
- Fantasies of a "problem patient" dying or moving away
- Increased authoritarian style or attempt to force treatment options or religious views on patients
- Ignoring the patient's need for cultural safety
- Denial of a patient's illness or pathological features despite evidence
- Emotional over-involvement or over-identification with patients (including sexual behavior; see guidelines regarding boundary violations)
- Avoidance behavior with certain patients
- Hiding behind the anonymity of rounds (i.e., not providing your name to the patient)
- Increased tendency to refer patients on, rather than deal with difficulties directly
- Deadnaming patients (i.e., using the name used prior to a gender transition) or using incorrect pronouns

---

AVOIDING BOUNDARY VIOLATIONS[24,25]

The following guidelines suggest approaches for avoiding complaints of sexual misconduct and preventing boundary violations. Read your licensing body or college disciplinary actions (online or in published bulletins) for sobering lessons on how even good doctors can fall down the "slippery slope" when they ignore or flout appropriate boundaries:

1. Avoid any behavior, gestures, or expressions that may be seductive or sexually demeaning to a patient.
2. Show sensitivity and respect for the patient's privacy and comfort at all times:

- Do not watch a patient dress or undress.
- Provide privacy and appropriate covers and gowns.
- Knock before entering the room.

3. Obtain permission to do intimate examinations, offer explanations as to the necessity of the examination, and answer anticipated questions concerning the examination. Do not examine a body part irrelevant to the required examination (i.e., a breast exam in an asthma check).
4. Use gloves when examining sensitive body parts.
5. Do not make sexualized comments about a patient's body or clothing.
6. Do not make sexualized or sexually demeaning comments to a patient.
7. Do not criticize a patient's sexual or gender orientation.
8. Do not ask or make comments about potential sexual performance except where the examination or consultation is pertinent to the issue of sexual function or dysfunction.
9. Do not ask details of sexual history or sexual likes and dislikes unless related to the purpose of the consultation or examination.
10. Do not request a date with a patient.
11. Do not kiss or hug a patient. Do offer appropriate supportive contact (like touching a patient's arm) when warranted and then only with consent.
12. Do not engage in any contact that is sexual (from touching to intercourse).
13. Do not talk about your own sexual preferences, fantasies, problems, activities, or performance.
14. Learn to detect and deflect seductive patients and to control the therapeutic setting.
15. Maintain good records that document the necessity for intimate examinations or questions of a sexual nature as well as the pertinent positive or negative clinical findings.
16. Patients have the right to have a third party present during internal/intimate examinations if they wish, with the exception of life-threatening emergencies. Document the name of this person. In some cases, the physician will be able to provide this third party. In cases where the physician is unable to provide such a person, patients should be informed that they may bring a person of their choosing with them. In non-emergency situations, physicians have the right to

insist that a third party be present during internal/intimate examinations, and to refuse to conduct this examination if the patient refuses consent for a third party to be in the room.

17. Work on enhancing your skills and comfort levels when taking a sexual history.

For an excellent review, see the BASHH National guidelines for consultations requiring sexual history taking.[26]

Avoiding and Dealing with Doctor–Patient Communication Problems[27]

- Empathy can be nurtured as well as compromised. Recognize under what circumstances it might be absent in you (e.g., overbooked clinics), and try to change what you can.[28] A review article in *JAMA* tracked mood states, interpersonal reactivity, and empathy over the internship year and demonstrated a decline in trainee empathy over that period.[29] Don't let this happen to you.
- Recognize whether patients of a certain age or type repeatedly produce intense feelings in you (e.g., anger, sexual attraction, or sorrow), and try to determine whether they have hit a nerve in you ("counter-transference") or whether they are projecting their feelings on to you to give you a taste of their negative experience.
- Pay more attention to the patient's experience and less to your own performance anxiety, which will diminish with clinical experience.
- Distinguish your or your patient's anger at the system from your anger with each other, so that it does not contaminate your interaction. Agreeing with a patient's upset will make you an ally rather than an adversary and may defuse conflict. Don't take it personally!
- Keep a record or journal of your emotional responses to key residency developmental or initiation issues – for example, the first death of a patient (see below), first delivery, first bearing of bad news – and refer to it when you are feeling emotionally numb.
- Ask your program about onsite resources for enhancing interviewing and communication skills (coaching, workshops, electives).

- Consider what a culturally sensitive, anti-oppressive assessment might look like.

For a good resource, see www.researchgate.net/publication/301321141 _Anti-oppressive_Approach_to_Assessment.

DELIVERING BAD NEWS TO PATIENTS[30]

One of the most stressful aspects of clinical care is revealing a bad prognosis to a patient. Here are some strategies for delivering bad news:

- Bad news is best delivered when you have time for the patient.
- Make sure that you and the patient are reasonably comfortable; sit down. A pleasant room and private setting are extremely helpful.
- Watch patients for all-important nonverbal cues as to how they are listening to you. Be prepared for strong emotions and acknowledge them.
- Straightforwardness and lack of prevarication are essential. Be clear, honest.
- Keep medical terms to a minimum.
- Give patients the chance to be prepared for what you say: give them a warning that you are about to tell them something very difficult.
- Patients must be given time to express their fears and worries.
- Offer any hope that is realistic. They will need to understand the news in their own terms and realize how it is likely to affect their future.
- Be well prepared for the session: try to have a plan for disclosure before the interview, be as informed as possible about the patient's problem, and know how to get answers for the patient if you cannot answer her questions. Know what the patient needs to do next.
- Be available and schedule a follow-up session even if you are about to refer the patient to a specialist. Patients will appreciate your ongoing concern.
- Do not be surprised if you are more worked up about the news than the patient is. Patients can show true resilience or complete denial in the face of seemingly disastrous news.
- Don't take calls, texts, or pages during this discussion.

The Wall

Patient after patient, note after note. Patients were shuttled in and out of the clinic rooms in 15-minute intervals. My brain had become lulled into a monotony of patients with knee and hip pain. I filled out templated notes on each patient. When did the pain begin? How would you rate your pain on a scale of one to ten?

The next patient was new to the clinic. I introduced myself and proceeded with my objective questions, thinking more of my note and the next patients I had to see than of the person in front of me. Ms. Z was 58 years old. She had severe end-stage osteoarthritis in her knees with remarkable deformities. I inquired about what she had tried for her knee pain. "No one ever told me to try physical therapy!" I took a step back and tried to explain the usual sequence of therapies that are recommended prior to having surgery. Within moments, she burst into tears. And my attitude of monotonous ambivalence disintegrated. I sat forward and placed a hand on her knee.

She explained that she lives alone and has no social support. Her knee pain has been unbearable, and she fears that she may not be able to support herself financially any longer. It took a split second of vulnerability to break down my wall, the wall that serves to protect my heart from the daily emotional stress of being a physician. This was the reminder that I desperately needed mid-way through my intern year: the crucial reminder of why I went into medicine.

Other Tips to Enhance Communication with Your Patient

- Do not expect the same level of stoicism from patients that you expect from yourself. Learn to recognize cultural and personality and more traditional sex-related differences in the expression of pain, anger, and grief.
- Make a point of chatting with your patients, and try to learn at least one fact about their lives that will make them more human to you (e.g., the man with dementia on 8D used to be a composer).
- Let positive counter-transference happen consciously and selectively but be aware of it (e.g., "That old lady in the emergency department hallway could be my grandmother").
- Remember your own experiences of illness, loss, discomfort, and vulnerability. These may differ from those of your patients, but the memory will help to link you in understanding.

- Do not be afraid to let your patients express their emotions. If you are afraid, find out why in therapy, in supervision, or in a resident support or Balint-style group rather than refer the patients for psychiatric treatment. Only when appropriate, consider acknowledging your feelings to your patient (e.g., "I am tired today because I was on duty all night").
- Get to know your patient's family when possible and try to be available for brief education sessions. This may help your patient cooperate with your treatment, which will diminish your workload.
- Identify your patients' psychosocial needs. After you have done the groundwork, you may want to recruit help from the departments of psychology or psychiatry, social work, or chaplaincy. But do not call them in simply because you do not want to deal with these needs. You must not dilute your responsibility to your patients.
- Study your referral patterns to see whether you avoid certain problems with patients.
- Keep informed about key psychosocial issues, which often manifest themselves in patients if you take the trouble to ask.
- Be sensitive to the patient's feelings of being undressed or exposed physically.
- Knock before entering a room.
- Maintain good eye contact with the patient; avoid taking excessive notes.
- Ask how the patient would like to be addressed (first name or title), and make sure he or she knows your name.
- Try to sit or stand at the same level as the patient so as not to be intimidating.
- If you have an accent or speech difference, speak slowly.
- Increase cross-cultural awareness by asking about your patient's background, learning new language skills, and reading. Where appropriate, use a professional translator or, if necessary, a family member. (Remember that a family member may edit, censor, or under-report certain information that they find embarrassing.)
- For a good discussion of the differences between "cultural sensitivity" and "cultural safety," go to www.equityhealthj.biomedcentral.com/articles/10.1186/s12939-019-1082-3.
- Don't get angry about non-compliance with medication or treatment.
- Find out from your local licensing body about how to handle a patient's request to tape your interaction with their cell phone.

- Explore the patient's fears, misconceptions, side-effects, and financial worries (re: drug cost) instead.
- All non-compliance has a differential diagnosis, just like the illness you're treating!
- Use open-ended questions, and don't interrupt. (The average doctor interrupts a patient within eighteen seconds!)
- Ask the patient about fantasies ("What do you think it is?"), feelings, fears, and expectations about the illness. Find out what has changed in their functioning and what their expectations of you are.
- Make your explanations short, clear, and concise. Don't use jargon. Provide printed material if available.
- Negotiate, rather than dictate, a management and treatment plan with the patient, as an authoritarian stance may lower compliance.
- Offer the patient and her family self-help group information for added support. See www.selfhelpgroups.org.
- Try to follow your patients right through their illnesses. You'll learn much more through offering continuity of care in both the inpatient and outpatient settings.
- Be open to a patient's wish to explore alternative forms of healing (like acupuncture or herbal medicine) as an adjunct to conventional care if it enhances his sense of control and self-care. Be mindful of what the standards and guidelines are in your jurisdiction with respect to complementary and alternative medicine, too. Check out the National Center for Complementary and Alternative Health website at www.nccih.nih.gov/health/whatiscam.
- Ensure privacy.
- For some physicians, specialized education in boundaries, communication, and professionalism are needed to enhance skills and prevent harm. Many organizations offer highly interactive programs, such as pbieducation.com, cpepdoc.org, CMPA, as well as many local hospital and university-based workshops and courses.
- Watch your language! Words like addict, alcoholic, handicapped, morbidly obese, "non-compliant," or reducing the person to their diagnosis (i.e., "the diabetic in room 3") are all obsolete. Seek out resources on empathic, person-centered language that cover the following:
  - Inclusive language in media
  - Sexual and gender identity terminology
  - Pronouns matter: know your gender pronouns

- Respectful disability language
- Putting people first in obesity

- Review rules for the use of social media, email, and other technologies in chapter 11.
- Chapter 8 provides tip on developing narrative competence – the ability to work with the stories your patients bring.

Advocacy and Social Justice

When considering humanistic and patient-centered health care more deeply, the concept of social justice should be kept at the forefront in terms of individual care, but also as linked to the care of vulnerable, stigmatized, or under-served populations in the context of public health. Social justice is based on the concepts of human rights and equity. Under social justice, all groups and individuals are entitled equally to important rights, such as health protection and minimal standards of income. The goal of public health is to minimize preventable death and disability for all.

Our contemporary understanding of social justice has been impacted by the 1948 United Nation's Universal Declaration of Human Rights, which underscores the conditions needed for social justice. These include equal liberties and opportunities, fair distribution of resources, and support for people's dignity and self-respect.

Residents are invited to review the social determinants of health to examine inequities in access to health care. For example, ask yourself the following questions: How does socio-economic status affect my patient's treatment options and treatment adherence? How does my institution address the issues of marginalized people? Where in my training am I exposed to education around social justice and the social determinants of health? How is accessibility to care contingent on a person's civil rights? How are specific health interventions realigned in specific populations, and what might their differential effects be? How are health care resources allocated and payment of new treatments determined? How can communication strategies be improved to reach populations that have been historically stigmatized, oppressed, or marginalized? Medical culture has been shaped by the same power differentials and inequities as society at large.

Oppression can be inter-personal (person to person), systemic/institutional, or internalized (as in internalized homophobia). We all have "implicit biases," which are attitudes or stereotypes that affect our understanding, actions, and decisions in an unconscious manner. These are activated involuntarily, without awareness or intentional control, and they can be either positive (or seemingly benevolent in our own minds) or negative. We are ALL susceptible.

An anti-oppressive framework is the method and process in which we understand how systems of oppression such as colonialism, racism, sexism, homophobia, transphobia, classism, geopolitics, and ableism can result in individual discriminatory actions and structural/systemic inequalities for certain groups in society at large and in health care settings. This emphasis in medical education is relatively recent, and we invite you to learn more about it and ask for updated training from your hospital, program, or medical school.

For a thoughtful review of how to incorporate anti-oppression principles into your patient interactions, go to www.healthcareexcellence.ca /en/what-we-do/all-programs/equity-diversity-and-inclusion-virtual -learning-exchange/2022-01-13-equity-diversity-inclusivity.

An excellent module exploring key principles as related to diversity, equity, and inclusion was created by the Internal Medicine Resident Interest Group in Social Advocacy at the University of Toronto; it is regularly updated. Its authors have formulated a living document that invites critique, comments, and suggestions. It (along with numerous other DEI resources) can be found at www.womenscollegehospital.ca/wp-content /uploads/2022/07/Guidelines-for-Inclusivity-abridged-03.8.2022-SM -with-links.pdf.

Your university and postgraduate office will likely have a diversity and equity office as well as working groups inviting resident participation. Become a part of this vital discussion as an impetus for educational and policy change at your institution. This will enhance safety for you as a resident from a racialized or other minority group but will also result in a more culturally sensitive, fully inclusive approach to teamwork and care for all patients.

One of the pioneers in working on issues of public health and social justice (broadly speaking) in medical education is Dr. Martin Donohoe. His classic textbook *Public Health and Social Justice*, a Jossey-Bass Reader, can still be found on the public health and social justice website (www .publichealthandsocialjustice.org). This site also contains terrific, historic links to full curricula, publications, resources, and video tapes, which can be used for group discussion.

What about My Patient's Mental Health?[31]

One of the real downsides of hospital-based training, endless rotations, and a lack of exposure to continuity of care is that residents come to see their patients' suffering or onset of mental distress as "somebody else's problem." Many order a "psych consult" or page the social worker if the patient even appears troubled or upset.

More commonly, residents and fellows learn to refer out if a patient has any psychiatric illness history at all. Psychiatric illnesses are sometimes seen as "not real illnesses," or not worthy of spending time on, or seen as "encumbrances" that complicate "real" medical care. This suggests a split between mind, brain, and body, which is clearly archaic and will prevent you from becoming a holistic, humanistic physician who can help your patients over time, no matter what challenges emerge.

US statistics suggest that 18.6 per cent of all US adults have a mental, behavioral, or emotional disorder (excluding developmental and substance abuse disorders), and 4.1 per cent of all US adults have a serious mental illness, which results in serious functional impairment. One in five children either currently or at some point during their life has had a seriously debilitating mental disorder. (Source: National Institute of Mental Health, www.nimh.nih.gov).[32]

The link between physical and mental health is becoming increasingly clear. Patients who have had an MI accompanied by depression have an increased mortality risk of 3 per cent to 17 per cent. A cancer patient with untreated depression increases his mortality risk by 39 per cent. Individuals who are diagnosed with schizophrenia have a 50 per cent greater risk of dying from cancer. A young individual with depression has a 20 per cent greater risk of Type II Diabetes.

The idea that a hospital or outpatient practice can separate out mental illness from ongoing medical care is unrealistic and misguided.

We need to identify mental illness early, prevent it where possible, destigmatize it, provide resources, and optimize the care of ALL of our patients. Teamwork is key and a flexible and accessible model of shared care or collaborative mental health between doctors and mental health specialists works best for most physicians and their patients.

Remember, all therapeutic (and collegial) relationships are built over time.

In June 2014, the Royal College of Physicians and Surgeons of Canada published a document called "Mental Health Core Competencies for Physicians." The principles and competencies are summarized in table 6.4 (used with permission) and are linked to each of the CanMEDs physician roles of medical expert, communicator, collaborator, manager, leader, health advocate, scholar, and professional. The goal is to diagnose and treat mental health disorders with empathy, clinic rigor, and in a timely fashion.

Patient Safety

The old Latin saying "primum non nocere" means "FIRST DO NO HARM." Although all doctors want to be helpful to their patients, error and miscommunication result in patient injury and death every year. Researchers from the Rand Corporation, Stanford, UCSF, John Hopkins, the ECRI Institute, and twenty-nine international stakeholders examined the existing literature on clinical error and patient safety and published their findings in 2013. They were able to recommend the effectiveness of patient safety strategies and to identify contexts and elements, which can inform rigorous discussion about patient safety.

For more information on quality improvement, go to www.rand.org.

Remaining Sensitive and Compassionate about Death

Residents frequently report that, although they are often called on to confirm the death of a patient, they receive no guidelines on how to do so from a compassionate as well as a medico-legal point of view. It makes sense to request seminars on death and dying, as they have been shown to increase levels of confidence and empathy in residents caring for the dying. (Check out www.epec.net for a CME program called "Education for Physicians on End of Life Care," by Linda Emanuel, MD. Many useful links are also provided.)

Death is confirmed by

- Dilated, fixed pupils
- No carotid pulse

Table 6.4. Mental health competencies[33,34]

Role	Principles	Competencies
Medical Expert	Physicians have a responsibility to provide comprehensive care, including mental wellness, to their patients. This includes understanding the mental health condition of their patients; to treat these conditions within their competence level; and to refer appropriately.	Physicians will have working knowledge of the symptoms, etiology, and basic treatment of mental health and addiction conditions that may influence a physical condition that they are treating.
	Physicians practice a "shared decision-making model" with patients and other supports (i.e., families) that the patient identifies as active partners.	Physicians will detect/recognize physical health conditions in patients who present with what appear to be mental health conditions.
		Physicians will recognize the signs and symptoms of basic mental health conditions most common to their specialty practice, i.e.:
	Consideration of, and respect for, diversity and cultural safety are embedded in daily practice and care planning and programs.	· Anxiety disorders · Mood disorders · Psychosis · Addictions · Grief · Situational stress · Cognitive impairment · Sleep disorders
	Care and recovery builds on the strengths, capacities, and reality of each patient.	Physicians will undertake mental health screening where applicable.
Communicator	Clear, honest, and respectful dialogue about mental health matters is a mutual responsibility between physicians and their patients.	Physicians communicate with their patients with respect and without stigma irrespective or their mental health condition.

Role	Principles	Competencies
	All colleagues and patients with mental conditions are treated with respect. Mental health promotion is emphasized in patient encounters.	
Collaborator	The physician trusts, values, and seeks out the contribution of other relevant health professionals; they collaborate and learn with other professionals to achieve better patient outcomes; they consider patients as an active partner.	Recognizes and respects the diversity of roles, responsibilities, and competencies of other professionals in relation to their own as it relates to mental health and addictions. Works with and learns from others to assess, plan, provide, and integrate mental health and addiction care for individual patients or groups of patients (shared, integrated care).
Health Advocate	Promotes holistic health and encourages active participation of patients and other health care professionals as "agents of change for mental health."	Identifies opportunities for advocacy, health promotion, and disease prevention to optimize the care of their patients with mental health conditions.
Scholar	The recognition and treatment of mental health conditions should be promoted throughout the medical education continuum and in research.	Identifies and integrates information and evidence related to the care of patients with mental health conditions in their specialty.
Professional	Physicians are aware of their own cultural attitudes and biases towards people with mental health conditions, and how these may impact patient care.	Recognizes through self-reflection the impact or their behaviors, attitudes, and knowledge gaps that may negatively impact the quality of care and health outcomes of their patients with mental health conditions.

- No heart sounds and breath
  sounds for over one minute

When You Have Confirmed a Death

✎ TIP

"As a senior resident, I find it invaluable to do a briefing with the trainees involved after every single death, expected or not."

- Take a quiet moment to
  acknowledge this patient's
  life and passage.
- Remember that it is an honor to be involved at the time of death
  of a human being, not a nuisance. If family members are present,
  express your condolences in an unrushed fashion. (During your
  training, learn all you can about culturally different interpretations
  of death, burial, and mourning, so that you can be sensitive with
  patients' families around the death of their loved ones.)
- If the family is not present, speak to ward nurses who knew the
  patient about the best way to contact the patient's family. If appropriate, notify the staff physician supervising care, who may wish
  to make the call. If you call the family, identify yourself and ask for
  the next of kin. State at what time the patient died and whether you
  were directly involved in her care. Ask if the person would like to
  come in to be with the body, and notify the nurses of that decision.
  Reassure the family member that the individual died peacefully,
  with good nursing care.
- Record in the patient's chart the date and time you were called and
  the above clinical data regarding confirmation of death.

Sample Charting

Called to pronounce death of Mrs X. Patient was unresponsive to verbal
and tactile stimulus. Pupils were fixed and dilated. No breath or heart
sounds heard.

No carotid pulse felt. Patient pronounced dead at 23:42, 6 Nov. 2022.

- Fill out the death certificate as soon as possible. Find out local
  regulations regarding signing the death certificate, for example, to
  distinguish coroner versus non-coroner cases. Speak to your chief
  resident or attending physician if in doubt.
- If a clinical autopsy or postmortem is medically indicated, clarify
  the reasons with your attending staff or treatment team and seek

written permission in a sensitive fashion from the next of kin or executor of the estate. Explain to the next of kin that an autopsy may prove useful in better understanding the patient's disease, but that family wishes will be respected.

- If the death has shaken or upset you, be sure to talk to a trusted colleague in order to gain support. Do the same for them. Model for students and junior residents that death can be talked about. You may also want to write in your journal or do a piece of reflective writing on what happened.

I Remember
by David Kopacz (dedicated to Samuel Shem)[35]

I remember Carl CD4=0 ring-enhancing lesions on his MRI
seizing the moment, in a bad way,
this stick of a man
teetered on the brink of death
then stepped back into life
he told me how he was going to buy some weights
get his strength back
buy some new clothes
then he asked me if I would come to his funeral when he died
overworked, scared, and guilty,
I said, "Yes."
I'm sure he's been dead for years
I remember the old black guy who had to urinate
he had cancer all over his body
because of his penile prosthesis the nurse wouldn't start the foley
twice during the night
I catheterized him he was crying quietly
saying "I have to go, I have to go."
4:37 a.m.
the beeper woke me
shoes still on, the nurse said I should hurry
he lay there dead
now, I mean now, while I am writing this, years later, now, I realize what he meant when

he said, "I have to go."
pronouncing him dead:
there is nothing like the hollow silence of the chest of the dead,
"yes, this man is
dead" then, telling the family them crying me feeling out of place
and
awkward
I remember Larry, 40 y.o. stroked-out alcoholic always pulling
out the NG tube
and hissing the only word I ever heard him utter,
"Bitch!"
I remember the young gay man, dying AIDS and his partner
Smashing Pumpkins playing "Space boy" on
their tape player
now that song always reminds me of death
I remember the latino, X-IVDA, current AIDS and his infected
wife
reverse isolation
I remember Maitreya's black man with AIDS and CMV retinitis
I was never sure if he knew I was there
that he was in a hospital
that he was dying in the hospital while I was there
his eyes roamed, disconjugate
the first FHV+ blood I drew
I remember the fifty-year old stroked-out black woman whose
blood I mingled
with my own
through a needle stick
perhaps that is the source of my affliction . . .
I remember the Middle-Eastern man with kidney failure and
granules of white on
his chest
all I could think of was "uremic frost"
Dr. Troyer leans over
tastes his fingers,
"sugar!" he says
and I see the spilled sugar on his tray
he took a long time to die
I remember the young Latino alcoholic man with foam coming
out of his mouth

like a champagne bottle
he died quickly
I remember long days and longer nights I remember rage, sad-
ness, and a helpless feeling
of being trapped I remember a dream about smashing a patient's
head into the pavement
I remember a patient in the VA ER tears running down his face
without any sign
of emotion
I admitted him to the psych ward
that was definitely not normal
I remember the patient who I was convinced would hit me
it seemed inevitable,
I was the doctor . . .
he was mad
I was the doctor
and I didn't know any better
I often remember saying to myself,
"I don't know any better."
I remember being at home for Christmas eating cereal tears running down my
face without any sign of emotion
that was definitely not normal

Whiz Kids:
Teaching, Learning, Doing Research, and Leading with No Time

Learning

TIP

Effective study seems virtually impossible when you are tired or overworked. Decreased sleep, anxiety, physical discomfort, and high noise and distraction levels have variable effects on the desire to learn, memory, reading capacity, concentration, and task performance. The housestaff member who has a weekend or evening off is unlikely to study because of a need for sleep or social contact; he or she may then feel guilty and inadequate. Try to study when you are relaxed, as you will learn and retain more. Medical information has never been easier or quicker to obtain online, so you can access it wherever you are, whenever you want![1] Your medical library can recommend apps and textbooks and other resources, free of charge. (But don't overdo checking things on your phone.)

"For internal medicine residents especially, it is important to keep up on developments in diagnosis and therapy. At the very least, it is important to keep track of journal articles via, e.g., email or RSS feeds, if not actually reading a journal regularly."

Be aware of your preferred learning styles and which one to use in different circumstances. (Most people's learning styles draw on one or two behaviors that they prefer to others.) Knowing this will help you to keep up learning throughout your medical career, and in selecting and accessing appropriate CME (continuing medical education) options.

Residency programs now emphasize competence-based medical education. CBME is an outcomes-based approach to the design, implementation, and evaluation of education programs and to the assessment of learners across the continuum that uses competencies or observable abilities. This model has been well documented in the literature to improve transparency and accountability in medical training and is particularly helpful in delineating a clear structure of expectations for residents. Further, learners participating in CBME-aligned curricula have shown increased confidence in their skills, ultimately progressing towards the end of residency with improved performance upon graduation and entry to practice.

Benefits of a CBME curriculum include more frequent assessment and feedback; well-defined learning paths; clarity on competencies needed to progress; personalized learning plans; preparation for independent practice; and early recognition and support of learners who are struggling.

Source: CFMS Transition to Residency Guide (www.cfms.org)

Basic Learning Styles

- Using examples from concrete experience (e.g., case studies)
- Observing, listening, and reflecting (e.g., after doing rounds)
- Working with abstract concepts, relying heavily on logic for analysis and theorizing (e.g., studying texts and debating with colleagues and teachers)
- Learning by doing, active experimenting, and practicing (e.g., making diagnoses, performing procedures, and working with patients)
- Using AI models/programs of care (including virtual procedures)

Continuing Medical Education

Definitions and Options[2,3]

The American Medical Association and the Accreditation Council for Graduate Medical Education (ACGME) define CME as follows:

Continuing medical education consists of educational activities that serve to maintain, develop, or increase the knowledge, skills, and professional performance and relationships that a physician uses to provide services for patients, the public, or the profession. The content of CME is that body of knowledge and skills generally recognized and accepted by the profession as within the basic medical sciences, the discipline of clinical medicine, and the provision of health care to the public.[4]

The Royal College of Physicians and Surgeons of Canada now requires credits for maintenance of certification, as does the College of

Family Physicians of Canada (www.cfpc.ca/mainpro/). Continuing medical education has become a mandatory part of maintaining licensing in most jurisdictions.

 TIP

"It is important to beware of the bias inherent in sources and teachers. Residents should feel free to ask presenters for disclosures, and beware of 'incentives' (dinners, etc.) from industry. There is a large body of literature showing that these things make a difference in prescribing practice."

Self-Directed CME Methods

- Reading journals, texts
- Computer (online) programs – often free through your university (or watch for discount coupons!)
- Clinical traineeships
- Teaching
- Publishing
- Literature searches
- Audio or videotapes, blogs, online CME programs
- Self-assessment and needs-assessment programs
- Research
- Self-audit of practice

Group CME Methods (Virtual or In-Person)

- Grand Rounds
- Conferences
- Audits of practice
- Structured formal examinations
- Journal clubs
- Workshops
- Self-assessment programs
- Quality assurance programs

The Call Cycle
by Emily R. Transue[5]

1. **On Call**
   Sometimes the busy moments
   Are the easy ones.
   Not the crazy times

When your pager keeps exploding
And the admits pour in
And the chaos un-concentrates
And you hope to hell you won't kill somebody
By mistake, distraction, oversight –
But the quiet moments are bad, too;
Too much time to think
To wonder when the next one's coming in
Whether you'll sleep the night through
Or get three hits at three a.m.
Time to be afraid of what you should've done and didn't
What you did do and should not have
In the wakeful silence, head on pillow.
The best times were
Just working, steadily,
Doing what is needed but not
More than can be done;
Riding the momentum of necessity,
Busy, numb.

2. Morning After

Green moss
Pebbles
A bit of broken glass;
Further off, a patch of yellow lichen.
It is so wet
And so clear
I'd swear that I can smell it through the glass,
That other world
Outside this window
Where linger at the elevator dawdles.
After all these hours here
The smell of hospital is in my pores.
I wish the window opened.
I'd like to breathe the air.

3. Afternoon After

Have you ever been so tired
You could cry, just from fatigue?
So tired that voices hurt your ears

And you'd like to curl up in a little ball
Under a take or a rock
And die
If dying means to sleep forever.

4. The Day Between

My family thinks
If you're not "on", you're "off".
It's hard to argue
Hard to explain
That a day of work
With sleep before and after
Is luxury enough.

5. Pre

This morning I rounded on
Two patients in my care a month each
On ventilators,
Patients who have never spoken to me.
A woman whose abdominal pathology
All of modern medicine has failed to diagnose,
Another whose lymphoma all of modern medicine has failed to
cure,
A third who will recover from her cellulitis,
Go home, shoot up again, come in again.
I was screamed at by the brother of a man
Who's dying of hepatic carcinoma at 41;
He yelled at me because he couldn't yell at God
Then I went to clinic, to see
A woman with diabetes without a home
Who's struggling against despair
And a man who wanted prescriptions
And someone to laugh at his jokes
And an alcoholic who needs a detox bed
But won't get one
Because the city has none empty.
I leave the radio off, driving home,
Because I cannot stand to hear another voice, another noise.
I sit on my sofa, still,
My mind a blank;

I am
An eggshell
Or a melon rind:
Scooped out,
Round and empty.
I've given all I have; there's nothing left.
I soak in a hot bath and go to sleep.

Making the Most of Your Learning Potential

Identify your own preferred learning style, as described above. Try to read up on a subject before a lecture or Grand Rounds to enhance learning. During teaching rounds, concentrate on taking away one new fact from each seminar. Learn something new every day.

At the beginning of your residency, reading about the cases you are actually treating provides a natural, well-timed motivation. Make a note of questions and knowledge gaps as you go. Carry useful pocket manuals or your access them on your smart phone, iPad, or laptop so that concisely organized facts are readily accessible. Subscribe to one or two good peer-reviewed, indexed journals in your field (either hard copy or online) and read the review articles. Find out what your hospital and university libraries provide in terms of journals, online resources, links, search engines and search assistance, and textbook/manual downloads. There's no point buying expensive textbooks when you can access most of them for free.

If a synopsis of your large specialty textbook is available, read it and answer any review questions it contains. Use the large textbook for a more thorough review of a topic.

When asked to prepare a Grand Rounds, pick a practical, non-esoteric topic that you want to learn about. Concentrate on evidence-based clinical articles. Ask to incorporate mini-rounds into morning rounds (e.g., a five-minute presentation on a useful topic every morning). Do not be afraid to ask questions during rounds; you are there to learn. Take advantage of all the experience in the room.

Insist on proper supervision by attending staff. Recently the Joint Commission of Accreditation of Healthcare Organizations and the

ACGME beefed up resident supervision rules, making it mandatory that medical staff be aware of these changes.

Carry a notebook or smart phone or iPad to jot down questions and useful facts, pointers, tables, and normal laboratory values. (Send yourself prompts, links, and reminders to your phone.)

Try to play a teaching role with juniors and medical students; this will force you to review and present data clearly.

 TIP

"I have found it helpful to focus as much as possible on learning, during residency, skills that will probably not change (physical exam, history taking, physiology) and maybe even short-changing learning information that will change (e.g., guidelines which I can look up, medication doses for uncommon medications, etc.)."

Identify gaps in your learning and arrange activities to fill them. Senior residents and program directors will have useful suggestions and resources. For instance, push for rotations in primary care, free or public health clinics, community and health centers; otherwise, your training may be incomplete for practice in a nonhospital setting (i.e., "the real world"). Arrange occasional individual teaching sessions with a mentor or tutor. You may have to request such sessions if your program does not offer them.

If your contract allows it, arrange to take time off every year for study, conferences, and exam preparation. Consider using this time to take a specialty review or exam preparation course.

Spend time developing an efficient internet search strategy. Conduct regular searches on topics of interest. Two excellent resources are the ACP Journal Club (Evidence-Based Medicine for Patient Care, at www. acpjc.org) and the Cochrane Collaboration (www.cochrane.org).

Exams!

One of the greatest stresses of residency involves preparing for, and then taking, the written and oral qualifying exams (the "boards") associated with internship, residency, or sub-specialty fellowship. Since you're already preparing, you might wish to take qualifying exams in both Canada and the United States to keep all your options open.

STUDY AND EXAM PREPARATION TIPS

- Find out what your program offers by way of mock oral exams, old exam questions (QBanks), online study guides, and exam review courses. Work through them alone or in your study group.
- Find out application deadlines for written and oral exams. And don't miss the deadline! As the exam draws near, form a study group with three or four friends whose study styles are similar to yours. You can meet virtually if scheduling in person is difficult.
- Consider every patient you see to be a potential case presentation for your exam. Discipline yourself to do a thorough history, physical, and case formulation about your patient. Practice presenting the case formally to a teammate from time to time.
- Remember to read about specific cases and actively protect study time throughout your residency.
- Emphasize problem solving rather than memorization, but remember to review rare disease entities and the basic medical sciences of your specialty (i.e., physiology, biochemistry), as you may be asked questions about these in the written and oral exams.
- Find out about Board reviews offered by your program or intensive exam workshops offered at other national centers.
- There are numerous apps that can give you the tools to create your own study flash cards and other apps that allow you to review Board prep content.
- Spend more time on topics you struggle with, rather than content you know well.
- Identify your exam-study style. Are you a "planner, crammer, or intermittent studier"? Weigh the pros and cons of that particular style.
- Arrange mock oral exams with senior clinicians in your department at least once a year and request detailed written and verbal feedback.
- Talk to recent candidates about the content and format of their exam.
- To avoid study burnout, reward yourself, for example, with an outing or special meal when you've had a productive session.
- For information on exam step 3 of the United States Medical Licensing Exam (USMLE), see www.usmle.org.

In Canada, exam links are

- LMCC: www.mcc.ca/examinations/
- College of Family Physicians of Canada: www.cfpc.ca/ExamInformation/

The specific specialty Boards generally publish or post "blueprints" showing what portion or emphasis of the exam will be on specific topics, so you can prioritize your focus accordingly.

- Check out the NEJM+ website for additional tips and strategies: www.knowledgeplus.nejm.org/
- If you don't pass, be kind to yourself. You can take the exam again.

TEST TAKING TIPS

1. Get to know the material.
2. Get enough sleep. Don't stay up late studying the night before.
3. Follow a normal routine the day of the exam.
4. Don't take those last few moments before the test for last minute cramming.
5. Do something relaxing the last hour before the test.
6. Take deep breaths!
7. Wear comfortable clothing.
8. Arrive early enough to sign in and take the time allotted.
9. Check the test brochure to be certain that you bring all needed documents (e.g., admission card or identification with picture).
10. Be familiar with the test format (i.e., take a computerized practice test and review the tutorial on the CD or web link supplied with the registration materials).
11. Be familiar with the types of questions (short answer, multiple choice) that will be asked.
12. Know how the test will be marked.
13. Watch the clock.
14. Use your time efficiently.

Changing Position

Being a left-handed surgery resident was more difficult than I had anticipated. But I was beginning to feel obtuse, awkward, and hesitant outside of the operative room as well. Figuratively and literally it was apparent that I was not fitting in.

A patient complication. A harsh senior resident. A failed exam. An argument with a friend after I went to him for help ("You've been so sensitive lately, and it's really annoying.") The physical exhaustion was eventually replaced by a mental and spiritual exhaustion. I didn't think I could continue.

The stresses of surgical residency are unique. For many, surgical residency represents our first experiences with personal failure. The fact that many of these failures are not preventable does little to appease our consciences. We are committed, high-achievers, and reconciling with our own shortcomings takes both effort and humility. We often work twice as long as our colleagues, and receive half the praise. Double standards for expectations can be pervasive, within our own department and throughout the rest of medical culture.

One day in the operating room, a staff suggested to me: "Why don't you try standing on the opposite side of the table. I think it will be easier for you." He was right. The steps of the operation flowed better. I gained confidence. I took pride in my work, and my performance improved.

I began to reposition and refocus myself from a mental and spiritual perspective, as well. The senior resident was a new mother, with a six-month-old infant at home. I studied for and repeated the exam with a friend who was also unsuccessful (we had been too ashamed and embarrassed to admit it to each other). The other resident who admonished me had his own stresses, and once we discussed them, he became my gym buddy. I focused on small successes, instead of ruminating on my failures. I felt better equipped to continue my residency. Though work was still difficult and expectations remained high, I had reclaimed the joy that had been fostered years ago when I was a medical student.

Breathe. Take a few steps. Reposition yourself to approach a challenge from the opposite direction. You may be surprised what you discover.

Teaching

One of the enduring ironies in postgraduate medical education is that staff physicians teach residents and residents teach medical students, but it seems in some programs that "nobody teaches anybody how to teach." (The old adage about procedures of "watch one, do one, teach one" is hopelessly obsolete.) As a result, the caliber of teaching residents receive varies significantly from school to school, hospital to hospital, and attending to attending.[6]

Teaching occurs at the bedside, on rounds, in conference rooms, in journal cl17ubs, on Grand Rounds, and at conferences, but most residents are hard-pressed to describe their own learning style (see above), much less which attributes make for an effective teacher. Residents generally emulate "good teachers" and promise themselves not to be like "bad teachers." Many postgraduate medical offices provide workshops and tutorials on teaching, and some staff physicians make a point of teaching about teaching. One useful program offered at centers across Canada and the United States is the Teaching Improvement Project System (TIPS). Many programs also have online modules on "the resident as teacher," as do specialty association resident sections on their websites. Increasingly, we are ALL being asked to be allies and to create a safe and inclusive learning environment for racialized, gender/sexual, and other minority learners. The UW (University of Washington) Medical Center has some wonderful resources: see www.sites.uw.edu/uwgme/equity-diversity-inclusion.

Here are some DEI topics to research, present, and discuss in rounds and medical educational conferences:

Sample Topics
- Teaching and Inclusivity
- Addressing Microaggressions in the Classroom
- Addressing Race, Culture, and Structural Inequality in Medical Education
- Beyond Cultural Competence: Critical Consciousness, Social Justice, and Multicultural Education
- Reducing Implicit Bias through Curricular Interventions
- Reducing Racial Bias among Health Care Providers

To deepen teaching skills, some residents choose to complete a concurrent Masters in Medical Education, if available through their program.

The following are practical suggestions for maximizing teaching and learning in a variety of settings.

Teaching

One of my senior residents liked to give PowerPoint presentations. Several times a week, she would bring her tiny Macbook to the hospital. We crowded around a table and listened to her talk. Another senior resident liked to hand out papers. By the end of our month together, my knapsack had seemingly doubled in volume and weight from the papers he printed.

I remember hardly anything about what they taught, only how they taught it. I do remember their styles and their actions: the resident who made sure to learn every nurse's name, and the one who made us present out cases in front of our patients, letting the patients jump in when we made a mistake.

And I remember techniques I saw them apply: a senior resident who could focus so intensely on a patient the rest of the world seemed to vanish, or the neurology resident who showed me how, if you landmarked just right and took a moment to visualize the space, your lumbar punctures would hit home every time.

When I became a senior resident, these were the people I modelled. I tried to do the things I'd liked, and avoid the things I didn't. At least, I figured, I'd only make new mistakes. I try to be careful around my students. I know that they're watching my actions, ready to make them their own.

How to Maximize Bedside Teaching

With the demands of documentation and constant EHR/EMR "clicking," it is not surprising that less than 50 per cent of resident time is actually spent at the bedside, but this time is vital for trainees to learn about patient interviewing, communication skills, and the art of the physical exam. Remember to do the following:

- Model respect for the patient's privacy and wishes; keep visits brief.
- Introduce the patient to team members by name and give the names of your team members. Express gratitude for her time and assistance in teaching.

- Tell your team members in advance what you want them to observe or examine regarding the patient, so as not to linger at the bedside unnecessarily.
- Discuss the patient's case in a confidential fashion and setting (i.e., never in the elevator or cafeteria).
- Observe students' or juniors' physical-exam and interviewing skills wherever possible and provide immediate, one-on-one feedback. Here's where you can emphasize the art of medicine in addition to technical proficiency.
- Your day is full of teachable moments. Seize the moment!
- Schedule five-minute mini-rounds on a useful topic during every morning round. Seize as many teaching opportunities as you can in the course of the day.
- Work to create a comfortable learning environment where ridicule, criticism, and unhealthy competition are not found. Be open to questions and feedback yourself.
- Introduce discussions of cultural safety and humility for minority patients and ask learners to consider the personal and historical obstacles they and their communities may have faced in health care settings. If they don't trust you from the get-go, there's a reason (see resources above).
- Provide suggestions for reading and learning more.
- Your specialty association website will likely have links on teaching.
- Go to www.mededportal.org (an AAMC initiative) for more information and resources on teaching.

HOW TO GIVE VERBAL FEEDBACK TO A TRAINEE

- Make your expectations known for medical students, interns, and junior residents at the beginning of the rotation and refer to these throughout.
- Always focus your comments on specific performance observations, behaviors, or events rather than making subjective generalizations.
- Find an approximate time and quiet setting for discussion.
- Never humiliate publicly. The days of accepting the use of SHAME and HUMILIATION as teaching techniques are gone,

and such behavior will likely result in remedial or disciplinary action or even termination.
- Focus on what needs to be changed. Be succinct and direct and don't provide too much information.
- Frame your comments in an empathetic, constructive fashion, emphasizing patient care, teamwork, and common goals for the patient – avoid put downs, blaming, or ego challenges.
- Make your comments solution-based. Try to have the trainee elicit specific actions, decisions, or changes that would result in improved performance.
- Ask the trainees what they plan to do differently next time. Remind them that we all continue to learn as we go.
- Give frequent feedback and follow up on previous discussions.
- Familiarize yourself with your program's resident evaluation forms so you know what specific elements to look for in a trainee's performance.
- See also PARO's Top Ten Teaching Tips and other suggestions for being a great teacher: www.mypara.ca/during-residency/.

Procedures

I have never been quick to learn procedures. Although I'm an internal medicine resident, I couldn't consistently draw a blood gas until the end of internship. The first joint aspirations I did drew nothing but blood.

I eventually became comfortable with everything but central lines. Something always went wrong and someone else always had to take over.

This changed after I spent time on call in the ICU with Mark, one of the fellows. The first time he saw me fail, he frowned, scrubbed in, and slid the line in immediately.

"I'm sorry," I said.

"You need to stop being so tense," he said. "You just have to practice."

After scrubbing out, he opened a fresh kit and walked through each step. When we reached a step where my hands failed, he made me repeat it until they didn't. This culminated in him watching me tie the knot which sutures the line in place.

"You do that, you'll stab yourself," he said. He took the suture and tied a perfect knot: slowly, so that I could see each step.

"Now, you do it," he said.

I fumbled my way through the tie, but got it.

He took the suture back from me and stuck the needle through my scrub top and another perfect knot.

"Now, do it a hundred times," he said.

Eventually, my lines began to go in smoothly, and I became a senior resident and began to teach interns. They fumble, the way I did; some more, some less. I always say the same thing.

"Relax," I say. "You just have to practice." Then I find the tools and we do it again.

Maximizing Conference Room Teaching

- Start and finish on time.
- Use audiovisual materials (including X-rays, scans, photographs) wherever possible to illustrate case material.
- Talk about real people, human beings with unique stories of illness, not lab results. (One interesting study in Israel had radiologists attach photos of the patients whose X-rays they were reading. This humanized the experience for them because they could imagine real people with real lives.)
- Try to keep presentations case-based rather than lecture-style, as this has been shown to motivate physician learning.
- Use the chalkboard, flipboard, overhead projector, or PowerPoint graphics to show lab results or draw other graphs.
- If a resident is presenting a case or a topic, let her finish with few interruptions, saving questions for the end.
- Summarize key points. Ask Socratic-type questions to stimulate discussion.
- Try to provide handouts, summaries, bibliographies, or links to review articles at the end of the learning session.

How to Give an Effective Audiovisual Presentation Using PowerPoint, Slides, and Overheads[7]

These tips apply to both in-person and virtual presentations. Make sure your review all the technical details of your virtual platform so as to allow the sharing of your screen and moderation of discussions without glitches and delays.

- Present only one slide or overhead per minute or you will overwhelm your audience.
- Do your selected images of people reflect the diversity of your learning community and the patient populations you serve?
- Number and order your slides carefully.

TIP

"I would encourage presenters to remember who their audience is, what that audience wants to hear vs. what the presenter wants to say (with emphasis on the former rather than the latter), and to remember that most people can remember, at best, three key points from a talk. Before I give a talk, I like to ask myself, 'If I could pick one thing for the audience to remember, what would it be?' Then, I try to really hammer that point home and remove unrelated points."

- Use bold print and no more than six lines per slide and six words per line to facilitate reading. Use bullet headings to focus attention.
- Keep graphs and figures simple.
- Consider using dual laptops or projectors to contrast images (e.g., before and after treatment) or text versus an image like a CT scan or X-ray.
- Try not to move backwards and forwards with slides. If you need to re-reference a slide have another copy of it placed appropriately in your line-up.
- If using a pointer, be incisive to refer to a specific point; don't wander.
- Bring a back-up memory stick with your presentation material saved to it.
- Arrive in the lecture theatre early to set up your laptop and to familiarize yourself with the microphone, audiovisual (AV) equipment, and light dimmer.
- Turn the lights back on during discussion time.
- Pay attention to timing: begin and end your talk promptly in the allotted time, leaving ample time for questions and feedback.
- Remember, you don't always need PowerPoint slides. You can also teach informally (off the cuff) and encourage dialogue, the sharing of narratives, and questions.

Other Tips on Organizing Your Presentation

- State the intent of your talk, outline the learning objectives, and make sure your presentation has a beginning, middle, and end.
- Engage your audience (attention wanes after 15 minutes).

- Keep content relevant, concise, and interesting without too much detail. Use appropriate humor to engage your audience.
- Repeat important take-home messages and summarize.
- Practice speaking clearly in a conversational style with good pacing, volume, and pitch. Don't read a script and, wherever possible, try to interact with your audience.
- Dress professionally for the occasion in comfortable, unrestricting clothing.

Becoming a Leader[8]

Being a physician can provide key opportunities to develop your leadership skills.[9] Many of you will have entered medicine with grassroots political or activist experience and a commitment to social justice, diversity, and equity, and improving health care systemically. Don't lose sight of that hard-earned expertise and passion!

The following discussion offers some suggestions for developing your leadership skills.

Much has been written about leadership and how it influences us as individuals and as a society. Many of us need leaders to give us a sense of direction, stability, purpose, and hope. Others do not gravitate towards leaders, maintaining their identity more autonomously. And then there are those who thrive by leading.

In general, leaders are average people who differ from their peers in some ways and mirror them in others. These are people who were born with an innate set of talents and skills (not as common as one might think) and/or who grew to develop such a portfolio over time. Regardless of their nature or nurture, leaders have a clear sense of their values and beliefs, have the social skills to attract and maintain relationships with others in a way that motivates action on those values and beliefs, and maintain a transparency, integrity, and genuineness that foster the trust of those who choose to follow.

How do you become a leader? Leadership can be demonstrated in any sphere of action, and on any scale, to bring about positive change and promote improved outcomes. For residents, the acquisition of leadership skills is an important aspect of their development as medical professionals. The following set of catch phrases can inspire the cultivation of leadership skills among new physicians.

Get involved. Many organizations could use your energy, ideas, and vision. Your program and its host university will have committees that welcome, and need, resident input; your provincial house-staff organization (PHO) is managed and led by residents and would welcome your input with open and grateful arms; your provincial or state medical association welcomes and needs resident input; and your national organizations (Canadian Association of Internes and Residents, AMA Resident and Fellow Section, the Committee of Interns and Residents [CIR], and your specialty society) have roles and purposes for resident input. You can also partner with international development agencies to offer your skills abroad; or consider working with Médecins Sans Frontières after graduation. All these organizations offer opportunities to put your ideas and personality to the test with lots of support, encouragement, and, in many cases, formal training.

Many organizations outside of medicine would also welcome your input and energy. Habitat for Humanity, Big Brothers/Big Sisters, the United Way, political parties, and non-governmental organizations also present opportunities for leadership development and for personal and professional growth.

Get passionate. Reflect for a while on your core values and beliefs: What is it that most creates energy or tension within you? Perhaps you are a passionate defender of socially accountable medicine. Perhaps you have a new idea that merits attention. Seek out the people and organizations who would appreciate your contribution and leadership. If a cause puts a fire in your belly, it will sustain your ability to lead. And so, identify your passions and get busy.

Get goal-oriented. Spreading yourself too thin will produce mediocre results. Pick one or two areas of leadership and apply yourself to them as best you can. Not only will this help you maintain balance in your life, it will also help you succeed in those things that you choose to take on. Be a finisher. Leaders didn't get to where they are by stopping halfway down the track.

Get honest and real. Get to know yourself really well. Most leaders can readily identify their critical strengths as perceived by themselves and others. They can also readily identify their vulnerabilities, flaws, and shortcomings – again, as perceived by themselves and others. Be yourself and be genuine: superficiality and phoniness are easy for others to detect. Learn to be comfortable in your own skin, how to use your own strengths and talents, and how to adapt your style of interpersonal engagement to meet the needs of others and the situation at hand.

Get trained. Leadership skills develop over time. Most successful leaders had the benefit of some form of formal leadership training. Typically, leadership courses offer assessment of personality traits and interpersonal styles as part of their curriculum. This process, although sometimes a little painful, is well worth the investment of time and course fees. Ask your provincial or national housestaff and medical associations for their recommendations for leadership training, and also consider opportunities such as the Royal College's Annual Resident Leadership Program and the CMA's Physician-Leadership Institute, which is open to residents from both sides of the border. The AMA offers executive leadership programs as well. You can also encourage your program director to develop a local leadership program as part of the core curriculum.

Get ready to learn from mistakes. As you develop leadership skills you will make mistakes. Despite your best intentions, you will bruise feelings, leave people out, subvert processes, create unintentional consequences, and perhaps even do harm. Seek lots of feedback on your leadership efforts, learn the techniques of reflective practice, and develop a process of modifying your own leadership strategies as you move forward.

Get a board of directors. Leaders identify mentorship as one of the most critical elements of a successful career. Everyone benefits from mentorship and by mentoring others. In general, mentors are individuals who negotiate a relationship that focuses primarily on the growth and development of the less experienced of the pair; and some mentors actively seek ways to promote the career development of their mentee. These relationships can be incredibly satisfying and often last for many years. Indeed, some people have a number of mentors, each of whom helps with a particular area of development (e.g., one for clinical research, one for grant writing, etc.). This collection of experts can be your personal "board of directors" and can enrich your career and life development.

Get the link between leadership and physician health. Leadership development is a tremendous opportunity to focus on your own resiliency. The insights gained in leadership development, particularly with respect to identifying your core values and beliefs, your interpersonal style, and your personality traits, are powerful and practical. When things are stressful and difficult, and your vulnerabilities become apparent, your leadership skills and traits can help you to cope well. In addition, your leadership skills can help promote a system of medicine that enhances the health and well-being of all involved, including all health professionals as well as the patients and families they serve.

(Reprinted, with permission, from Puddester, D. (2009). *CanMEDS Physician Health Guide*. Royal College of Physicians and Surgeons of Canada, Ottawa.)

What about the Hidden Curriculum?

New residents and other medical trainees are encouraged to question the wisdom or legitimacy of what they are asked to learn. Curricula are, after all, designed by senior faculty and overseen by licensing bodies, specialty organization, colleges and institutions, and provide "standards of practice." Most of us refer to "The (official) Curriculum" as the formal, stated, and intended body of knowledge we are all meant to master. This is the actual course of study, and consists of teaching, evaluation of teaching methods, syllabi, and other material used in any educational setting from lecture halls to labs, to seminar rooms, the bedsides and clinics. The Informal (or delivered) Curriculum is "what actually happens." As Delese Wear of NEOMED reminds us, it consists of "idiosyncratic, popup, and often unplanned instruction that takes place between anyone who is teaching (attendings, residents, or other health care professions) and trainees. It reflects what teachers believe trainees should acquire in terms of knowledge, skills, values, and attitudes."[10]

The Hidden Curriculum, in contrast, involves what is taught inadvertently. This concept originally comes from the educational rather than the medical literature, and it contains messages both ideological and subliminal from the formal and informal curricula. The hidden curriculum is transmitted by individual human behaviors, but also by the structures and practices of institutions, including hospitals and universities. Dr. Fred Hafferty, who first applied notions of the hidden curriculum to medicine, described it as "understandings, customs, rituals, and taken-for-granted aspects of what goes on in the life-space we call medical education."[11] It thus consists of unexamined assumptions, values, rules, protocols, privileges, manifestations of power and domination, practices, messages, indifferences to inequity, use of language, and prioritization of what is important and less important in the knowledge to be transmitted.

Residents often have trouble defining the Hidden Curriculum, but they generally do not have difficulty identifying it when they encounter it. The Hidden Curriculum manifests through negative role modelling, unprofessional behavior, and the message "do what I say and not what I do" from preceptors and supervisors. In the face of the Hidden Curriculum, learners feel discomfort as their experiences and feelings are discounted, and they may feel silenced or powerless in the face of power inequities.

 TIP

"If possible, it is helpful to continue to read a newspaper, news website, or non-medical magazine to keep up with the world outside of medicine. If nothing else, it helps us relate to our patients. Some suggestions: Globe and Mail, New York Times, Economist, New Yorker, Harper's, Bloomberg Business-week, London Telegraph."

Here are some questions to help you discuss how the Hidden Curriculum manifests and plays out in your own learning environment:

1. How do we know what we know? What material is included and what is excluded in what we are taught? (The latter is often referred to as the "Null Curriculum.")
2. How does power play out in any encounter between learner and teacher, doctor and patient? What is the pecking order in this service, ward, or clinic?
3. When have I felt discounted, silenced, or ridiculed in my training? How does this represent a microcosm of the overall learning environment?
4. What gets labeled as important in teaching versus "soft," "touchy-feely," or dispensable?
5. How do institutional policies, assessment techniques, and the language we use (including disparaging slang or jargon) illustrate the hidden curriculum?
6. How are my own values challenged by the values of my institution?
7. How has unprofessional behavior been manifested by powerful individuals and then addressed by my institution?
8. What messages about race, class, gender, sexuality, physical able-ness, and privilege are given explicitly, implicitly, or in a contradictory manner?
9. How does our current curriculum model societal expectations,

rules, inequities, and power structures? Who has a voice and who doesn't?

10. What are examples of hypocrisy and mixed messages in my learning? How are these addressed?

11. What attitudes would I like to see changed in my learning group, class, residency program, profession? How are time and space allocated to particular themes, subject matter, and how does this illustrate the importance or non-importance of these subjects?

12. How is money spent at my institution? How does that suggest what is important?

13. How are dissent, feedback, and helpful criticism handled in my learning environment?

14. When have I personally experienced or witnessed anti-Indigenous and other forms of systemic racism, sexism, homophobia, transphobia, ableism, and class assumptions within medical settings? What does that tell me about the culture I now work in?

The Real World

One of the first clinics I went to in medical school was with an internist locally famous for his diagnostic skills. People said he'd read every issue of *NEJM* cover to cover. And unsurprisingly, he started the observership by pulling a sheaf of photographs from an envelope and asking me to identify the physical findings in each one. Each picture was followed by a question about the physiology of the disease.

But on our way down the hall to see his first patient, the questions changed.

"Who was Madoff?" he asked.

"Sorry, what?" I asked. I couldn't think of a Madoff's sign or any appropriate medical eponym.

"Madoff," he repeated. "The financier who took everyone's money."

And then, later. "Who is Dennis Kucinich?"

This time I was prepared, albeit puzzled.

"You must learn all of Harrison's," he told me afterward, "but it is not enough. Your patients do not read medical textbooks, and if you cannot relate to them, you will never take a good history."

I've noticed this many times since. The best clinicians I've ever met are often the ones with the broadest interests: the old internist who quoted T.S. Eliot on the wards, or the generalist who stopped me before we went into a patient's room so that we could watch the patient through the window, saying, "Come, Dr. Watson. Let us observe."

Expanding Your Worldview

The Roman playwright Terence wrote, "Homo sum: humani nil a me alienum puto."

His insight remains true today: "I am human. I think nothing human is alien to me." He reminds us that nothing human should be foreign or alien to us.

As physicians, we are honored to bear witness to all forms of human struggle and to not judge or avoid them. No matter what your specialty, increasing your knowledge of cultural and psychosocial issues can only help you become a more consummate healer who provides optimal, person-centered care. Consult an up-to-date behavioral medicine textbook or do a Medline search on the topics listed below. Incorporate these subjects into rounds, teaching, and case management. Don't be the kind of practitioner who refers anything "complicated" to the social worker or psychiatrist. You can never know enough about human suffering and resilience.

Invite guest consultants to discuss them as well. Explore the arts and humanities to broaden your worldview about human experience and suffering. Read broadly as the above resident narrative suggests! They help us challenge assumptions and biases while providing an aesthetic and often provocative experience.

> TOPICS RELATED TO PSYCHOSOCIAL AND CULTURAL ISSUES
>
> As you become more experienced, you'll see that arbitrarily or dismissively separating mind from body and mental illnesses from physical illnesses or ignoring social determinants of health does

a huge disservice to our patients and to ourselves as humanistic, holistic practitioners. Make a point of reading and learning about the following topics:

 TIP

"I am very fond of the 'On Being a Doctor' section in *Annals of Internal Medicine*, and the 'Best Of' collections."

Aboriginal and Indigenous health advocacy
Alcohol and substance abuse
Alternative therapies
Anti-oppression frameworks
Anxiety
Artificial intelligence in medicine
Arts for health (i.e., music and art therapies)
Attention deficit, enuresis, and other childhood problems
Bias (explicit vs. implicit)
Body image/"Body fascism"/Fat-shaming
Brief psychotherapy
Bullying and harassment
Child and sexual abuse
Climate change (and related health impacts)
Colonialism (and its impact on Indigenous communities and culture)
Compliance and non-compliance with treatment (now called "adherence")
Complementary health
Corrections facilities and prison health care
Cost-benefit decision analysis
Cultural aspects of care
Cultural safety
Cultural humility
Death and dying
Dementia
Depression and bipolar disorder
"Difficult" patients
Disability studies
Diversity, equity, and inclusion
The doctor–patient relationship

Drug abuse
Eating disorders
Empathy
End-of-life care and decisions (including MAID – Medical
   Assistance in Dying)
Epidemiology
Environment, global warming, ecological crises
Ethical issues in care including euthanasia
Exercise and health
Family violence
Gay and lesbian, bisexual, and transgendered health issues
Gender issues (including non-binary identification); sexism in
   medical care
Geriatric care
Grief and mourning
HIV-AIDS – medical and psychosocial care
Homelessness
Human trafficking
Illness behaviors, malingering
Inter-professional studies and practices
Intersectionality
Insomnia
Leadership
Life-cycle issues
Medical and health humanities (see chapter 8)
Medical Assistance in Death (MAID)
Medicare, "Obamacare," disability insurance, universal health care
Medical History: What can we learn from the past?
Multiculturalism
Narrative in medicine
Neuro-diversity
Obsessive-compulsive disorders
Occupational health
Pain diagnosis and management
Palliative care
Pandemics
Patient safety and clinical error
Patriarchy and privilege in medicine

Personality disorders
Pharmaceutical industry practices and influence
Phobias
Population and minority health
Power and authority in care and learning
Prayer and healing
Pregnancy
Prevention (health)
Professionalism and unprofessional behavior
Psychiatric emergencies
Psychiatry and medicine (models of collaborative or shared
    care)
Psycho-geriatrics
Racism (including structural racism in medical culture and
    practice)
Rural and Northern medicine
Schizophrenia
Sexual assault
Sexual dysfunction
Smoking cessation
Social justice
Social determinants of health
Spousal abuse (male and female, including same-sex relation-
    ships)
Stigma
Stress management
Suicide
Truth and Reconciliation
Women's health and health research

The Medical Humanities/Health Humanities and Narrative-Based Medicine

As we built our health humanities website at the University of Toronto (www.meded.temertymedicine.utoronto.ca/health-arts-humanities), we realized that many of the problems faced by residents and fellows in their education revolve around issues that do not get named or discussed. These include the impact of physician encounters on patients and the important role of non-cognitive attributes in future healers including exploring feelings as a part of learning and tolerating ambiguity and uncertainty. And what about embodied, working definitions of empathy, reflective capacity, cultural sensitivity and diversity, and the hidden curriculum?

The medical humanities, often called "health humanities" to be more inclusive of other professions, have been defined as "an integrated, interdisciplinary philosophical approach to recording and interpreting human experiences of illness, disability, and medical intervention."[1] In short, the medical humanities are expressly concerned with the human side of medicine. They incorporate several fields, including philosophy, history, the arts, literature, anthropology, sociology, and bioethics.

The discipline of health humanities encourages a way of thinking, rather than content-based knowledge. They encourage critical thinking (the ability to ask, How do I know what I know?). They help foster narrative competence – the ability to work with stories, to listen optimally, and to co-construct the meaning of illness and healing with patients over time (see below). They foster visual literacy – the ability to work with non-verbal cues. And reflective capacity – the ability to step back

> ## *Reflexivity – Three Questions to Ask Yourself*
>
> - Who am I? How am I formed by privilege (or past depriva-
>   tions)? What are my beliefs and values? How aware am I of my
>   blind spots, prejudices, and implicit assumptions?
> - What am I? What is my working definition of professionalism?
>   What does it mean to be a doctor, and how is my profession
>   perceived by contemporary society?
> - Where am I? What context am I working in? What are the needs
>   of my patients and community? How do I keep in mind the
>   social determinants of health and principles of social justice?
>   What public health issues are predominant where I practice?

and to learn from past experience (reflection on action) so that it can be applied in the here and now (in action).

Humanities scholars themselves also benefit from a critical dialogue with their health care counterparts. They can be enriched by an ongoing dialogue with colleagues from clinical disciplines by having direct access to clinical teaching settings, which link to their study of critical theory. They can be invited to help shape the discourse around perceptions of health and illness in our learning community and in the society at large. A more central focus of medical humanities is on increasing the role of humanities in the provision of good patient care.

The result can be a university-wide community of scholars – what you could call "medicine watchers" and clinical practitioners from multiple disciplines who share (or robustly critique) contemporary and historical views on human experience, suffering, and dignity. Critical dialogue invites us all to be accountable in improving the way we care for patients and teach learners.

The offerings by medical and health humanities divisions in medical schools are rich and diverse. Most North American medical schools have a mix of elective and mandatory teaching offerings. They can include watching films, learning to interpret paintings, performing close reading of literary texts, doing reflective and creative writing, keeping a personal reflective portfolio, organizing seminars about the interface between the arts and medicine, and exploring the arts for health movement. They often invite trainees to develop an artistic practice themselves, which can afford new forms of creative expression and reflection, but also encourage learning with BOTH sides of the brain. They come to honor both thoughts and feelings, the subjective and the objective, in their learning process. These endeavors can help reduce the gap between biomedicine, evidence-based medicine, and the human sciences, such as philosophy, history, sociology, and anthropology. They facilitate interdisciplinary and inter-professional teaching and research, model a patient-centered approach to medical care, challenge biomedical arrogance, and equip doctors to meet the moral challenges of practice not covered expressly (or adeptly) by medical education.

A recent AAMC scoping review calls for full integration of humanities-based teaching within medical school and residency curricula as a humanizing force in medicine: www.aamc.org/what-we-do/mission-areas/medical-education/frahme. Updates on new approaches and teaching ideas are provided regularly.

Finally, the humanities also help counteract burnout and cynicism. Reflective, creative practitioners take better care of their patients, but they also take better care of themselves, because they have new tools to challenge their assumptions and to sustain their personal values and sense of purpose while providing optimal care.

Some Tips on Creating Humanities-Based Programming during Your Residency: Phase 1

Here are some suggestions for offering other arts and humanities-based learning opportunities during your residency. Narrative-based medicine is discussed below.

Start with hospital-based initiatives and make sure colleagues and administrators know about your work. Hold monthly, interdisciplinary, lunchtime meetings with engaging speakers tackling "out of the box" subject matter.

As examples, at the University of Toronto, we've organized sessions given by a family doctor studying to be a professional buffo clown, a toxicologist discussing poisons in opera, a nurse-dancer addressing the need for movement for children in hospital and how that might impact hospital design, and a social worker offering "on the spot training" for mindfulness in the hospital setting. Cast a broad net. Invite students, residents in other specialties and faculty from both health and

arts disciplines. Advertise events in your university newspaper, hospital bulletin, and through social media. Serve snacks (if you can!). Ask
participants to fill out evaluations of the sessions. Keep these in order
to demonstrate impact and to fine-tune your programming. Consider
starting a newsletter, blog, or website to promote your activities.

Form partnerships with non-medical colleagues. Contact the heads
of the English, history, philosophy, bioethics, music, and film studies
departments and invite them and their colleagues and students to your
monthly meetings. Find out who has a particular interest in health, disability, and the study of illness narratives and ask them to present or to
be a discussant.

Form partnerships with other health care humanities organizations
nationally and internationally to obtain further guidance in establishing your local presence. Join listservs. For example, both the NYU Literature, Arts, and Medicine Database (www.medhum.med.nyu.edu/)
and the Literature and Medicine affinity group of the American Society of Bioethics and Humanities (www.asbh.org/) have been extremely
helpful in assisting learners internationally to choose literary content for teaching students and for canvassing what's being done in
the field.

Infuse your own department or faculty with humanities projects,
and seize opportunities to introduce arts-based content into existing
residency curricula and lecture content. Encourage other residents to
give a Grand Rounds on an art-based theme. Organize a trainee art
exhibit in the lobby of your hospital or a yearly humanities essay con-
test. Introduce a poem or short text into morning rounds and link it to
the subject matter or diagnosis at hand. Submit a workshop to a faculty
development or CME conference.

Form a listserv or start a blog and build a virtual humanities community for students, residents, and faculty. You'll discover that many of
your colleagues (including those in non-clinical fields like research) are
using arts-based teaching innovations but believe that they are working
in complete isolation! They will be delighted to find like-minded educators and scholars at their own university and will also support future,
more formal initiatives and funding requests. Provide links to other
health care humanities websites and organizations and ask to be listed
on their websites as well. Post narratives and educational resources
(like lists of films and texts useful in teaching). Become a go-to resource
for colleagues in curriculum design and inter-professional learning. As

you build links with colleagues, prepare a list of possible electives that can be offered to residents. Make sure these electives meet the standards of your school and ensure that they are included on your website and in program syllabi of offerings for students and residents. Keep evaluations as evidence of your impact. Hold social events several times a year. A movie night for residents works well, as does the showing of episodes of specific TV series such as *House* or *Nurse Jackie*. (A list of top medical films is provided below.) Allow other residents to suggest content or to be discussants. Such meetings build morale, foster community, and help advertise your other initiatives. Attendees may then volunteer to help you with specific tasks related to your program-building (publicity, research, writing letters of support, etc.).

Offer to consult to your faculty on developing the potential links between the humanities and faculty well-being, professionalism, reflective capacity and inter-professionalism. Prepare and post resources of readings, films, writing exercises and websites that may be useful in teaching, personal learning, or research. Hone your qualitative research skills and link with interested local consultants. The impact of most humanities-based initiatives cannot be captured by standard bio-medical research protocols. Nonetheless your dean will likely request proof for the relevance of your work, its impact on learning, and for publications in peer-reviewed journals.

Next Steps

Curating Content, Assessing Learning Needs, and Deepening Your Program's Offerings: Phase 2

Here's a model of "curating content" relevant to the post-grad learner in your program.

It can be challenging to build arts and humanities-based sessions within the formal residency curriculum, given that teaching and work schedules are already oversubscribed. In many medical schools such sessions remain optional or elective and, as a result, may be perceived as less important than "obligatory content" by trainees and faculty.

As mentioned above, you should aim to facilitate regular teaching in official settings – Grand Rounds, case conferences, resident retreats, and core teaching seminars and half days. You can curate content based on resident interests and learning needs.

A curator (from Latin *curare*, meaning "take care of") is a manager or overseer of diverse yet thematically linked visual or narrative content. This model has been adopted successfully in educational fields outside of medicine, particularly with respect to digital learning.

Here are suggestions for applying this model of curricular innovation at your medical school and within your residency program:

- Ask faculty at the residency or PGME level what content or sessions would be helpful to them in fleshing out the new or existing curriculum. Compile a list of specific themes that seem to have been neglected (e.g., "narrative-based ethics," "structural racism in health care," or reflection on balance and well-being during medical school).

The best opportunity for impactful and sustained change comes during phases of accreditation and curricular reform or re-design. Present curricular suggestions at these times to fix identified problems or fill requirements for curricular reform.

- Establish a team roster of arts and humanities lecturers and ask that they send you a "ready to go" lecture title and brief description of the class they wish to teach based on the faculty "wish list" obtained in Point One above. Post this menu on your website, if you have one, or through social media and distribute to teaching faculty. Aim to include artists, humanities scholars and non-physician clinicians as well as medical teachers on your team to drive home the role of humanities in creating inter-professional dialogue and critical exchange. Inter-professionalism and collaborative problem solving are emerging priorities in most medical faculties, yet students report that regular teaching sessions can fall flat. Collective close reading of narrative, visual, or film texts and onsite reflective writing have been used successfully in multiple teaching sessions and with learners from several clinical fields.

As an example, we curated five inter-professional narrative Grand Rounds for an ICU unit in Toronto. Discussing and writing texts for that group of doctors, nurses, pharmacists, chaplains, patient advocates, students, and residents became a proxy for examining communication and clinical problems, power differentials, and team building without actually pointing fingers or naming names.

- Wherever possible, have one representative of more than one clinical and scholarly discipline at teaching sessions to model critical and inter-professional or interdisciplinary discourse around medical themes. This reminds students and residents that there are multiple critical lenses with which to examine and understand illness, human suffering, and the provision of health care. Involve artists and humanities scholars in course and seminar design and delivery wherever possible, and help make connections between these scholars and educators at the medical school. (We facilitate such connections through our website.)
- As part of your curating, formulate overarching learning goals for ALL sessions, as this suggests curricular coherence and rigor. Convey those goals to all arts and humanities faculty. (This bears repeating to medical colleagues who may be skeptical about what you are doing.) It's helpful to explicitly link teaching to professional attributes as linked to the CanMEDS professional roles and to create writing prompts around these roles. As an example, for ADVOCACY, we suggest writing a personal story about a time where you did or did not stand up for a patient.

In the US, these physician roles, attributes, and obligations are identified and can be illustrated by well-selected literary, journalistic, film and video clips and art pieces and visual image. Suggested arts-based content can be found at the end of this chapter.

With respect to professionalism, the ACGME specifies the following:[2]

> Residents must demonstrate a commitment to carrying out professional responsibilities and an adherence to ethical principles. Residents are expected to demonstrate: (1) compassion, integrity, and respect for others; (2) responsiveness to patient needs that supersedes self-interest; (3) respect for patient privacy and autonomy; (4) accountability to patients, society and the profession; and, (5) sensitivity and responsiveness to a diverse patient population, including but not limited to diversity in gender, age, culture, race, religion, disabilities, and sexual orientation.

More Tips

- Be flexible (at first) as to scheduling of content, for example providing a last-minute Grand Rounds if asked, or reading and discussing a poem as a part of a more conventional lecture. Provide easy access to online PowerPoints and video recordings prepared by your faculty to support adaptation of your content for mandatory lectures.
- Find a catchy name for your initiatives so that colleagues keep what you are doing in mind and follow the thread over time. Examples: The Art(s) of Medicine, Humanizing Medicine with the Health Humanities, CINEMA MEDICA, Resident Reflective Writing Group, and the like.
- Be sure to collect resident evaluations of each session so that you can demonstrate the efficacy, impact, and popularity of your seminars. Repeatedly remind students (from all disciplines) that a career in medical humanities is possible and that specific electives (outside of the curriculum with arts-based projects and research) are also available to deepen their experience. This paves the way for increased trainee demand for core humanities-based content, helps with educational succession planning, and encourages a demand for humanities-related curricular change within the faculty over time. Residents you help train (and those who go on to pursue masters and doctoral studies in the humanities) are likely to weave the humanities into their own teaching approaches, writing, and research, thus creating a growing community of scholars.
- The medium is the message. Incorporate multiple media formats into teaching sessions to model arts-based learning. Include video, TV shows, YouTube, and film clips, musical reflections, and pieces of visual art. Use short literary pieces (no more than three pages) that can be read or performed onsite, within the class. Residents may not read or view content provided in advance, so use materials strategically and spontaneously onsite to capture full impact and immediacy.
- Aim for half of your session to be a presentation and the rest to incorporate discussion, reflective writing, or small group exchange. This format will stand out as more active and interactive when compared with more conventional lectures and may be rated more highly than standard lectures. Arts-based exercises (e.g., the onsite creation of a graphic medicine panels or comics) have also been popular with students.

As you and your team meet with other residents, ask where humanities-based content could best accompany or enhance other mandatory teaching sessions in the regularly scheduled residency curriculum. For example, students and residents at the University of Toronto have created a companion curriculum of short literary pieces and patient videos that match ALL lectures, learning blocks, and clerkship rotations during medical school. These are "pulsed out" regularly by email from the student-run humanities blog called ARTBEAT but are also readily available to faculty wishing to add a poem, short, or video clip story to flesh out discussion around specific topics (like "delivering bad news"). This curated content organized around both specific lectures and more general medical themes can be found at www.utmedhumanities.wordpress.com/the-companion-curriculum/.

- Attend curricular planning and other postgraduate medicine administrative meetings regularly to explain your curatorial model. Offer your services repeatedly so as to stay on the faculty radar (and to act as an ever-present lobbyist for curricular change). Make explicit the link between humanities-based teaching and physician wellness by reminding colleagues that reflective practitioners take better care of their patients and themselves.

Your ultimate goal is of course to have humanities-based content infiltrate the standard residency curriculum as mandatory, fully intrinsic, and highly valued. Many humanities programs have yet to demonstrate the efficacy of teaching approaches in ways that suit the deanery and the quantitative model of biomedical research. Being a flexible, nimble curator and helpful consultant who tracks results, impacts, and evaluations can be a useful strategy to demonstrate the relevance of your humanities work and the impact of arts-based teaching innovations over time.

What Is Narrative-Based Medicine? Getting the Real Story from Your Patient

Narrative-based medicine suggests that patients will tell us their story, their way, if we are willing to receive it (and don't interrupt them). There are practical ways to improve your narrative competence.

Practical Strategies for Practicing a More Narrative-Based Medicine

Physicians from all specialties and clinician colleagues from all disciplines have become intrigued with what Rita Charon has called "Narrative Medicine" and what her colleagues in the United Kingdom have called "Narrative-Based Primary Care." Many physicians report that they agree with the principles of narrative-based primary care but wonder how they can realistically incorporate strategies into a busy office "without opening up a whole can of worms." There are ways to improve your narrative competence – that is, your capacity to interpret, co-construct, and bear witness to the stories your patients bring you. Don't just take a history. Receive a story!

Here are some simple, practical strategies to try and then integrate into your doctoring style.

- Charon starts her first patient visits with, "What would you like me to know about you?" before jumping into questions about symptoms. Try asking a more open-ended question like this in a new assessment. You can allow a few minutes for the patient to present their concerns and still move into a more systematic, structured inquiry after that. If you need to contain the story, you can employ your usual time-management strategies, but make a point of telling the patient that you want to pick up the thread next time. Ask, "Have I missed anything?" at the end.
- The average doctor interrupts a patient within eighteen seconds. Make a point of letting the patient finish her thought before launching into the next question or comment.
- Consider asking your patient to write a one page "Impact of My Illness" document, which you will read and discuss with them and keep in the chart. This may be the first time your patient was ever asked how the illness has changed or interrupted the story they had imagined for themselves.
- Add a final S to your SOAP (Subjective Objective Assessment Plan) notes – for Suffering. You don't have to write this down, but ask yourself if you have allowed room for the patient to talk about their distress or real concerns in each visit.
- Find out one thing you didn't know about your patient's story in every visit. Who are they when they aren't ill? What are their interests, hobbies, the names of their grandchildren? Did you know that man with Alzheimer's used to be a composer?

- Look for a metaphor or key word that emerges in your meetings that is unique to your working alliance. It may be found through a humorous exchange, but can become a symbol of the story you are constructing together over time.
- View non-collaboration (or non-compliance and non-adherence) as a blocked narrative, not as patient stubbornness. Get the real story. Non-compliance has a differential diagnosis like every other problem in medicine. You are definitely a character in that plot. Spending the time now will save both of you time later.
- Consider how a patient's experiences of discrimination (racial, sexual, ableist, classist, homophobic, or transphobic) have shaped their views of and trust in the health care system. Ask them to talk about it at their own pace.
- The next time you are troubled by a patient encounter, take three minutes to write down what happened. Write it the way you would tell a colleague, as a story with a beginning, middle, and end. Having it down on the page will allow you the distance to see how your own story (expectations, time pressures, unresolved grief) has collided with your patient's. Most people are surprised how much story emerges in only three minutes and how it can facilitate personal reflection.
- In a time of high-tech record-keeping, make a point of maintaining eye contact and not typing while the patient is speaking. Your body language conveys (or annuls) your receptiveness to a story. Think of other barriers to storytelling in your office (e.g., where or how chairs are placed, your answering non-urgent calls during appointments, and so on). Change what you can!
- The next time you feel bored with a patient, think about the question you haven't asked. Ask yourself what your unexamined assumptions about the patient are and revisit the moment in your shared story where the assumption took hold.
- Regarding assumptions (implicit or explicit), give yourself a writing prompt: "People with tattoos are ..."; "Obese people are ..."; "Single mothers are ...". Stereotypes are really the unexamined stories we tell ourselves without realizing it.
- When you're not sure what is going on with a patient, ask them, "What do you think is going on?" This is the story he is telling himself over and over about his symptoms. It may or may not give you a clue about etiology, but at the very least it will enlighten you as to his fears and worst-case plot scenarios.
- Patients tell stories differently to doctors than they do to anyone else. Ask them, "How would others describe you?" If what they

tell you doesn't match what you're seeing in your visits, then you've missed something important in their story.

- From time to time, ask your patient, "What's the one thing you haven't asked or told me?" Chances are that's the story that matters most.
- Before you see your next patient, take a moment with their chart. Take a deep breath. Ask yourself, "Where did we leave the thread of our story the last time?"
- A symptom is not a story. A lab result is not a story. They may be the punctuation, but there's always more.

There are several training programs in narrative-based medicine, such as the University of Toronto's digital certificate programs (www .narrativebasedmedicine.ca), in addition to programs such as Columbia University's master's degree in narrative medicine (www.sps.columbia .edu/academics/masters/narrative-medicine) if you're looking to develop specialized skills in this area. In addition, there are annual conferences, such as the University of Iowa's Examined Life Conference (www.examinedlifeconference.com), that offer learning opportunities about reflective and creative writing as well.

Sources

The above humanities lesson plan is excerpted with permission from Allan D. Peterkin and Anna Skorzewska (Eds.). (2018). *Health humanities in postgraduate medical education.* Oxford University Press, Oxford.

Strategies for practicing narrative-based medicine come from Allan D. Peterkin. (2006). *Portfolio to go: 1000+ prompts and provocations for clinical learners.* University of Toronto Press, Toronto.

Humanities and Arts-Based Learning: Some Additional Resources

As well as familiarizing yourself with updated psychosocial articles, consider the use of literary classics for learning, as these can facilitate individual reflection and group discussion on ethics issues of care and on the complexity of human relationships. They can also inoculate you against cynicism about the profession.

Here are some seminal books on what it means to be a doctor and on how history has shaped (and disparaged) our profession:

A Short History of Medicine – E. Ackerknecht
Toward an Aesthetic Medicine: Developing a Core Medical Humanities Undergraduate Curriculum – A. Bleakley, R. Marshall, and R. Broemer
The Making of Modern Medicine: Turning Points in the Treatment of Disease – M. Bliss
Histoire de médicine et la chirurgie de la grande peste à nos jours – P. Boussel
Stories of Sickness – H. Brody
The Healing Art: A Doctor's Black Bag of Poetry – R. Campo
ABC of Learning and Teaching in Medicine – P. Cantillon (ed.)
Doctoring: The Nature of Primary Care Medicine – E.J. Cassell
The Nature of Suffering and the Goals of Medicine – E.J. Cassell
Narrative Medicine: Honoring the Stories of Illness – R. Charon
Stories Matter: The Role of Narrative in Medical Ethics – R. Charon and N. Montello
Final Exam: A Surgeon's Reflections on Mortality – P.W. Chen
This Side of Doctoring: Reflections from Women in Medicine – E.L. Chin
The Call of Stories – R. Coles
The Picture of Health: Medical Ethics and the Movies – H. Colt, S. Quadrelli, and F. Lester
Medicine in the Twentieth Century – R. Cooter and J. Pickstone
Disability Study Reader – L. Davis
History of Medicine – J. Duffin
Attending: Medicine, Mindfulness and Humanity – R. Epstein
The Wounded Soldier – A. Frank
Better: A Surgeon's Notes on Performance – A. Gawande
The Checklist Manifesto: How to Get Things Right – A. Gawande
Complications: A Surgeon's Notes on an Imperfect Science – A. Gawande
The Yellow Wallpaper – C.P. Gilman
Narrative-Based Medicine: Dialogue and Discourse in Clinical Practice – T. Greenhalgh and B. Hurwitz
The Anatomy of Hope: How People Prevail in the Face of Illness – J. Groopman
How Doctors Think – J. Groopman
Doctors' Stories: The Narrative Structure of Medical Knowledge – K. Montgomery Hunter
A History of Medicine – B. Inglis

Body Language – N. Jain, D. Coppcock, and S.B. Clark
Medical Thinking: A Historical Preface – L.S. King
The Illness Narratives: Suffering, Healing, and the Human Condition –
    A. Kleiman
Medicine: An Illustrated History – A.A. Lyons
Body of Work: Meditations on Mortality from the Human Anatomy Lab –
    C. Montross
Incidental Findings: Lessons from My Patients in the Art of Medicine –
    D. Ofri
Singular Intimacies: Becoming a Doctor at Bellevue – D. Ofri
The Courage to Teach – P.J. Palmer
The Greatest Benefit to Mankind – R. Porter
On Doctoring: New, Revised and Expanded Third Edition – R. Reynolds
    and J. Stone
The Doctor Stories – R. Selzer
Letters to a Young Doctor – R. Selzer
*The Development of Modern Medicine: An Interpretation of the Social and
    Scientific Factors Involved* – R. Shryock
Empathy and the Practice of Medicine: Beyond Pills and the Scalpel – H.
    Spiro, E. Peschel, M.G. Curnen, and D. St. James
Literature and Medicine: An Annotated Bibliography – J. Trautman and
    C. Pollard
*Bedside Manners: One Doctor's Reflections on the Oddly Intimate Encoun-
    ters between Patient and Healer* – D. Watts
*Teaching during Rounds: A Handbook for Attending Physicians and Resi-
    dents* – D. Weinholts and J. Edwards.
The Doctor Stories – W.C. Williams and R. Coles

Journals of the Medical Arts and Humanities

Here are some top journals that explore what makes medicine an art.
Articles are written by doctors, artists, and patients, and by humanities
and social science scholars; they apply a critical, creative lens to health
care in general and to medical education and culture.

Ars Medica: A Journal of Medicine, The Arts and Humanities – www
    .ars-medica.ca
Bellevue Literary Review – www.blreview.org
The Healing Muse – www.upstate.edu/bioethics/thehealingmuse
Journal of Medical Humanities – www.link.springer.com/journal/10912

Literature and Medicine – www.muse.jhu.edu/journals
/literature_and_medicine/
Medical Education – www.mededuc.com
Medical Humanities (BMJ) – www.mh.bmj.com

Many North American medical schools have created partnerships with local art galleries, where learners participate in facilitated visits and discussions of art works with artists, gallery educators, and physicians with training in visual teaching strategies.

For a weekly dose of visual reflection and thoughtful discussion of selected art works, sign up at www.rxmuseum.org.

Films, Documentaries, and Videos

Films provide a great medium for socializing, sparking discussion, building community and morale. Films encourage personal reflection about the work we do as healers and how illness and medicine are constructed and perceived culturally. Here are some classic films and videos to facilitate group discussion of physician identity, and the doctor–patient relationship. The second list explores themes of racism, discrimination, and social justice.

- *And the Band Played On*
- *Article 99*
- *Awakenings*
- *Breaking the Waves*
- *Celebration (Festen)*
- *The Citadel*
- *Cleo from 5:00–7:00*
- *Common Threads: Stories from the AIDS Quilt*
- *Dallas Buyers' Club*
- *Dancer in the Dark*
- *Death of a Salesman*
- *Death Takes a Holiday*
- *The Diving Bell and The Butterfly*
- *The Doctor*
- *The Elephant Man*
- *Frances*

- *Happiness*
- *Hospital*
- *Ikira*
- *I Never Promised You a Rose Garden*
- *Kingdom*
- *The Last Angry Man*
- *Lorenzo's Oil*
- *The Lost Weekend*
- *Magnificent Obsession*
- *Magnolia*
- *Marnie*
- *M*A*S*H*
- *Milk*
- *Murmur of the Heart*
- *My Left Foot*
- *One Flew Over the Cuckoo's Nest*
- *Ordinary People*
- *Philadelphia*
- *The Prince of Tides*
- *Resurrection*
- *Scenes from Silver Lake*
- *Sicko*
- *Side Effects*
- *The Snake Pit*
- *Spellbound*
- *Sunday Bloody Sunday*
- *Sybil*
- *Terms of Endearment*
- *Titicut Follies*
- *White Corridors*
- *Whose Life Is It Anyway?*
- *Wild Strawberries*
- *Wit*

FILMS AND DOCUMENTARIES ON SOCIAL JUSTICE, GEO-POLITICS, CLIMATE CHANGE, AND RACISM

- *American History X*
- *An Inconvenient Truth*

- *The Angry Inuk*
- *Bowling For Columbine*
- *Do the Right Thing*
- *Fahrenheit 9/11*
- *Food Inc.*
- *I Am Not Your Negro*
- *Kanehstake: 270 Years of Resistance*
- *Menace II Society*
- *Once We Were Warriors*
- *Schindler's List*

For a wonderful resource matching more current films and documentaries to specific clinical topics, go to the NYU Literature, Arts and Medicine Database at www.litmed.med.nyu.edu/Main?action=new. Residents and students also enjoy discussing episodes of TV shows. Consider using a favorite (or controversial) episode from *Grey's Anatomy*, *House*, *In Treatment*, *Nurse Jackie*, or *Scrubs*.

Branching Out: Arts and Health Humanities Associations and Organizations

These associations hold annual meetings where you can network and find out about research and publishing opportunities.

- Association for Medical Humanities/UK – www.amh.ac.uk/
- American Society of Bioethics and Humanities – www.asbh.org
- The Canadian Association for Health Humanities – www.cahh.ca
- Creating Space: The Annual Canadian Health Humanities Conference (info is posted and updated on www.cahh.ca)
- The Health Humanities Consortium – www.healthhumanities consortium.com/
- Consider joining the HealthHumSimplelist Listserv, which is sponsored by the Health Humanities Consortium, and Case Western Reserve University Department of Bioethics.
- To join, contact the list administrator at healthhum-manager@ simplelists.com.

Conclusion

The health humanities and arts-based learning can provide a source of reflection and renewal in your daily work and may help you maintain a sense of purpose and pleasure as you help your patients construct meaning about their illness experiences and suffering. The field is growing exponentially in both Canada and the US and requires new, diverse voices to deepen scholarship and impact. Some scholars in the field emphasize the need to improve patient care and foster physician reflexivity and wellness.

Others now embrace "critical health humanities," which welcomes an interdisciplinary lens to health humanities drawing on critical theory, including feminist, postcolonial, queer, anti-oppression, and cultural history approaches to practice and research. This focus on structural influences on personal patient narratives and experiences then deepens the connection between health humanities and the social determinants of health.

Keep in mind that you can pursue a masters or PhD in any of the health humanities disciplines and that this can become an academic trajectory for which you can attain academic promotions.

Not Just a Job

Professionalism, Ethics, Regulation, and the Law

In 1996 the Royal College of Physicians and Surgeons of Canada introduced an innovative framework called CanMEDS for medical education, which established core competencies for all doctors. Seven key roles of the doctor were identified:[1]

- Medical expert
- Communicator
- Collaborator
- Health advocate
- Manager
- Scholar
- Professional

A new version of CanMEDS was released in 2015. Of importance, the manager role was re-conceptualized and new competencies were designed to describe a new leader role more on this important shift later in this chapter. Further consultations and revisions regarding these roles are now underway, using the lenses of Diversity, Equity, and Inclusion.

The role of the professional is of critical importance to the profession, and the Royal College and the College of Family Physicians of Canada defined this last role as follows:

> As Professionals, physicians are committed to the health and well-being
> of individual patients and society through ethical practice, high personal

standards of behavior, accountability to the profession and society, physician-led regulation, and maintenance of personal health.

Physicians serve an essential societal role as professionals dedicated to the health and care of others. Their work requires mastery of the art, science, and practice of medicine. A physician's professional identity is central to this Role. The Professional Role reflects contemporary society's expectations of physicians, which include clinical competence, a commitment to ongoing professional development, promotion of the public good, adherence to ethical standards, and values such as integrity, honesty, altruism, humility, respect for diversity, and transparency with respect to potential conflicts of interest. It is also recognized that, to provide optimal patient care, physicians must take responsibility for their own health and well-being and that of their colleagues. Professionalism is the basis of the implicit contract between society and the medical profession, granting the privilege of physician-led regulation with the understanding that physicians are accountable to those served, to society, to their profession, and to themselves.[2]

The Royal College also identified the following key competencies related to professionalism:[3]

- Demonstrate a commitment to patients by applying best practices and adhering to high ethical standards
- Demonstrate a commitment to society by recognizing and responding to societal expectations in health care
- Demonstrate a commitment to the profession by adhering to standards and participating in physician-led regulation
- Demonstrate a commitment to physician health and well-being to foster optimal patient care

The ACGME (Accredited Council for Graduate Medical Education) has also identified core competencies for residents:[4]

- Patient care and procedural skills
- Medical knowledge
- Practice-based learning and improvement
- Interpersonal and communication skills
- Professionalism
- Systems-based practice

With respect to professionalism, residents must demonstrate an ability to treat all people with respect, compassion, sensitivity, and dignity. Self-interest is surpassed by a dedication to serve the needs of patients, and there is an acceptance and understanding that residents are accountable to patients, colleagues, and society as a whole. The professional competency is built upon these three sub-competencies:

- Demonstrating professional conduct and accountability
- Demonstrating humanism and cultural awareness
- Maintaining emotional, physical, and mental health, and pursuing continual personal and professional growth

Source: NEJM Knowledge+[5]

In the 1990s the American Board of Internal Medicine (ABIM) commenced a similar project to advance the evaluation of professionalism as a fundamental component of clinical competence. This subcommittee defined professionalism as "the attitudes and behaviors that serve to maintain patients' interests above physician self-interest."[6] In 2002, this work resulted in the publication of *Medical Professionalism in the New Millennium: A Physician Charter*,[7] which has since been endorsed by over 100 organizations and continues to influence the evolution of medical education, training, and practice. The Charter emphasizes three fundamental principles: primacy of patient welfare, patient autonomy, and social justice. These specific professional responsibilities are cited in the Charter:

- Commitment to professional competence
- Commitment to honesty with patients
- Commitment to patient confidentiality
- Commitment to maintaining appropriate relations with patients
- Commitment to improving quality of care
- Commitment to improving access to care
- Commitment to a just distribution of finite resources
- Commitment to scientific knowledge
- Commitment to maintaining trust by managing conflicts of interest
- Commitment to professional responsibilities

The ABIM developed a superb online curriculum including case vignettes, strategies for fostering and evaluating professional attitudes, signs of unprofessionalism, and a comprehensive bibliography (www .abimfoundation.org/what-we-do/physician-charter).

Finally, the following statement, published in *JAMA*, elegantly defines the patient-physician covenant and how it must be guided by both professional and ethical principles:[8]

> *Medicine is, at its center, a moral enterprise grounded in a covenant of trust. This covenant obliges physicians to be competent and to use their competence in the patient's best interests. Physicians, therefore, are both intellectually and morally obliged to act as advocates for the sick wherever their welfare is threatened and for their health at all times.*
>
> Today, this covenant of trust is significantly threatened. From within, there is growing legitimation of the physician's materialistic self-interest; from without, for-profit forces press the physician into the role of commercial agent to enhance the profitability of health care organizations. Such distortions of the physician's responsibility degrade the physician–patient relationship that is the central element and structure of clinical care. To capitulate to these alterations of the trust relationship is to significantly alter the physician's role as healer, carer, helper, and advocate for the sick and for the health of all.
>
> By its traditions and very nature, medicine is a special kind of human activity – one that cannot be pursued effectively without the virtues of humility, honesty, intellectual integrity, compassion, and effacement of excessive self-interest. These traits mark physicians as members of a moral community dedicated to something other than its own self-interest.
>
> Our first obligation must be to serve the good of those persons who seek our help and trust us to provide it. Physicians, as physicians, are not, and must never be, commercial entrepreneurs, gate-closers, or agents of fiscal policy that runs counter to our trust. Any defection from primacy of the patient's well-being places the patient at risk by treatment that may compromise quality of or access to medical care.
>
> *We believe the medical profession must reaffirm the primacy of its obligation to the patient through national, state, and local professional societies; our academic, research, and hspital organizations; and especially through personal behavior. As advocates for the promotion of health and support of the sick, we are called upon to discuss, defend, and promulgate*

medical care by every ethi-
cal means available. Only by
caring and advocating for the
patient can the integrity of our
profession be affirmed. Thus
we honor our covenant of trust
with patients.[9]

 TIP

"It's worth reflecting on the true source of stress. People often get upset at patients or other trainees when they are really upset about systems issues (e.g., pressure to admit or discharge; pressure to cover calls)."

Ethics vs. Legal Considerations

Medical residents have growing concerns about the risks of litigation during or after their training, and understandably seek ways to protect themselves. Educators in medical ethics and professionalism suggest that this focus is sadly misplaced and that residents should concentrate on learning ethical ways to preserve their relationships with patients and to act in their best interests as professionals. Because ethics and legal principles naturally overlap, it is generally assumed that the ethical physician should rarely be sued, although the application of the law to specific issues and case dilemmas can vary among provinces and states.

Most residents have taken courses and discussed ethics as undergraduates, but formal learning about ethics and professionalism during residency varies considerably from program to program.[10] As most training programs shift to competency-based learning paradigms, there have been new studies of opportunities to evaluate and enhance ethics training as a critical component of professional identify formation.[11] As well, undergraduate teaching may not prepare them for the hidden curriculum,[12] the not-so-obvious implicit learning culture where mixed messages about ethical positions, patient care, and collegial relationships conflict with official statements and orthodox messages about professionalism.[13,14,15]

Residents make decisions about ethics and physician–patient relationships daily, and the lack of formal help or instruction in these areas can add further stress, often referred to as moral distress,[16] to resident life. Trainees face conflict when they try to respect patients' autonomy if they believe that their own is compromised. (Conversely, they like it when patients readily agree, and this at times may benefit the doctor more than the patient.) Residents whose views differ from those of their patients or who witness malpractice will experience dissonance and confusion. Ethical disagreements with attending physicians, particularly concerning treatment, often are not voiced, and this represents a significant stressor.[17] Residents sometimes perform treatment as mandated by superiors, even if they strongly disagree, which contributes to significant moral distress. Always pay attention to times where you've felt silenced or coerced and reflect on what you did in the acute situation; then identify specific options or solutions for the next time this happens.

This chapter is intended to sensitize you to ethics issues and legal considerations and is designed to allow you to contemplate your role as a medical professional. It is by no means a comprehensive summary of the issues, nor does it offer legal directives.

Ethics Issues

All residents are required to engage in a curriculum that advances their knowledge of ethical principles that are foundational to the development of their competency as a professional. There are many models of curriculum, ranging from seminars to certificates, that touch on important topics. The award-winning Ethics Certificate program at Vanderbilt University[18] covers these core issues:

- Approaching ethics at the bedside: theories and principles, ethics infrastructure
- Informed consent, decision-making capacity, surrogacy, and advanced directives
- Financial conflicts and resource allocation
- End-of-life, withdrawal of care, and medically ineffective care (futility)
- Unique ethical considerations for trainees
- Mistakes and disclosure of errors
- Vulnerable populations

While you may not wish to complete, nor have access to, a comprehensive certificate program, you are encouraged to reflect on each of these topics[19] during your training in any specialty, seeking supervision when appropriate. Always distinguish what is expedient for the doctor/

system from what is good for the patient. Remember that decisions and actions deemed "legal" are not always ethical.

Moral Aspects of Medical Practice

Residents often experience conflict between their wish to heal ("benefi-cence") and patients' wish for autonomy and self-determination. In addition, residents' views of illness and of cultural or moral issues may differ dramatically from those of patients. Issues related to abor-tion, gender affirming surgery, medically assisted death, and care of migrants and refugees have become hot-button issues in certain juris-dictions. Residents must learn to recognize these inner conflicts and how they relate to the patient, and to ascertain, and then respect, the patient's wishes, rather than adopt an authoritarian, omnipotent stance. If residents cannot appreciate a patient's position, either they should say so, explaining what this may mean to their physician–patient contract, or they should help the patient find alternative care. They then remain responsible for their patient's care until another physician is found.

INFORMED CONSENT PROCESS

Informed consent exists to protect the patient, not the hospital or the caregiver. It consists of three key elements (see below).[20] Ask your teaching hospital to provide resources on what is expected of you as a resident.

- It must be voluntarily given – patients must be free to give consent, or not, and must offer their decision in the absence of coercion or duress.
- It must be given by a capable person – you are expected to take reasonable steps to ensure your patient has the ability to fully understand, analyze, and communicate their opinions and deci-sions clearly.
- It must be sought after the patient has been properly informed about the procedure, test, or intervention, its anticipated risks and benefits, the anticipated risks and benefits of not proceeding, and risks and benefits that may be unique to their life's circumstances.

Patient Refusal of Treatment

A patient has the right to refuse treatment if his reason is adequately explored and is not based solely on misunderstanding, misinformation (e.g., from physician-patient conflict), or coercion from external sources. The likely consequences of failure to give treatment should be presented to the patient. In most hospitals a patient is then asked to sign a statement affirming that treatment has been refused in full knowledge of these consequences. It is important to remember that this choice should not automatically be equated with incapacity or a suicidal tendency in the patient, although these possibilities must be explored. Take the time to find out what the patient's beliefs, fears, cultural safety concerns, or misperceptions are.

Management of the Patient Who Is Incapable

Incapable (formerly "incompetent," a triggering term for many) patients lack the capacity to make decisions about their own care and well-being. They cannot understand information relevant to a decision, consider choices logically, make a choice consistent with their own values, or communicate that choice. Most incapable patients have chronic neurological conditions that affect cognition, insight, and memory, such as dementia or post-stroke or post-traumatic syndromes. Some psychiatric illnesses (like acute psychosis) also affect insight and judgment. Legislation defining who can declare a patient incapable or incompetent varies; in some areas it is any physician, whereas in others it must be a psychiatrist. Chart documentation always includes a mental status exam and a commentary on the three criteria for informed consent (information, comprehension, and voluntariness). Verify the appropriate procedure with the hospital's social services department. Also check to see if the patient had previously completed a living will or advance directive.

If informed consent cannot be given because of a lack of capacity, the resident, with the help of a social worker, will want to initiate the proceedings for naming a substitute decision-maker or health care proxy, the details and designations of which vary from province to province and from state to state. The substitute decision-maker or health care proxy is an appointed person, who must be able to determine what the patient would have wished if able to choose, not what is best for the estate, the family, or the proxy. Ideally this person is someone who loves and respects the patient and may be a family member, but it cannot be assumed that the spouse or sibling will best serve the patient's interests.

Withholding of Information

Physicians have traditionally used "therapeutic privilege" to withhold potentially harmful or devastating information from a patient, often at the request of the family. Today this is seldom deemed appropriate by lawyers and ethics consultants because the competent patient has the right to know about diagnosis, treatment, prognosis, alternatives, and risks. Our colleagues in bioethics tell us that the question is not whether to tell, but how to tell. The physician is ethically bound to convey difficult news compassionately and to deal with the results, while continually offering information and support to the patient.

Confidentiality

The resident should not release information about a patient to anyone without clear authorization or express approval, which should be documented in the chart. This also means not chatting about patients where you might be overheard – in the elevator, hallway, or cafeteria. Caution with respect to protection of and access to medical records must be emphasized to all staff, especially with respect to technologies, such as computerized records, email, fax machines, and cellular telephones, virtual care platforms, and other systems that may be accessed by unauthorized individuals. Your hospital will likely have online teaching models about privacy, sharing information, and who constitutes the "circle of care."

"Implied consent" traditionally referred to a physician divulging details about a patient to family members or other members of the treatment team, but even this practice should be explored with the patient and recorded. Residents are often casual in the way they discuss some patients with each other (i.e., in an elevator or in the cafeteria), because of the potential for learning involved or an unconscious need to vent their feelings. This practice is increasingly being viewed as unethical because it may violate a patient's consent about what is said about him or her, and to whom.

In the United States, up-to-date information on the Health Insurance Portability and Accountability Act (HIPPA) can be found at www.hhs .gov/hipaa/index.html and www.ama-assn.org/practice-management /hipaa/hipaa-privacy-security-resources. In Canada, information on the Personal Information Protection and Electronic Documents Act (PIPEDA) and other documents related to patient privacy can be found at the office of the Privacy Commissioner of Canada at www .priv.gc.ca/en/privacy-topics/privacy-laws-in-canada/the-personal-information-protection-and-electronic-documents-act-pipeda. This is an area under considerable evolution, and there may be additional duties and responsibilities set by your province or state.

Exceptions to absolute protection of a patient's medical privacy vary locally, but include the following situations:

- Responding to a subpoena to give evidence in court (where files and documents can be held as evidence)
- Responding to a court order or search permit to produce a patient's chart (not simply a visit from a police officer or sheriff)
- Reporting, to appropriate authorities, child or elder abuse, gunshot wounds, unsafe drivers and pilots, certain venereal diseases, and workplace accidents
- Reporting, to appropriate authorities, a patient's imminent danger to self or others (suicide, homicide, rape, kidnapping, violent behavior, etc.)

If you have any questions about your duty or obligation to breach confidentiality you ought to seek advice from your program director, medical regulator, residency association, or indemnifier (who often have access to legal advisers or medical practitioners with considerable familiarity with these issues).

Management of the Patient with a Poor Prognosis[21]

Every resident during training is faced with decisions about continuing treatment as opposed to palliation and non-resuscitation of terminally ill patients, and residents must become familiar with making such distinctions. These decisions can be challenging and, at times, will be heart-wrenching and difficult. Each institution you work in will have a policy on resuscitation and how to document decision making, so become familiar with it. In Canada and elsewhere, medical assistance in dying (MAID) has been in place for many years and is undergoing considerable change.[22] Further, Canada is anticipating including mental illnesses as grievous and irremediable medical conditions in the next few years, setting the stage for additional changes in the provision of MAID services. Providing high quality end of life care is important and nuanced, and it will become more familiar as you move through your residency. We encourage you to become deeply familiar with this area of practice as soon as possible in your residency.

General guidelines from various medical,[23] nursing, and hospital associations for non-resuscitation include the following:

- An assessment that the condition is irreversible and estimates of how long the patient might live without intervention, as well as of the consequence of no-code status (i.e., a "do not resuscitate" order)
- An assessment of the patient's competence and ability to understand risks, benefits, consequences, and options with respect to a no-code status
- Consultation with an appropriate family member if the patient is incompetent
- Documentation of the attending physician's approval and a second opinion from another physician or clinical ethics consultant if there is doubt about the suitability of a no-code status
- A clear order written in the chart to clarify the no-code status

Management of Medical Resources

The management of medical resources is a controversial issue beyond the scope of this discussion, and its ramifications differ considerably between socialized medical systems (as in Canada, with initiatives such as Choosing Wisely[24]) and private ones (as in the United States, where the American Medical Association has a considerable portion of their Code of Medical Ethics dedicated to the financing and delivery of health care).[25] The resident should, however, remember the fundamental principle that every human being is entitled to appropriate care, regardless of diagnosis, race, creed, or ability to pay. Residents must be prepared to advocate for patients who are subject to systemic discrimination, marginalization, and/or stigmatization, which may at times lead to disagreement with supervisors and their hospital hierarchy. Your focus should be on individual patients and bedside decisions rather than macro-level policymaking.

Patient Safety: A Top Priority

An increasing and well-placed focus on comprehensive care of patients looks at errors, safety risks, and best protocols for patient safety. Medical indemnification organizations, such as the Canadian Medical Protective Association, offers its members a detailed collection of resources on patient safety at www.cmpa-acpm.ca/en/education-events /good-practices, including information on the fundamental elements of safe patient care, the role of having a just culture of patient safety, and practical case studies for your consideration.

National organizations, such as Healthcare Excellence Canada (www.healthcareexcellence.ca), are also expanding the view of patient safety to include interventions that reduce the harm from care that is offered without cultural safety or humility. In the United States, the ACGME[26] has also expanded their common program requirements to address issues of diversity, equity, and inclusion, clearly linking such initiatives with patient safety and improved quality of care.

The World Health Organization also has good resources on patient safety and reminds us of the common safety issues that occur in North American health care systems including medication errors, infections, surgical and treatment complications, and diagnostic errors.[27]

By learning how to practice medicine safely, within a just culture, and mindful of the importance of culture, you will improve the health and well-being of your patients, reduce your medico-legal risk of complaint or litigation, and contribute to improved outcomes of the health care system.

LEARNING MORE ABOUT PROFESSIONALISM
AND ETHICS ISSUES, INCLUDING QUALITY
IMPROVEMENT AND PHYSICAL, PSYCHOLOGICAL,
AND CULTURAL SAFETY

The following suggestions are offered for learning more about medical ethics:

- Consult the CanMEDS and ABIM websites listed above.
- Request and attend ethics case conferences, Grand Rounds, lectures, and retreats.
- Arrange debates or seminars around emerging trends and controversies. For example, how will recent Canadian court decisions about the legality of medically assisted death affect your patients, practice, and your sense of being a doctor?
- Try to incorporate ethics issues into your regular case presentations or into other residents' discussion groups to stimulate discussion. For example, explore what we mean by "culture" and "cultural competence" in health care culture. What does "cultural security" or "cultural safety "mean for an Indigenous patient?
- For an excellent resource, consult an article by Elana Curtis and co-authors, entitled "Why cultural safety rather than cultural competency is required to achieve health equity: A literature review and recommended definition."[28]
- Introduce ethics concerns into daily work. For example, should we be having free lunches on behalf of pharmaceutical companies, or is this a conflict of interest?
- Seek guidance and examples from more senior residents and attending physicians.
- For tips on ethics integration in teaching see an article by Fraser Howard, et al., entitled "Integrating bioethics into postgraduate medical education: The University of Toronto model."[29]
- Consider pursuing additional training in ethics, quality, or safety, such as a certificate program or advanced degree.
- Contact the hospital's ethics consultant about the particular difficulties of a case.

- Pay attention to your own levels of discomfort when you sense something is unethical and try to discuss these feelings with a colleague. Do not dismiss such feelings or let them add to your anxiety.
- Consult the books by Jonsen et al.[30] and Beauchamp et al.[31] in the notes; they are practical, case-oriented pocket guides to medical ethics and legal matters.
- Refer to the CMA's Code of Ethics and Professionalism (www .cma.ca/cma-code-ethics-and-professionalism) or AMA's Code of Ethics (www.ama-assn.org/delivering-care/ethics/code -medical-ethics-overview).
- Consider finding and attending an ethics seminar, workshop, or refresher course offered by a university's continuing medical education program.
- Prepare a Grand Rounds on an ethics topic, and consider alternative models of presenting such as a debate.
- Call the National Reference Center for Bioethics Literature at Georgetown University (1–800-MED ETHX or visit www.library .georgetown.edu/bioethics) for reference help.
- Read broadly to stretch your thinking.

Readings in Medical Ethics

Here is a list from the "Great Books in Medical Ethics" course offered by the Evanston, Illinois, Hospital Department of Medicine. Goodreads (www.goodreads.com) also has curated reading lists on medical ethics and professionalism that are updated regularly by readers. Literary events such as the Examined Life Conference (www.examinedlifeconference .com) at the University of Iowa also identify new voices speaking on important ethical topics. Consider forming a journal club to explore ethical issues raised by these classic literary works. (See the last chapter for additional titles.)

The Doctor's Dilemma – George Bernard Shaw
The Hippocratic Oath
Cancer Ward – Alexander Solzhenitsyn
The Death of Ivan Illych – Leo Tolstoy
An Enemy of the People – Henrik Ibsen

A Very Easy Death – Simone
  De Beauvoir
The Plague – Albert Camus
"A Country Doctor" – a story
  by Franz Kafka
"Ward Six'" – a story by Anton
  Chekhov
Tender Is the Night – F. Scott Fitzgerald
Frankenstein – Mary Shelley
Erewhon – Samuel Butler
The Power and the Glory – Graham Greene
The Imaginary Invalid and The Doctor in Spite of Himself – Molière
Man's Search for Meaning – Victor Frankl
The Elephant Man – Bernard Pomeranz
The Physician in Literature (excerpts) – Norman Cousins
Equus – Peter Shaffer

 TIP

"I always schedule at least one day off
the week after an ICU/ CTU rotation to
give myself a long weekend if possible."

Hippocratic Oath[32]

[You may disagree adamantly with some of its content, but it is
interesting to consider this historical document and to compare it
with subsequent physician oaths.]

*I swear by Apollo, the physician ... that according to my ability and judg-
ment, I will keep this oath and stipulation: to reckon him who taught me
this art equally dear to me as my parents, to share my substance with him
and relieve his necessities if required; to regard his offspring as on the same
footing with my own brothers, and to teach them this art if they should
wish to learn it, without fee or stipulation, and that by precept, lecture and
every other mode of instruction ...*

*I will follow that method of treatment which, according to my ability
and judgment, I consider for the benefit of my patients, and abstain from
whatever is deleterious and mischievous. I will give no deadly medicine to
anyone if asked, nor suggest any such counsel; furthermore, I will not give
to a woman an instrument to produce an abortion.*

*With purity and holiness I will pass my life and practice my art. I will
not cut a person who is suffering with a stone, but will leave this to be done
by practitioners of this work. Into whatever houses I enter I will go unto
them for the benefit of the sick and will abstain from every voluntary act
of mischief and corruption; and further from the seduction of females or
males, bond or free.*

*Whatever, in connection with my professional practice or not in con-
nection with it, I may see or hear in the lives of men, which ought not be
spoken abroad, I will not divulge ...*
Hippocrates, 5th century BC

Legal Considerations

Although ethically sensitive residents and effective communicators are
less likely to be sued successfully, there are, nonetheless, several measures they can take to protect themselves from legal action. Here is a list
of the most common allegations leading to medical malpractice suits
and strategies for avoiding them:

- Failure to diagnose or treat
- Failure to obtain appropriate consultation
- Improper or inaccurate communication among healthcare workers
- Unnecessary, improper, or negligent intervention or treatment
- Failure to respond to patient inquiry or emergent request
- Untimely or premature discharge from hospital
- Failure to obtain legal consent (i.e., prior to anesthesia)
- Equipment malfunction
- Abandonment or discharge from care without arranging appropri-
  ate follow-up or referral

Avoiding Litigation

There are things you can do to avoid complaints of malpractice. Here
are some tips.

- Know the standards and guidelines set by your medical regulator –
  they are all published on their websites, and they will send you
  notification of any updates. You will find that by following these
  expectations, your risk of complaint and litigation will be minimized.
- The most common reason for receiving a complaint or being sued is
  poor communication and physician attitude (i.e., arrogance, inter-
  rupting, not listening). Become a master communicator – you can
  never take too many workshops, receive too much feedback, learn
  new skills to apply in complicated situations, and adapt your skills
  to meet any changes expected by society.

- Practice the best medicine you can – the provision of high quality, safety-sensitive, culturally safe, and humble care will serve your patients (and you) well.
- Avoid coercion, misrepresentation of facts, or leaving conflicts unresolved with patients. Address a patient's dissatisfaction openly and calmly (see chapter 6). Physicians with good communication skills and good relationships with their patients are rarely sued, even if they have made an error in judgment.
- If in doubt about a diagnosis, treatment, or procedure in a particular patient's care, always obtain support for your decision from the senior resident, the attending physician, or a consultant. Document this information in the chart. Your residency malpractice insurance or union (resident association) guidelines may require you to discuss all aspects of care with your attending physician, but it is particularly important to record this information when discharging patients. Such guidelines may also come from your program and local licensing authority.
- Document all "transfers of care," that is, when signing over post-call, post-shift, or on leaving rotations. Residents worldwide have perfected safety-maximizing protocols for reliable, systematic transfers of care. See table 9.1 from Resident Doctors of Canada or RDoC (www.residentdoctors.ca/wp-content/uploads/2017/09/)

Table 9.1. Recommendations for transitions of care

Resident Doctors of Canada believe that patient safety can be enhanced by improved handover education. They recommend that:

1. Each patient handover should incorporate direct verbal interaction between care providers. Given the complexity of the handover process, using both verbal and written communication will ensure safe and accurate transfer of patient care.
2. Handover should take place in a quiet area where distractions are minimal. Sufficient time must be allotted for the handover.
3. The handover process should employ evidence-based tools and be standardized for each clinical setting. There are a variety of mnemonics and aids that may be adapted to the particular needs of a clinical setting.
4. A formal handover curriculum should be an accreditation standard for medical education, reflecting the core competencies of the CanMEDS framework.
5. Physicians require both didactic and interactive training in handover. The interactive component is especially important, and supervised evaluation of handover should be part of the training curriculum. A senior or chief resident, faculty member, or program director should regularly observe each resident's handover performance and provide formal feedback.

Source: https://residentdoctors.ca/

Policy-Statement-Handovers-EN.pdf). Call your hospital's director of professional services, residency director, union representative, or union lawyer if inadequate supervision or co-coverage is available to you during call or emergency department duty and document this exchange.

- If you make an error in an order, treatment, or procedure, do not attempt to hide it. Discuss it directly with the senior resident or attending physician or hospital manager to learn how and when the information should be divulged to the patient and family. Be sincere in your apologies. Do not alter medical records (the EMR will demonstrate or date and time-stamp these attempts in any case). For useful sample guidelines on disclosing adverse events, go to www.cmpa-acpm.ca/en/advice-publications/browse-articles/2015/disclosing-harm-from-healthcare-delivery-open-and-honest-communication-with-patients. Here you can access a checklist on "communicating with your patient about harm."
- Be sure to obtain proper consent from a patient before a procedure or treatment is started. If you do not, you could be charged with assault and battery. Because the attending physician ultimately is responsible for consent if he or she performs the surgery, determine what information he or she wants given and how it should be given.
- Do not release any information to a third party without written, documented consent. Ask the hospital's legal department under what circumstances patients have the right to see their own charts. (Patients should have the right to do so. Usually, a physician must be present to explain the aspects of care detailed in the chart so there are no misunderstandings.)
- Always double-check the orders of juniors and medical students before signing them, because you are responsible for the consequences.
- Verify how much your attending physician expects to be involved in patient care and decision making and the kind and frequency of documentation expected from you (e.g., once a week in a rehabilitation setting vs. several times a day in an intensive care unit).
- Make sure you have adequate malpractice protection that covers you for the full period of the statute of limitations (the designated number of years a patient can sue a physician after the particular intervention) in your province or state. Investigate whether you are covered for moonlighting rather than assuming you are insured outside the hospital.
- When preparing written prescriptions, print or print out drug names, indications, dosing, and timing instructions. Avoid

abbreviations, sloppy handwriting, and vague directions like "prn." When handing in a prescription, spell the patient's name and the drug name carefully.[33] Avoid oral (verbal) orders, as they put you, patients, and nursing staff at risk. The AMA House of Delegates, in one of its annual meetings, stressed that "medication errors expose patients to additional but preventable risks leading frequently to prolongation of hospital stay and in some cases contributing to morbidity and mortality, medication errors being the most common case of non-op adverse events (19.4%) and the second most prevalent and second most costly reason for medical malpractice litigation."[34] Most of us use electronic medical records (EMRs) and print prescriptions using our office computers. It's still important to double-check the name of the patient with date of birth and the name and dosing of medications.

- Maintain good rapport with patients. Avoid making inappropriate or angry comments. Improve cultural sensitivity around ethnic groups.
- Obtain a patient's permission before discussing care with family members.
- Discuss the benefits, risks, and statistical results of a particular procedure or treatment with your patient, and document the discussion in the chart.
- The EMR/EHR will date and time all patient visits, orders, and interventions. Document if you were instructed by your senior resident or attending physician.
- The electronic record will demonstrate any attempts you make to change documentation or attempts to access patient information to which you do not require access (i.e., checking out VIP patients in your hospital).
- Always search and record potential drug contraindications or allergies, or previous drug interactions. Hospital pharmacists can help you with this.
- Keep your charting and dictations up to date.
- Do not agree to partake in research protocols unless they have been cleared by the university and/or hospital ethics committees.
- Verify hospital and local guidelines on curatorship, commitment, use of restraints, and consent issues. Learn whether the age of majority differs from the age of consent to treatment. When a patient is a legal minor, try to have the patient's consent to notify

his or her parents. If the treatment is potentially controversial, you may have to obtain parental or guardian consent yourself. Consider obtaining an external consultation.

- Have controversial and sensitive procedures witnessed (e.g., pelvic exams and procedures such as lumbar puncture post-trauma that may result in complications). Document the name of the attendant.
- Be aware of legally sensitive areas such as rape, child abuse, custody, and potentially violent behavior when interviewing patients.
- Review reporting protocols and make sure you prepare very precise documentation because you may have to give evidence in court.
- Request periodic lectures from your hospital's legal department on specific topics that apply not only to residency, but also to eventual hospital or community-based practice.
- Master skills in virtual care, including being up to date on the most recent standards and guidelines and discerning when a patient ought to be redirected to face-to-face care.

Working with Your Regulator

You may be named in a complaint or notification to a medical regulator. Increasingly, patients are making complaints to regulatory bodies about residents, with the most common issues being deficient patient assessment and unintended negative outcomes. Most complaints did not result in severe physician sanctions; however, those that did were linked to clinical error, poor communication, and lapses in professionalism.[35] This can be a stressful experience, and one that is unfamiliar. Here are some tips to help:

- Keep your file with the College or Board up to date, including your contact information and payment of any fees.
- Open correspondence from them immediately, including email correspondence. They may be alerting you of a new standard or guideline, a complaint matter, or other time-sensitive issues. If you need support, reach out to your resident association, your program director, chief resident, indemnification organization, physician health program, or other trusted support – avoiding opening the letter will only make things worse.
- Take time to process what it is your regulator is asking of you. Review all medical records in detail, consult with the involved

supervisor, speak with your program director, and have any response you submit reviewed by your indemnification organization.

- Tell the truth, always.
- Never alter the medical records. Amendments that are appropriately labeled, dated, and signed are acceptable but the original record must never be altered. Be mindful that most EMRs allow for external auditing that can readily identify inappropriate modification or access of the record.
- Respond in a timely fashion and share only the facts. It is possible your response will be read by the patient and their counsel, as well as a committee of the regulator. A humble, factual, sincere, and respectful tone is helpful.
- If called to an interview, treat it like you would attending court – tips on that topic follow.
- If you made a mistake, say so, and describe your appreciation of the harm done to the patient. It is appropriate to apologize and express regret, and also appropriate to describe the steps you have taken to learn from the incident, including participating in remedial efforts (i.e., additional coursework, remedial rotation).
- Taking good care of yourself will help you participate in a regulatory process better. Lean into your courage and contact your physician health program; review resources on manag ing the stress of medico-legal actions, such as www.cmpa-acpm .ca/en/advice-publications/browse-articles/2012/medico-legal-problems-and-patient-safety-incidents-the-emotional-impact.

Working with the Court

Residents may sometimes be asked to testify about patients they have seen, treated, or assessed. Here are several tips for testifying.[36]

- In Canada, call the Canadian Medical Protective Association for guidelines if you are a member. In the United States, speak to your housestaff representative, hospital risk manager, or malpractice insurer.
- Determine whether it would be more appropriate for your attending physician to appear as the person finally responsible for the patient's care.

- Clarify details of your expected appearance (fees, date, time, and location) with the lawyer who has consulted you.
- To avoid wasted time, request that you be called just before your appearance in court and ask whether a detailed written report would be adequate instead of an appearance.
- Discuss with the lawyer who requests your testimony what evidence is expected from you and how to address the judge. Let her know if you have objections to the usual procedure of swearing in witnesses with the Christian Bible.
- Bring copies of reports, X-rays, and other documents, because the originals may be kept as evidence. Be prepared with a brief summary or notes.
- Be prepared to state your credentials; you must establish your credibility. Expect to be challenged.
- Stay calm and present a serious demeanor. Do not become angry, irreverent, or comical. Use simple terms and do not bluff if you do not know the answer to a question.

OATH FOR NEW DOCTORS[37]

I swear to fulfill, to the best of my ability and judgment, this covenant:

I will respect the hard-won scientific gains of those physicians in whose steps I walk, and gladly share such knowledge as is mine with those who are to follow.

I will apply, for the benefit of the sick, all measures which are required, avoiding those twin traps of overtreatment and therapeutic nihilism.

I will remember that there is art to medicine as well as science, and that warmth, sympathy, and understanding may outweigh the surgeon's knife or the chemist's drug.

I will not be ashamed to say, "I know not," nor will I fail to call in my colleagues when the skills of another are needed for a patient's recovery.

I will respect the privacy of my patients, for their problems are not disclosed to me that the world may know. Most especially must I tread with care in matters of life and death. If it is given me to save a life, all thanks. But it may also be within my power to take a life; this awesome responsibility must be faced with great humbleness and awareness of my own frailty. Above all, I must not play at God. I will remember that I do not treat a fever chart, or a cancerous growth, but a sick human being, whose illness may affect his family and his economic stability. My responsibility includes these related problems, if I am to care adequately for the sick.

I will prevent disease whenever I can, for prevention is preferable to cure. I will remember that I remain a member of society, with social obligations to all my fellow men, those sound of mind and body, as well as the infirm ...

Source: Louis Lasagna, 1964. "A Modern Hippocratic Oath." www. aapsonline.org/ethics/oaths.htm.

Written in 1964, this was an effort to update the Hippocratic Oath. What would you change today? Or better yet, have a stab at writing your own contemporary physician oath and discuss it with colleagues.

10

Taking Care of Business

Managing Your Finances

The complete details of budgeting and investing and of planning and setting up a practice are beyond the scope of this chapter. In Canada, more information can be obtained from the Canadian Medical Association, provincial residency associations, and the MD Management Limited network. This network also offers superb tax, financial set-up, and financial counseling seminars, preferred loans, and other services to Canadian medical residents in training. In the United States, the American Medical Association offers some practice-related workshops.[1] Student loan repayment protocols, for example, change over time; they are published in *The Physician's Guide to Financial Planning*. Further financial information can be obtained from unions, the Committee of Interns and Residents (CIR), the American College of Physicians (ACP), the American Association of Medical Colleges (AAMC), the American Medical Students' Association (AMSA), and occasionally at the hospital or state association program level. There are also some wonderful grassroots resources, such as *Physician Financial Independence,* a Facebook-hosted, 30,000-member strong, source of peer support focused on helping physicians achieve financial health.

This chapter touches briefly on the following areas: budgeting, education debts, moonlighting and its tax implications, insurance, obtaining loans, and getting help from other professionals. Run your decisions by a financial expert. Try to set yourself defined, time-specific goals and then track them over time. Keep all of your documentation organized, up to date, and let your spouse or executor know where your loan, banking, credit card, investment, insurance, and tax information is stored. Check your credit rating at least once a year.

Budgeting

A budget consists of income and expenses, both fixed and variable. A monthly budget should be updated regularly with your partner and include the following items:

Income Sources

- Salary: your own and spouse's
- Pensions
- Bonuses
- Investments: dividends, interest, rent
- Research or other grants
- Alimony
- Child support
- Moonlighting
- Other income

Fixed Expenses

- Housing: mortgage, rent
- Utilities: phone, heat, water, electricity, internet
- Property: taxes, maintenance costs, and insurance
- Health care: medical insurance and deductions, medications, dental care, family health coverage
- Loan payback (e.g., on student loans)
- Insurance: life, disability, catastrophic health event policies, malpractice
- Income taxes
- Transportation: public versus own vehicle (insurance, maintenance, licensing, parking)
- Childcare
- Board examinations, licensing, professional, and medical society fees
- Other expenses
- You may wish to establish an emergency fund for unforeseen expenses

Variable Expenses (Areas to Control)

- Conferences, CME, books
- Retirement investment

- Other loans (car, personal, credit cards, line of credit)
- Food: groceries and takeout
- Household expenses
- Clothing, laundry, cleaning
- Pocket money
- Transportation
- Vacations
- Gifts
- Charities
- Repairs (household)
- Entertainment (concerts, films, clubs, television, publications)
- Emergency funds
- Retirement contributions (start early!)

Table 10.1. Your net worth

Assets		
Cash or equivalent		
	Bank accounts, savings	$_____
	Bank accounts, checking	_____
	Life insurance cash value	$_____
	Other	$_____
Securities		
	Stocks, common and preferred	$_____
	Mutual funds	$_____
	Bonds	$_____
	Other	$_____
Real estate		
	Home	$_____
	Cottage	$_____
	Other buildings	$_____
	Land	$_____
	Other	$_____
Other investments		
	Medical practice	$_____
	Retirement savings plan (RRSP, IRA, etc.)	$_____
	Home ownership savings plan	$_____
	Other business ventures	$_____

(*Continued*)

Assets

Other property

	Home furnishings (appliances, furniture)	$_____
	Cars	$_____
	Boats, planes, recreational equipment	$_____
	Jewellery	$_____
	Collections (art, stamps, etc.)	$_____
	Other	$_____
Debts owed to you		$_____
Miscellaneous		$_____
Total assets		

Liabilities

Mortgages outstanding

	Home	$_____
	Other buildings	$_____
	Land	$_____
	Other	$_____
Loans outstanding		
	Banks, savings and loan	$_____
	Broker	$_____
	Insurance policy loan	$_____
	Other (student)	$_____
	Other	$_____
Taxes		
	Income tax (federal and provincial or state)	$_____
	Property	$_____
	Other	$_____
Bills outstanding		$_____
Miscellaneous		$_____
Total liabilities		$_____
Net worth (assets minus liabilities)		$_____

Education Debts

Some provinces in Canada allow a six-month grace period after completion of medical school before repayment on government loans is due, but there is some variation. Check these regulations with your university's registrar, postgraduate medical office, the Canadian Medical Association (www.cma.ca), or an accountant familiar with medical residents' issues.

Education debts can be a source of extreme stress for medical residents in the United States, where traditionally loans had a two-year interest-deferment period during internship and a ten-year payback limit after completion of medical school. Since residency lasts from four to six years, these conditions can be a source of considerable stress. (Strikingly, primary care physicians in the first three to five years following residency often have expenses that exceed earnings.) Residents can request a forbearance to not make payments during residency, but interest charges have generally started after the two-year period. AMSA, the CIR, and the American Medical Association have been lobbying effectively to change the legislation governing these conditions including the length of the payback period. (For updates, see the Resident Resource section of the AMA website, www.ama-assn.org, and visit the AAMC loan repayment/foreigners and scholarship website database at www. aamc.org.) In Canada, you may be able to extend your repayment period to a maximum of 19.5 years. It's also essential to investigate debt-repayment incentives offered in underserviced, northern, and rural areas in both Canada and the United States.

Medical Moonlighting and Its Tax Implications

Moonlighting (or working shifts outside of your hospital or residency hour obligations) can provide a lucrative source of added income, but the following factors should be weighed:

- Whether the residency program policies approve of moonlighting; be aware that some programs will undermine your attempts at lobbying to limit residency hours by pointing out that residents voluntarily seek out extra (moonlighting) hours.
- Provincial or state restrictions on moonlighting (e.g., hospital vs. outpatient settings, applicable hours); the Accreditation Council for Graduate Medical Education (ACGME), for instance, prohibits work within one period of a regular residency scheduled shift.
- Whether your malpractice insurance provides coverage outside the hospital and whether the moonlighting establishment will offer such coverage
- The need for and availability of supervision

- Potential scheduling conflicts with residency and home life
- Licensing regulations (e.g., your eligibility to prescribe drugs outside of a training milieu)
- Earnings from fees (your employer will deduct a percentage for overhead from your billing, the rates usually ranging from 25 to 40 per cent)
- Get the overhead rate stated in writing and signed by an authorized official.
- Keep a record of your billings and ask your employer for official receipts.
- Determine availability of support, secretarial services, and referral sources.
- You should not be coerced to do moonlighting; work in the setting where you are actually training.
- Pay attention to your energy levels – do not moonlight if it exhausts you or interferes with study time.

Self-Employed Physicians

Moonlighting will allow you to increase tax deductions and credits because you are a self-employed physician. These deductions and credits can include the following:

- Rent and administration charges
- Salaries and employee benefits
- Medical supplies
- Office taxes and insurance
- Office supplies and expenses
- Office telephones, computers, and other equipment
- Medical journals, textbooks
- Office repairs and maintenance
- All other expenses that help you earn income (e.g., cleaning bills)
- Convention expenses
- Continuing medical education expenses
- Entertainment expenses
- Malpractice insurance/CMPA coverage in Canada
- Professional services
- Travel expenses (a percentage of your car expenses related to your practice)
- Office at home

- Interest and bank charges; any interest that you must pay on loans used for business purposes or for earning income and any bank charges related to these loans
- Leasing fees (automobile and equipment)
- Depreciation of furniture and textbooks
- Moving expenses to relocate after residency

Other Tax Deductions

Your accountant will advise you as to how purchasing government bonds and pension and retirement investment plans (i.e., Registered Retirement Savings Plans in Canada, and Individual Retirement Accounts in the United States, with other recognized savings vehicles like the TFSA) can reduce your tax load.

If you are not moonlighting (i.e., not self-employed), your tax deductions and credits may be limited to the following: tuition, monthly student deduction, equipment and textbooks, exam and insurance fees, and moving expenses (in the first year of residency), besides the standard deductions and credits detailed on tax forms.

Other tax areas to explore with your accountant depend on your particular circumstances and include childcare, interest on mortgages (in the United States), investment losses, medical expenses (in excess of a certain percentage of your income), charitable or political donations, sales tax credits, child education plans, and spousal income sharing.

Insurance

Make sure you explore and fully consider all insurance options. Check your housestaff agreement for details. Purchase coverage while you're healthy!

Life Insurance Terms and Definitions

- Whole life: provides a fixed amount of insurance protection and an accumulation of savings in exchange for a regular premium until the insured's death.
- Limited payment life: whole life insurance for which the premiums are level but paid over a specified period (e.g., 20-pay life, single-premium life)

- Endowment policy: combines life insurance and savings as in whole life; however, the policy has a specified maturity date. If the policy holder lives to this maturity date, he or she can opt to receive the face value as a lump sum or to receive payments for life or over a specified number of years
- Critical life: covers you for acute or new onset life-threatening illnesses (as delineated in the contract) and offers a lump-sum for those conditions.
- Participating: policy holders are given a share in the total profitability of the insuring company; this is commonly called a dividend but is in reality a refund on premium overpayments.
- Non-participating: policy holders have no rights to share in the profits of the company; the premium is fixed and is calculated on the basis of an estimate of interest rates, administration costs, and future mortality.
- Double indemnity: the beneficiary receives twice the face value of the policy if the insured's death is the result of an accident.
- Term (or temporary) insurance: called "pure" because it has no cash-surrender or loan value; policies are insured for specified periods, and benefits are paid only if death occurs within the term of the policy.
- Level term: the face value remains constant over the life of the policy.
- Decreasing term: the face value of the policy decreases each year, but the premium remains the same.
- Renewable term: can be renewed after a prescribed period of time.
- Convertible term: this may be converted to permanent coverage within a prescribed period without evidence of insurability.
- Review all options closely with your financial planner.

Most residents in Canada and the United States are provided a combination of life, health, and disability insurance through their hospitals, housestaff associations, or university. Ask your hospital resident representative about your coverage, and if none is available, contact your provincial or state medical association about available programs.

Buying Life Insurance

- Look for the lowest-cost renewable term insurance available.
- Do not be dazzled by the projections of "cash value" accumulations. These are usually based on assumptions favorable to the company.

- Whole life insurance is expensive and very rarely makes financial sense. This option should be carefully reviewed with your financial planner.
- Provincial and state medical association group plans may provide term insurance at one-half to one-fifth the cost of similar individual policies.
- Ask your association representative to comment on any deficiencies or agent claims existing in the group policy.
- Discuss your life insurance needs with the provincial or state medical association's insurance adviser to see what coverage (if any) you need. Many single physicians starting out in practice need none at all or just enough to cover their debts. Once they marry and have a family, their needs change. You should reassess your needs annually to cover any changes in your lifestyle.
- Even though they do not need any life insurance coverage, some physicians obtain the minimum unit amount from their local medical association to protect their future insurability. Failure to do so would jeopardize their ability to obtain future coverage if a medical problem develops.

Disability Insurance

Discuss your disability insurance needs with your provincial or state association's insurance adviser to determine whether you are adequately covered. You may be covered by the hospital for a portion of your income, but you might want to supplement this with an additional amount before starting out in practice. When you begin practice, estimate your expected income over the first two years and obtain the appropriate amount of disability coverage. As your income increases, your coverage can increase until it reaches the maximum allowed. Initially you may elect a low qualification period (e.g., fourteen days) before receiving payments, but as your finances become more stable you can increase the length of this period and reduce the cost of premiums. Be sure to maximize benefits while you are healthy, as premiums and exclusions to coverage increase with any illness.

Compare your medical association's disability plan with those of private companies. You may find that some of these companies will not sell insurance coverage if you participate in your medical association's plan. Physicians who want more coverage than the association plan allows buy some coverage from a private company before buying more from the association. Before buying such a policy, however, ask your provincial or state association to review the private company's proposal. Your choice will depend on your annual earnings and the amount of protection you want. See the insurance agent of the medical association annually to reassess your needs.

Buying Disability Insurance

- Buy the insurance while you are healthy; you will not usually qualify after you become ill, diagnosed with specific medical conditions, or disabled.
- Check with your hospital representative to see whether you are already covered.
- You may want to supplement your present coverage through your medical association policy or a private plan.
- Medical association plans may be 30 to 60 per cent cheaper than private plans.
- Be wary of agents' "scare tactics" and "smoke and mirror tactics."
- Select a short "elimination period" until your finances are well established.
- Premiums are neither tax-deductible nor creditable, but benefits are not taxable.
- Ask your medical association's representative to comment on any deficiencies a private agent claims exist in the group policy.

Malpractice Insurance

In Canada, one body – the Canadian Medical Protective Association (CMPA), a mutual medical defense organization – provides professional liability protection to its members. CMPA coverage is mandatory for Canadian physicians. In the United States, details of malpractice coverage should be explored through state medical associations or the hospital or moonlighting establishment for which you are working.

Other Insurance

Risk management, automobile, health insurance after residency, and homeowner's insurance are further options to be explored with your broker.

Obtaining a Loan or Line of Credit

- Banks are in business to make money from lending. They are not lending you money as a favour. Shop around! Residents are a great risk for banks. You should not be paying banking fees, annual fees, or credit card renewal fees.
- Be businesslike when dealing with your banker; see her by appointment and prepare complete and accurate documentation. You may want to suggest in the interview that you might want to do all your banking (personal and professional) at one branch if the deal is favorable.
- Ask for the prime rate on loans with variable interest rates. Make the banker justify any higher rate.
- A fair rate to expect is prime + ½ per cent to prime + 1½ per cent for a variable rate in a stable economy, but you may be able to negotiate better rates. A fixed rate is more expensive but may be useful if you expect interest rates to rise.
- Establish a line of credit on which you can draw during the first six months so that you pay interest only on the funds you use.
- Bear in mind that banks also try to woo professionals and will match the offers made to you by their competitors, so feel free to shop around. Some medical organizations, unions, hospital systems, and universities have made arrangements with specific banks to offer bespoke services to their members, often with additional benefits and supports unavailable to the general public. Reach out to them to see what is currently available, and also check out the resources below.
- You may wish to consolidate your student loans into a professional line of credit, thus securing a lower interest rate and allowing for tax deductions on interest charged.

Help from Other Professionals

Residents need help from other professionals, especially as they finish training and consider starting up a practice. Obtain references from your provincial or state medical association or from colleagues. The CIR also provides such information.

What a Good Accountant or Financial Planner Can Do for You

- Help you design and follow a monthly budget and help you strategize paying down your debt
- Set up a record-keeping system for your practice when you start
- Provide you with monthly and formal financial statements that will summarize the financial health of your practice
- Help you budget and plan for the post-residency period
- Prepare income tax returns (some local medical associations offer income tax preparation services for residents at a reduced rate)
- Advise on financial investments
- Comment on the suitability of and timing for incorporating your practice
- Discuss retirement, estate, and tax planning

Choosing an Accountant

The ideal accountant should have the following:

- Experience with a medical practice
- Ability to communicate in a clear, concise, and professional manner
- Ability to provide responsible leadership for your financial affairs

Other Considerations

- Once the accountant sets up a bookkeeping system, make sure you have a good understanding of how it works. There are numerous easy-to-use apps and programs you can review.
- Ensure that the system is being maintained properly so that you are not paying the accountant for jobs that you could do yourself.
- Take your accountant with you when you consult with other financial advisers or grant permission for them to communicate. He or she will have a good understanding of your financial affairs and will be able to interpret any advice and its implications.

What a Good Lawyer Can Do for You

Ask the housestaff union for the name of the lawyer it retains to assist residents, usually free of charge, for matters related to residency (e.g., contract abuses). A good lawyer can also

- Help you create a will (no matter how young you are)

- Review contracts from potential employers (and help you to ensure that what was promised in a job interview is delivered contractually
- Draw up formal contracts between you and your coworkers when you start practice.
- Advise on lease agreements, mortgages, deeds, by-laws, and so on about the location of your practice
- Advise on personal matters such as wills
- Advise on investments, taxes, and so forth
- Assist you in writing a will or living will
- Create a trust or corporation to protect assets and reduce tax load

Important Considerations in Dealing with a Lawyer

- Avoid choosing a friend as a business lawyer, as it may be awkward to change lawyers later.
- Ask your family lawyer, colleagues, or accountant to recommend a business lawyer.
- Ensure that the lawyer can communicate with you in a manner you can understand.
- Make the most of the time spent with the lawyer by making sure that your material is well organized and that you are providing all the information he or she needs to do the job well.

Post-residency Help

What an Investment Specialist or Stockbroker Can Do for You

- Look after or make buy-and-sell transactions
- Provide prompt, accurate execution of orders
- Provide a record of your holdings
- Make reliable market forecasts
- Provide timely technical and fundamental research
- Give insight into your investment needs

What a Real Estate Agent Can Do for You

- Connect you with a good mortgage broker
- Show you what is available for purchase and give expert appraisals
- Help you choose the best location for your office
- Help arrange details of leases

- Advise you on investment property
- Refer you to another agent on matters that are outside his area of expertise

What a Good Business Management Consultant Can Do for You

- Help you identify tax-credited educational investments for your children
- Help set up a medical practice, including choosing a good location, training staff, and so on
- Offer expertise and problem solving on various aspects of the practice such as collections, income distribution, and partnership terms
- Help you prioritize financial costs (home purchase, debt payment, forming investment and credit strategies, etc.)
- Provide practice surveys and business analysis
- Give specialized consultation on financial investments, personal and family budgeting, and so forth
- Advise on risk management, automobile, and homeowner's insurance – these are further options to be explored with your broker

Other Sources

- For information on AMA Practice Management Workshops for Residents, see www.ama-assn.org. They publish a very helpful document called "Succeeding from Medical School to Practice," at www.ama-assn.org/ama/pub/about-ama/our-people/member-groups-sections/resident-fellow-section/succeeding-medical-school.
- MD Management and the CMA publish a guide called "New in Practice – What Medical Residents Need to Know Before Entering Practice."
- The AAMC has excellent resources on finances during residency. See www.students-residents.aamc.org/financial-aid/handling-finances-during-residency.
- Your specialty association website may have a finance section or resident-specific advice. One good example for emergency docs can be found at www.emra.org.

11

Knowledge Is Power:
Social Media Guidelines and
Helpful Resources

This chapter will review various sets of guidelines for the use of new technologies in learning and in communicating with colleagues and patients. The plea to use common sense rings loud and clear in all of them.

The use of social media has revolutionized our culture, including medicine and health care. Patients, because of their access to the internet, become better informed around illness and treatment than they were before. This phenomenon has been called "Doctor Google," and represents both a challenge and advantage to the care of patients.

The Federal State of Medical Boards (US), in its model policy guidelines for appropriate use of social media and social network in medical practice, highlights that physicians must protect themselves from unintended consequences and maintain the public trust by protecting the confidentiality and privacy of their patients, avoiding requests for online medical advice, acting with professionalism, being forthcoming about their employment, credentials,

 TIP

"The internet has democratized access to medical information, a.k.a. Doctor Google. Just as it's easier for residents to look up information on any condition, it's easier for patients as well. It can be tempting to dismiss patients' own research, but they're often looking at the same sites we are. Finding out what patients have found online, talking about the specific information they found, and leading them toward other resources can often go a long way toward assuaging patient fears and engaging patients in their own care."

and potential conflicts of interest, and that they be aware that information they post online may become available to anyone and could be misconstrued. Indeed, patients often become curious about their health care providers, and seek access to information on their personal lives. This becomes relevant when, for example, residents use social media to date, network, log personal information, or post photos or other images. The guidelines suggest that doctors are discouraged from interacting with patients on personal social networking platforms.

Social networking websites can be useful places for doctors to gather and share their experiences, and to discuss diagnosis and treatment. It is recommended, however, that these networks are secured and password protected. Patient privacy and confidentiality must be protected at all times. Information that could be used to identify a patient should never be included in electronic exchanges that might contravene privacy laws, such as HIPAA in the US (PHIPA, in Canada). Doctors who choose to write about patient encounters or their experiences as professionals must diligently disguise identifying data. When they post content online, they should remember that they are always representing the medical community and their standard of professionalism.

To review their university and hospital institutions' policies on the use of social media, the Canadian Medical Association published a policy paper called "Social Media and Canadian Physicians: Issues and

 TIP

"What has emerged over the past ten years is a semi-public sphere. In terms of disclosure, Facebook is somewhere between a phone call and the front page of a newspaper. But every electronic communication falls somewhere along that spectrum."

 TIP

"It is essential to keep accurate records of any communication with patients, just as one would write a note after any clinical encounter."

 TIP

"Any information that could identify a patient is considered confidential. This information can only be communicated along secure lines of communication. What constitutes a secure line varies from jurisdiction to jurisdiction and sometimes from hospital to hospital. Residents should consult their hospital's privacy officer to find out the exact rules in a particular jurisdiction."

Rules of Engagement."[1] Their recommendations are provided in the following section, and the CMA offers updates on social media utilization on the Physician Wellness Hub portion of their website.

Key Issues

Patient Confidentiality

- The privacy and security of individual patient information is paramount and should never be shared beyond the circle of care. This principle is also enshrined in CMA policy. In communicating with an individual patient in anything other than a face-to-face environment, a secure electronic communication platform must be used. Identifiable patient information, including images, should never be posted online or shared in electronic communications of a general nature.

- When using social media, physicians should endeavor to use the most stringent security and privacy settings available for the particular platform.

- Physicians with employees should make them aware of issues concerning patient confidentiality in their own use of social media. Consideration should be given to instituting a social media policy for the office or practice.

- Social networking sites cannot guarantee confidentiality. Anything written on a social networking site can theoretically be accessed and made public. For example, the Patriot Act in the United States makes it possible for the US government under certain conditions to access any information posted on a social networking site or website hosted by a US service provider, even if this information is located within the "private or direct message" area of the site.

 TIP

"As a rule of thumb, don't email, text, or post online anything you wouldn't be comfortable seeing on the front page of a newspaper in an exposé of what residents say when they think nobody is looking."

 TIP

"It's best to avoid putting any information that can identify a patient into a text message. Just like an email, text messages are insecure and their content can be reproduced by any recipient. And if the wrong person receives the message, a serious privacy violation might take place."

Professionalism

- Having an online profile or identifiable presence on social media can have the same degree of positive or negative impact on a physician's social reputation as being active in any other public venue. In fact, having access to a global audience can magnify this reputation.
- The most effective use of social media often involves communicating information that is both personal and professional. However, physicians must retain the appropriate boundaries of the patient-physician relationship when dealing with individual patients. The same standards of professionalism that would apply in face-to-face physician-patient interactions also apply in electronic interactions.
- If a physician is an employee of a health care institution or organization that has social media guidelines in place, he or she should review these and act accordingly.

 TIP

"In general, most email addresses are considered insecure. Most hospitals will grant residents a secure email address via which they can send identifying information about patients to other people with a secure address. Of course, information should only be sent if the recipient has a reason to receive it (e.g., it is being sent to another physician involved in that patient's care)."

 TIP

"It's annoying to perform a patient assessment or a complicated procedure only to be paged midway through. Many residents now text each other where once they might have paged. Texting has advantages over paging: it's asynchronous, which means that residents can respond at their leisure, and one can put a lot more information into a text message than into a short pager callback number."

 TIP

"As a matter of politeness, I refrain from checking my smartphone for anything in front of a patient. I treat my smartphone like I treat my pager, like I treat any bodily function: It's best done outside the patient's room, ideally in private."

Online Communication Issues

- Electronic communications are not anonymous and are always stored in some form. As such, it is possible to trace the author of a comment, even if posted anonymously.

- Once their material is published online, authors of comments on social media sites no longer control how and where the information is disseminated, and these comments can sometimes lose context.
- Postings to social media sites are subject to the same laws governing how patients and members of the public seek information about health and increase the sense of engagement patients have in their own care. Through a variety of websites, and fueled by the growing availability of electronic patient health records, patients are increasingly sharing information with other patients about their health conditions and their health care providers.

 TIP

"Patients may sometimes want to communicate electronically. Requests for this will only increase. After all, virtually every other profession now conducts large amounts of business online. If you are going to communicate with patients by email, for example, it is often helpful to get a signed consent and document that you've discussed the risks and benefits with the patient, as with any medical procedure. Again, it can be helpful to contact the privacy officer at your hospital, as many hospitals have policies around electronic communication with patient and may even have standard consent forms for physicians and patients to sign."

The New Media, Professionalism, and Confidentiality

The rapidity with which we can share information about ourselves and others is a mixed blessing. Here are some tips for avoiding professional breeches:

TOP 10 TIPS FOR USING SOCIAL MEDIA IN PROFESSIONAL PRACTICE

The Canadian Medical Protective Association has published the following helpful guidelines on using various social media platforms.

1. HAVE AN OBJECTIVE AND SELECT THE RIGHT PLATFORM

Physicians should have clear objectives for their professional social media presence so they can select the most appropriate social media site. If your goal is engagement, then platforms such as Facebook and Twitter may be appropriate. If the aim is teaching and learning, then private physician networks may be the best choice. To disseminate health information to benefit the public, blogs may be considered. If the goal is advocacy or a call to action, media interviews with potential social media exposure may generate the desired outcome.

2. AVOID SOCIAL MEDIA FOR ONE-ON-ONE DISCUSSIONS

Doctors must remember that social media can be used to engage in public communication, but it is not appropriate for private conversations. Social media may be ideal to connect with patients collectively on issues such as general health promotion or office administration, but you must not communicate specific patient health information to an individual over social media. While some sites appear to facilitate private conversations through direct messages, content communicated via social media is unprotected and publicly accessible. Confidentiality of patient information can be placed at risk.

3. ESTABLISH CLEAR BOUNDARIES

Whatever platform you use, you need to keep clear boundaries between your professional and personal social media use. For example, if using Facebook both professionally and personally, it's best to have a separate account for each. And, the high standard of behavior that physicians are held to (by statute and professional necessity) also extends to your social media use.

4. RECOGNIZE THAT THE REACH IS WIDE AND THE AUDIENCE UNKNOWN

Because social media has a broad reach, it can be difficult for physicians to know their audience and tailor their messages. As a result, your information should be general in nature and directed at a non-scientific audience. With no physical barriers to the internet, the information may be used by Canadians or people in other countries.

5. CONSIDER THE IMPACT OF YOUR COMMUNICATION STYLE AND REACH

Communication principles that apply when speaking to patients, stakeholders, or the media also apply when using social media. You should use clear language, have supporting examples that respect privacy and confidentiality when giving an opinion, provide credible sources and research, address all sides of an issue, and present information professionally. Remember that information shared via social media can have a significant and lasting impact. When contributing to social media, keep in mind that the information reaches far and wide, and is permanent.

6. GENERATE INTEREST, PARTICIPATION

The very nature of social media is to invite people to review, share, respond, and contribute to information. Comments, reactions, support, and contrary views are all part of the landscape and should be delivered respectfully. Each participant brings their unique perspective to the discussion. In other words, social media is a two-way street and you should be prepared to be part of a dialogue, when appropriate.

7. BE AWARE THAT LIBEL, SLANDER, AND DEFAMATION APPLY

Defamation – that is, making false statements that can harm the reputation of an individual or an organization – carries the same consequences whether it appears online or in traditional media. When defamatory statements are published or spoken online or otherwise, you may face allegations of libel or slander. As well, you should be aware of the potential for cyber libel – when something posted on the internet is both untrue and damaging. You must also realize that plagiarism and copyright infringement can lead to legal action.

8. DEVELOP A SOCIAL MEDIA POLICY

Physicians should determine how they will use social media – to engage patients or disseminate information, or both. When it's appropriate, physicians may choose to answer certain questions or respond to comments in a discussion; however, they should be mindful of the content and the audience.

When you state in a policy or guideline how you intend to use social media, it sends a clear message to patients and others on what to expect. Guidelines should be communicated and apply to staff, patients, colleagues, and other health care providers working in your office.

9. MANAGE PRIVACY AND MINIMIZE BREACHES

Some social media platforms allow physician-only groups to participate and share expertise in a way that mimics Grand Rounds in hospitals, where doctors gather to discuss cases. Physicians must recognize these online practitioner communities are still virtual spaces and can be subject to security breaches.

When using social media, you must always consider what security measures and procedures should be adopted to avoid privacy breaches. This includes using appropriate protection and privacy settings to avoid communicating patient health information.

10. FOLLOW LICENSING BODY AND COLLEGE GUIDELINES

Medical regulatory authorities (colleges and licensing boards) recognize that physicians are using social media in their practice and have created material to guide physicians on how to engage online while meeting legal and professional obligations. The material includes information on how to respect professional boundaries and the importance of exercising caution when posting information that could identify a patient.

Source: https://www.cmpa-acpm.ca/en/advice-publications/browse -articles/2014/top-10-tips-for-using-social-media-in-professional -practice

What about Patient Advocacy?

Residents often ask about how to advocate for people and causes using social media. Here are some guidelines:

Remember not to use patient names or details or any unique or identifying information without your patient's written consent and their final approval of what you'd like to post.

You can use social media for advocacy in several different ways: listening to and amplifying the stories of those with particular experiences, informing people of issues they were previously unaware of, organizing supporters for a specific cause, and lobbying for more direct action. Sometimes, sharing a day-to-day experience in health care can have a meaningful impact. For example, the story of working with patients in the ICU during a pandemic raises the profile of the need for widespread vaccination. Additionally, physicians use social media to mobilize around community issues like a hospital or clinic closing, but this can point to larger issues and encourage debate around health equity. This can then allow physicians to capture timely subjects in the news cycle and offer their unique perspective. Physicians can also influence public policy. Patient stories are often more memorable than facts and data and may compel legislators to act.

Other Communication Technologies Used in Patient Care

Email

Most doctors now communicate with patients by email, but parameters, expectations, and patient consent should be explicit. The following guidelines are thorough and state of the art.

Email Communication Guidelines from the AMA

(a) Establish turnaround time for messages. Exercise caution when using email for urgent matters.
(b) Inform patient about privacy issues.
(c) Patients should know who besides the addressee processes messages during the addressee's usual business hours and during the addressee's vacation or illness.
(d) Whenever possible and appropriate, physicians should retain electronic or paper copies of email communications with patients.
(e) Establish types of transactions (prescription refill, appointment scheduling, etc.) and sensitivity of subject matter (HIV, mental health, etc.) permitted over email.
(f) Instruct patients to put the category of transaction in the subject line of the message for filtering: prescription, appointment, medical advice, billing question.
(g) Request that patients put their name and patient identification number in the body of the message.
(h) Configure automatic reply to acknowledge receipt of messages.
(i) Send a new message to inform patient of completion of request.
(j) Request that patients use the auto-reply feature to acknowledge reading a clinician's message.
(k) Develop archival and retrieval mechanisms.
(l) Maintain a mailing list of patients, but do not send group mailings where recipients are visible to each other. Use the blind copy (BCC) feature in software.

(m) Avoid anger, sarcasm, harsh criticism, and libelous references to third parties in messages.

(n) Append a standard block of text to the end of email messages to patients, which contains the physician's full name, contact information, along with reminders about security and the importance of alternative forms of communication for emergencies.

(o) Explain to patients that their messages should be concise.

(p) When email messages become too lengthy or the correspondence is prolonged, notify patients to come in to discuss or call them.

(q) Remind patients when they do not adhere to the guidelines.

(r) For patients who repeatedly do not adhere to the guidelines, it is acceptable to terminate the email relationship.

Medico-legal and Administrative Guidelines

(a) Develop a patient-clinician agreement for the informed consent for the use of email. Most teaching hospitals have a templated form. This should be discussed with and signed by the patient and documented in the medical record. Provide patients with a copy of the agreement, which should contain the following:

  i.   Terms in communication guidelines (stated above).
  ii. Provide instructions for when and how to convert to phone calls and office visits.
  iii. Describe security mechanisms in place.
  iv. Hold harmless the health care institution for information loss due to technical failures.
  v.   Waive encryption requirement, if any, at patient's insistence.

(b) Describe security mechanisms in place including

  i.   Using a password-protected screen saver for all desktop workstations in the office, hospital, and at home.
  ii. Never forwarding patient-identifiable information to a third party without the patient's express permission.
  iii. Never using patient's email address in a marketing scheme.
  iv. Not sharing professional email accounts with family members.
  v.   Not using unencrypted wireless communications with patient-identifiable information.

vi. Double-checking all "To" fields prior to sending messages.

(c) Perform at least weekly backups of email onto long-term storage. Define long-term as the term applicable to paper records.

(d) Commit policy decisions to writing and electronic form.

(e) The policies and procedures for email be communicated to all patients who desire to communicate electronically.

(f) The policies and procedures for email be applied to facsimile communications, where appropriate.

(g) The policies and procedures for email be applied to text and electronic messaging using a secure communication platform, where appropriate.

Source: AMA Policy Finder[2]

Telemedicine and Virtual Care

The COVID-19 pandemic catapulted most physicians into the world of providing virtual care by phone, video, or email. There is no turning back, as many patients and providers have come to prefer these modalities when medically appropriate and safe.

Here are some basic protocols to review and discuss with your attending staff. Establish how you will be supervised for the virtual care you provide on your own to outpatients.

The Virtual Playbook

Excerpts from the *Virtual Care Playbook* are reprinted with the generous permission of the Canadian Medical Association.[3]

SCOPE OF PRACTICE: WHAT PROBLEMS CAN BE SAFELY ASSESSED AND TREATED

Physician regulators all adhere to the same concept when it comes to virtual visits: a physician must not compromise the standard of care. That means that if a patient seen virtually provides a history that dictates a physical examination manoeuver that cannot be executed remotely, the physician must redirect the patient to an in-person assessment.

For this reason, the scope of virtual practice is currently limited to encounters that require only history, gross inspection, or data that patients can gather with cameras and common devices, such as glucometers, home blood-pressure machines, thermometers, and scales. In practical terms, you can safely use virtual care to

- assess and treat mental health issues
- assess and treat many skin problems (photos submitted in advance provide resolution that is much better than the resolution of even a high-quality video camera)
- assess and treat urinary, sinus, and minor skin infections (pharyngitis, too, if you can arrange throat swabs)
- provide sexual health care, including screening and treatment for sexually transmitted infections, and hormonal contraception
- provide travel medicine
- assess and treat conditions monitored with home devices or lab tests (e.g., hypertension, lipid management, thyroid conditions, and some diabetes care; in-person consultations will still be needed for some exam elements)
- review lab, imaging, and specialist reports
- conduct any other assessments that do not require palpation and auscultation

In contrast, the problems that are currently **not amenable to virtual care** include any new and significant emergency symptoms, such as chest pain, shortness of breath, and loss of neurologic function. They also include ear pain, cough, abdominal/gastrointestinal symptoms, musculoskeletal injuries or conditions, most neurological symptoms and congestive heart failure.

Note that the normal requirement for physical examination can be waived if doing so is truly in the patient's best interests, such as

- during contagious disease outbreaks
- when the patient has temporarily limited mobility or lack of transportation

"Webside" Manner

It is easy to overlook the fact that conventional physician offices provide many visible cues that assure patients that they are in a professional office to see a medical doctor. Most of those cues are absent in virtual care.

In addition, because video connections do not allow patients to see either the doctor's screen or the doctor's surroundings, the patient will not know where your gaze has gone when you are not looking them in the eye. That impairs your ability to engage sufficiently to win patient trust, which is particularly important when you do not have an existing relationship.

Still, accumulating research provides reassuring evidence that patient outcomes and satisfaction after virtual visits are equal to conventional encounters.

Key Recommendations

- Place your workstation in a location that protects the patient exchange from being seen, overheard, or interrupted by others. That includes ensuring that there is no visibility of your screen(s) through a window.
- Use a professional, neutral backdrop and good lighting, and wear a white coat. While many doctors resist wearing white coats, older research shows that patients of all ages prefer their doctors to wear white coats, and it reinforces for them that you are a health professional.
- If you use a separate web camera, position it so that the camera is directly above the computer window with the patient's video image. This allows you to always be looking directly at the patient.
- Eliminate all distractions from your computer and surroundings. In particular, turn off all visible and audible computer notifications, which create noticeable distractions.
- Make an extra effort to engage with the patient at all times and assure them that they have your full attention. This includes eye contact, body language, and attentiveness.
- Collect and create patient education texts and weblinks to share after the encounter to replace what you can show to patients when you are seated in the same room.

"The Virtual Visit from Beginning to End" by Mark Dermer

This terrific resource from the *Virtual Care Playbook* has been adopted by the CMA, Royal College and the CFP. Provide the patient with the following for the virtual visit, which includes everything your office does for a conventional visit:

1. record and update patient demographic elements
2. verify the patient's health insurance card
3. note the reason for the visit
4. add any photos submitted in advance (particularly for skin complaints and sore throats)

Also collect consent to use video conferencing if this is the patient's first time. Ideally, these tasks should be delegated to office staff to complete before the video connection begins.

At the beginning of the video connection with the patient, perform the following verifications, disclosures, and consent actions.

•   Authenticate the patient's identity. If it's a first encounter, ask the patient to hold up a piece of valid government-issued photo ID to the camera to confirm who they are. But, if you already know the patient by sight, that will suffice.
•   Confirm that the patient is in a province, territory, or state where you hold a license and billing number. Physicians usually must be licensed where the patient is located, and governments do not issue billing numbers to doctors without licenses in their jurisdiction; ask the patient which city and province or territory they are in, and record that in the chart.

Ask the patient the following things:

1. Ask whether they are in an appropriately private location. If they are, record their response in the record. If not, arrange for them to quickly change locations (parked cars are a common fallback) or reschedule the visit.
2. Ask whether other persons are present off camera (always assume that they are, particularly with mature minors).
3. Disclose the risks of a virtual visit and obtain verbal consent. Record consent in the chart.
4. At the conclusion of the virtual visit, make extra effort to confirm the patient's understanding of the assessment and plan, then arrange to send any prescriptions to pharmacies and any requisitions or referrals to the patient or the appropriate office or facility.

5. Complete the encounter note for the virtual visit, following the same standard as for a conventional visit.
6. Bill the government health plan the appropriate fee code(s) for the virtual visit. The health plan or your provincial or territorial medical association can advise you on billing rules and any specific fee codes for virtual care.
7. If necessary, complete, process, and submit any forms associated with the visit.[4]

Excerpted from the *Virtual Care Playbook* by Dr. Mark Dermer. (2020), CMA, Royal College, CFPC. More detailed resources covering all aspect of using virtual technology (from selecting optimal technology and obtaining patient consent, to specifying the scope of practice and adopting tips for maximizing communication) can be found at:

https://www.cma.ca/virtual-care-playbook-canadian-physicians (Canada)
https://www.ama-assn.org/system/files/ama-telehealth-playbook.pdf (US)
and the American Telemedicine Association: https://www .americantelemed.org

Artificial Intelligence in Medicine – Future Shock

New AI technologies will increasingly affect how we practice medicine because they bring forth so many opportunities and efficiencies by

- speeding up documentation and other administrative tasks
- automating the reading and interpretation of x-rays, scans, and lab results
- predicting specific clinical outcomes
- using data sets to identify patterns, support sequences of decisions, and facilitate more accurate diagnosis
- identifying new preventive and treatment measures based on genetic data
- optimizing medication selection and fostering new treatment approaches/innovations based on AI modelling
- allowing patients to wear or use home-based diagnostic devices with data delivery in real time

- facilitating robotic surgeries
- analyzing costs, efficiencies, errors, and patient satisfaction levels
- allowing for 3D modelling in the teaching of anatomy and surgical simulation and preparation
- enhancing existing virtual and remote telemedicine approaches
- creating "smart" clinics and hospitals by streamlining connectivity of all systems

High-Tech Conclusions

Always weigh the pros and cons of using existing or new technologies to communicate with or treat patients. Be prepared to discuss the information (and seemingly legitimate misinformation) patients find online in an open and non-judgmental way. Think of it as an opening to deeper dialogue and for more education and connection.

Never allow technology (or expedience) to compromise the doctor-patient relationship or your maintenance of appropriate professional boundaries. Always clarify the parameters, limitations and expectations related to virtual linkages (for example, you cannot possibly reply 24/7 to emails). Sometimes, you need to see a patient in person to really know what's going on medically and psychologically. The more often we are removed from the bedside or clinic, the less humanistic our practices may become. And the more "plugged in" we become as physicians, the less we may be able to achieve balance, well-being, and freedom in our personal lives.

Always trust your clinical intuition, knowledge, and judgment alongside your compassion. There's no substitute for the Art of Medicine, even in the midst of rapidly advancing medical science.

12

I'm Finally Done: Now What?
Thoughts on Transitioning into Practice

In Greek mythology, Procrustes was a robber who pretended to be an inn-keeper on the road to Athens. Travellers seeking success in that city would stop at the inn, where Procrustes would tie them to a bed and adjust them to its length, cutting off the limbs of those who were too tall and stretching those who were too short. He was eventually killed by the hero Theseus.

Residency is truly a modern "Procrustean voyage," where confor-mity, even to deforming principles, can be the price of success. Musi-cal, creative, playful, spontaneous, even romantic aspects of our lives may be cut off if we're not careful. There is no modern-day Theseus to intervene to preserve our integrity, to remind us of our need to remain whole. Our superiors and patients often expect too much of us.

Residency can be a time of great personal growth as well as stress and doubt. The completion of residency marks a departure from the many years of study and training and a shift towards independence and autonomy, away from attending physicians, senior residents, and the hospital hierarchy. Choices have to be made fairly with your part-ner and family about fellowships, subspecialties, private versus hospi-tal practice, urban versus rural practice, and moves to new locations. Personal priorities have to be re-examined in the light of having more free time after years of living in an externally imposed structure. Debts wait unpaid. Residents sometimes feel emotionally numb at the end of their training, wondering if they will be able to maintain competence and empathy. They also experience mixed feelings of nostalgia or even loss over moving on, and of pride and accomplishment, tinged with panic, in having become full-fledged physicians.

Various factors can make starting a practice a bit unnerving, particularly in the context of a world upended by COVID-19, climate emergencies, and strong political tensions. Many patients have unrealistic expectations about their health and of their physicians, resulting in a marked increase in litigation against physicians. Malpractice claims in North America have gone through phases of escalation and stability, and the impact of the pandemic is yet to be fully appreciated. In Canada, patients may consult an excessive number of physicians because health care is perceived to be free of charge. At the same time, provincial or state programs are being cut, hospitals closed, and the job mobility of new physicians curtailed. Physician unemployment in some specialties is problematic, with the RCPSC reporting up to 20 per cent of new specialists were unable to find work at the time of their certification.[1] In the United States, many patients and some physicians have come to see their exchange as being based on profit and consumerism, and overseen by corporate insurance or managed-care companies that dictate policy and, indeed, what is to be considered acceptable treatment. Thankfully, physicians have benefited by applying their leadership skills to challenging issues affecting the profession and are increasingly leading positive and transformative change.[2,3]

There are other reasons to remain optimistic about the future of residency training and medicine in general in North America. New areas of focused practice are emerging according to the Association of American Medical Colleges,[4] such as onco-immunology, nocturnists, lifestyle medicine, clinical informatics, and virtual care. Surgical and radiological advances open more opportunities for minimally invasive and remote procedures. The holistic medicine movement with proponents such as Andrew Weil, MD, and Jon Kabat-Zinn, MD, have established the value of mind–body connection, mindfulness, meditation, and how the physician–patient relationship has its own capacity to heal. Artificial Intelligence is burgeoning. We are more aware of our past and how power inequities led to unexamined manifestations of historical oppression and systemic discrimination within health care. Dedicated colleagues across North America are seeking to transform medical education and practice with these inequities and exclusions in mind (and heart).

Best of all, doctors are insisting on taking better care of themselves and are spending more time with their loved ones, and this makes them better physicians and happier, more resilient human beings.

Options after Residency

The Fellowship and Research Option

Fellowships, which last from one to three years, fall into three categories: clinical, research, or combined.

A fellowship can provide an opportunity to develop a subspecialty, publish, and enhance the possibilities of an academic appointment. (In some university centers a fellowship, with resultant publications, is required before an academic appointment is granted.) It may allow you to sample a new university setting or city, postpone setting up practice, and clarify career plans. Discuss these issues with your mentor, residency director, or university fellowship officer. Matters to consider in negotiating a fellowship are similar to those in residency selection and include the following:

- Application procedures and interviewing
- Selection criteria (e.g., residency completion, provincial or state licensing) and degree of competition
- Benefits, funding, and salary (existence of a financial ceiling if one bills for patients seen)
- Office space and secretarial services
- Teaching, clinical, and call duties
- Publication expectations
- Assignment of credit or authorship for work done
- Possibility of grant renewal or ongoing funding
- Obligation to remain with the research department for a stipulated period on completion of the fellowship
- Availability or guarantee of a staff position after fellowship

Fellowship Funding

Many trainees begin doing research in medical school and residency and choose to continue after residency. The principal sources of fellowship funding in Canada are the Canadian Institutes of Health Research

(CIHR), Health Canada, and the Natural Sciences and Engineering Research Council. Provincial funding is also available for specific projects, and the Royal College and College of Family Physicians in Canada also offers grants. Funding in the United States is diverse and you may wish to carefully research options that may be offered by health care systems, foundations, corporations, governments, and universities.

Current information on most fellowships available in the United States appears in the education issue that the Journal of the American Medical Association publishes every August (also available online). Information on federal research funding can be obtained from the National Institutes of Health, and Health Resources and Services Administration. Another resource is the American Physician and Scientist Association, at www.apsa.org. The number of subspecialty positions has actually been increasing in the United States over the past several years. Index Medicus has a listing of articles discussing pertinent topics relating to fellowships (administrative, pedagogical, and so on). It may be worthwhile doing a search of current literature in your area of interest. The AMA-FREIDA program also has a fellowship databank (see www.freida.ama-assn.org).

The fellowship office at the university at which you hope to train can provide information on deadlines, addresses, and the application procedures of provincial and state funding bodies. In addition, write to specialty associations because they often offer funding or scholarships, and their databanks provide information on fellowships in North America. Other potential sources of funding include the following:

- Employment under attending physician grants
- Hospital research institutes
- Residency extension (postgraduate year 5 or 6)
- Junior staff appointments
- Philanthropic agencies such as the National Cancer Institute or Heart and Stroke Foundation
- Private industry (e.g., pharmaceutical companies)
- Self-funded clinical fellowships where one bills for patients seen
- Other foundation awards
- Scholarships and grants available through state, provincial, and national bodies

Additional Degrees

Many physicians consider taking additional degrees after finishing residency. While it may be the last thing on your mind, additional education can help shape your career by helping you develop unique skills. Traditionally, MBA degrees were a stepping stone for those interested in clinical administration and leadership. More popular today are programs focused on physician leadership. These range from local certificate programs all the way to master's degrees in health leadership. Organizations such as the Canadian Society of Physician Leaders and the American Association for Physicians Leadership keep track of growth opportunities, including specific training programs.

Some physicians complete a master's degree in education or medical humanities, often with an eye to specializing in educational scholarship. Alternatively, many universities offer certificate programs in medical education that help busy clinicians enhance their talents as an educator.

Physician-coaches are increasingly common, serving a unique role in helping their peers develop their careers and enhance their leadership journey. Programs in coaching range from focused workshops and certificate programs all the way to master's degrees. The Institute of Coaching at Harvard Medical School is ensuring the field of coaching in medicine is based in scientific integrity and, increasingly, coaches are being accessed to help physicians enhance their talents and address any gaps in their skills.

Finally, physicians are incredibly creative people. Many physicians have turned to advanced degrees in creative writing, the humanities, narrative medicine, music, visual arts, and theatre to stretch their potential and nourish their minds.

While choosing to return to school may not be a simple or easy decision, additional education can be a gift and enhance your career significantly.

Academic Medicine

Many graduate specialists emerging from residency or fellowship training choose to embark on full-time university-based academic careers. In weighing the advantages of a given academic position, consider and clarify the following:

- What academic rank will be offered in the position (i.e., lecturer vs. assistant professor), and what mechanisms permit promotion?
- Will you be assigned some other title (i.e., "Clinical Associate"), and what are the advantages or disadvantages of this interim status?
- Will tenure be available, and how is it granted?
- Are cross-appointments with other departments permitted or encouraged?
- What grants or financial resources are held by the department, and how might your income be guaranteed?
- Will sabbaticals be available, and at what frequency?
- How is parental leave respected and supported?
- What are the mission statement of the medical school, hospital, department, and division? Are they compatible with your goals?
- How much time will be allocated or protected for research versus clinical service?
- What are the details of the research environment: lab personnel, office space, provision of materials and supplies (such as computer software)?
- What support (i.e., coaching, mentoring, administrative functions) will be available for research start-up?
- How much inpatient or outpatient clinical work is expected, and what opportunities for teaching will be available?
- How do financial considerations add up, such as salaries, billing ceilings (and where surplus money goes when you surpass a ceiling), income split between salary and clinical work, benefits (insurance and leaves of absence), office selection and office staff, moving expense reimbursement?
- What are the interview procedures (see chapter 2)?

During final negotiations for the academic post, seek a written offer summarizing the above points. Discuss the offer with family, your spouse, friends, and possibly your lawyer, as they will all help you clarify ambiguities in the offer and uncertainties in your own mind.[4]

Locum Tenens

Many graduating residents feel unprepared to settle down in one practice or academic setting. They may wish to work part-time, travel, pay off student loans in a hurry, or explore cities where they might wish to settle eventually. The advantages of *locum tenens* (Latin for "place holder") positions include the large variety of practice settings, flexible scheduling, low office overhead, and low start-up fees and living expenses. You can find locums by word of mouth, through medical journals, licensing bodies, provincial or state medical association registries, or your professional specialty association. Many medical placement agencies exist in the United States and Canada. See www .locumtenens.com and www.physicianwork.com. Visit your provincial or state medical association website for listings as well.

When negotiating with the placement agency or a specific medical facility, find out the mechanism of payment (hourly or daily, rates or fee for service), the overhead percentage deducted from your salary, and whether there is a minimum time commitment. Inquire whether you will be provided with provincial or state licensing, housing, and health and malpractice insurance. Don't be afraid to shop around or to negotiate firmly for benefits. The family physician shortage across North America puts you in a good position to bargain, and cross-province and state licensing is currently being made more accessible and reciprocal.

International, Humanitarian, and Volunteer Medicine

Many graduates decide to work part-time in a free, low-cost, or community-based clinic as a way of giving something back and enhancing skills for hands-on, low-technology primary care. Most provinces and states can provide lists of public-health or community clinics. The Red Cross holds health fairs across the United States, and recruits volunteers for health screening programs. Other physicians seek experience abroad in Third World countries. Often contacts can be made through Canadian or American medical schools that have affiliate programs overseas or through agencies such as CUSO (Canadian Universities Services Overseas), the World Health Organization, and the Pan American Health Organization. Here are a few specific resources for medical opportunities abroad:

- International Development Research Center (www.idrc.ca)
- Global Health Council (www.globalhealth.org)
- Health Volunteers Overseas (www.hvousa.org)
- International Medical Corps (www.imcworldwide.org)
- Médecins Sans Frontières (www.msf.org)

- Doctors of the World (www.doctorsoftheworld.org)
- Doctors Without Borders (www.msf.org)

Clinical Practice Options

Trying to decide where and how to set up a practice may prove daunting for the graduating resident. Options include group versus private versus hospital-based settings, salaried versus fee-for-service positions, HMOs, and public- versus private-sector institutions.

A new physician can join an already established group practice and pay overhead or buy into the partnership. Retiring physicians often sell their practices. See "Things to Consider," below.

Practice opportunities are usually listed in medical journals, on national, provincial, and state association websites, or sent to physicians by recruitment agencies (headhunters). Hiring a physician recruiter is one option. They work like a headhunter (a term that is sure to be abolished) and can help you in three ways:[5]

- They filter information and avoid a "web of confusion." They will do the legwork, field calls and inquiries, and match your preference and specifications to a potential employer.
- They maximize exposure to an inner circle of hospitals and clinics that don't advertise and will be selective about whom they share your CV with.
- They will take your working style, personal preferences, family needs, hobbies, and recreational interests into account and help you to select an appropriate job in an appropriate setting. They have links to realtors, chambers of commerce, etc.

Information on the geographical distribution of physicians in the United States can be found in AMA's annual publication "Physician Distribution and Medical Licenses in the United States." The AMA also publishes a useful resource on transitioning to practice which can be accessed at www.ama-assn.org/medical-residents/transition-resident-attending /transitioning-practice. Talk to your medical accountant about all options and financial and contractual obligations before signing on. Consider attending one of the AMA's annual practice management workshops for residents, which tour the country. Topics include "Starting Your Practice" and "Joining a Partnership or Group Practice." Information and up-to-date publications can be obtained from www.ama-assn.org. Your specialty association website may have guidelines on entering practice as well. Another useful resource is www.drcareers.ca.

THINGS TO CONSIDER ABOUT WHERE AND HOW YOU WANT TO PRACTICE

- Family needs and preferences (job options for your spouse, schools for your children, community resources)
- Provincial/state licensing requirements restrictions (you'll need to apply for licensing and billing privileges at least nine months in advance of setting up practice)
- Type of practice:
  - Solo, group (single of multi-specialty)
  - Hospital or university-based
  - Salaried or fee-for-service
  - Government/community clinics
  - HMO, PPO, or MSO (in the United States)
- Geography (city vs. rural; weather; proximity to other families)
- Financial issues (cost of move, practice set-up, affordability of community re: housing and cost of living)
- Contractual issues:
  - Salary, benefits, insurance coverage, bonuses, partnership options (remember to bargain hard!)
  - Service, on-call, and administrative responsibilities
- Collegiality, friendliness, and supportiveness of work setting
- Job satisfaction of physicians and support staff (i.e., a functional work setting!)
- Need for your clinical services or local competition levels (how long until your practice fills up?)
- Future prospects: Can you grow in this job and this community?

A Note on Side Gigs

Side gigs (www.physiciansidegigs.com) seem to be increasingly common in medicine, particularly for those in their early years of practice. Some find side gigs a useful way to pay off debt while others find it exposes them to joyful activity that is completely unrelated to their medical practice.

Some side gigs are directly related to medical practice. Course creation, medico-legal chart reviews, acting as an expert witness, completing medical surveys, serving on medical association committees or boards, or providing additional virtual care services all fit into this space. Be sure to approach this work like any other opportunity – do your homework, have a contract, set and maintain clear boundaries, and be mindful of any real or perceived conflict of interest.

Some gigs are entirely different and may include commercial ventures, like selling products or complementary and alternative health services. We encourage you to consult with your regulator and/or lawyer prior to moving too quickly into this space. Boundary issues and regulatory standards will require careful review and attention to minimize any conflict or tension in this sort of work.

What you choose to do with your spare time is, of course, up to you ... but we do encourage you to have an open and honest conversation with yourself about your capacity to take on additional work.

Summary

As you finish your residency, pat yourself on the back and celebrate with your loved ones, but remember that your learning does not stop there. You will require continuing medical education as long as you call yourself a physician. Give yourself permission to explore all your options: if you tire of clinical practice, you can conduct research, write, broadcast, consult, lobby, invent, administer, mediate, coach, create, or become politically active around issues such as climate change, systemic discrimination, housing and food insecurity, or the stigmatization and neglect of certain populations. You can work, teach, or consult in other countries.[6] You can join academia and become the kind of professor who humanizes the experience of learning for both students and residents. Your vocation within medicine can change and grow as you do. Career counseling and medical executive coaching is now available to doctors to help them explore options. Doctors used to think they were set for life – now we realize we need to establish career goals on a regular basis, re-invent ourselves, and try new challenges just like any other professional. We have to redefine and rediscover both pleasure and purpose in our work, throughout our careers.

Whatever your choice, remember the satisfaction of providing optimal, empathic, ethical care, of making accurate diagnoses, of helping someone feel better and regain a sense of dignity in the face of illness. Remember the honor of knowing what your patients have told you and no one else, and of being present at the key moments of their birth, life, and death. Remember to thank your colleagues along the way. Always find that balance between lifestyle and service that our predecessors could not imagine or attain. As Sir William Osler reminds us, "The practice of medicine is an art, not a trade; a calling, not a business; a calling in which your heart will be exercised equally with your head."[7]

Other Well-Being Resources

Baum, N., Blau, J., Moskowitz, P., & Paprocki, R. (2017). *The Three Stages of a Physician's Career – Navigating from Training to Beyond Retirement.* American Association for Physician Leadership, New Orleans.

Bower, K., & Riba, M. (2017). *Physician Mental Health and Well-Being.* Springer, New York.

Goldman, L.S. (Ed.). (2000). *The Handbook of Physician Health: The Essential Guide to Understanding the Health Care Needs of Physicians.* AMA Press, Chicago.

Gerada, C. (2020). *Beneath the White Coat: Doctors, Their Minds, and Their Mental Health.* Routledge, New York.

Hertling, M. (2015). *Growing Physician Leaders.* Rosettabooks, New York.

Dr. Michael Myers has written a number of books focused on physician health and well-being, including *How's Your Marriage?*; *Why Physicians Die by Suicide*; and *Becoming a Doctors' Doctor: A Memoir.* Information at michaelfmyers.com.

Ogborn, M. (2022). *Sudden Leadership: A Survival Guide for Physicians.* Friesen Press, Altona, MB.

Puddester, D., & Patel, H. (2013). *The Time Management Guide: A Practical Handbook for Physicians by Physicians.* Royal College of Physicians and Surgeons of Canada, Ottawa.

Simonds, G. (2018). *The Thriving Physician.* Studer Group Pensacola, FL.

The Resilient Physician (www.TheResilientPhysician.com; 1-888-629-2313) is a bimonthly newsletter "dedicated to today's physicians, medical families, and medical organizations," and contains practical tips on improving the quality of life for doctors and their patients.

Recommended Conferences

The CMA (Canadian Medical Association), AMA (American Medical Association), and BMA (British Medical Association) hold an International Conference on Physician Health every two years. Visit their websites for further information.

Notes

1 Body, Mind, and Soul

1   2021 report on residents. (2021). Association of American Medical Colleges, Washington, DC.
2   CAPER annual census of post-M.D. trainees, 2020–2021. (2021). Association of Canadian Medical Colleges, Ottawa.
3   Blachly, P.H., Osterud, H.T., Josslin, R., et al. (1963). Suicide in professional groups. *N Engl J Med*, 268: 1278–82.
4   McCue, J.D. (1982). The effects of stress on physicians and their medical practice. *N Engl J Med*, 306: 458–63.
5   National Academy of Sciences. (2019). Taking Action Against Clinician Burnout: A Systems Approach to Professional Well-Being.
6   West, C., Dyrbye, L., & Sinsky, C. (2020). Resilience and burnout amongst physicians and the general US working population. *JAMA Netw Open*, 3(7). DOI:10.1001/jamanetworkopen.2020.9385.
7   Mari, S., Meyen, R., & Kim, B. (2019). Resident-led organizational initiatives to reduce burnout and improve wellness. *BMC Med Educ* 19, 437. https://doi.org/10.1186/s12909-019-1756-y.
8   Pattani, R., Wu, P., Irfan, A., & Dhalla, M.D. (2014, Jul). Resident duty hours in Canada: Past, present and future. *Canadian Medical Association Journal*, 186(10): 761.
9   Mari, S., Meyen, R., & Kim, B. (2014, June). Resident-led organizational initiatives to reduce burnout and improve wellness. *Annals of Surgery*, 259(6): 1041–53. DOI: 10.1097/SLA.0000000000000595.
10 Canadian Medical Association, National Physician Health Survey. Ottawa, 2021.
11 Ibid.

12 Zoorob, D., Shah, S., La Saevig, D., Murphy, C., Aouthmany S., et al. (2021). Insight into resident burnout, mental wellness, and coping mechanisms early in the COVID-19 pandemic. *PLOS ONE*, 16(4). https:// doi.org/10.1371/journal.pone.0250104.

13 Couyarraze, S., et al. (2021). The major worldwide stress of healthcare professionals during the first wave the COVID-19 pandemic – the international COVISTRESS survey. *PLoS One*, 16(10): e0257840.

14 Global Climate and Health Alliance. (2021). The Limits of Livability.

15 Doctors of BC. (2021). Violence Prevention Guide for Community Clinics.

16 Cohen, J.S., Leung, Y., Fahey, M., et al. (2008). The happy docs study: A Canadian Association of Internes and Residents well-being survey examining resident physician health and satisfaction within and outside of residency training in Canada. *BMC Research Notes*, 1: 105.

17 Block, L., Wu, A.W., Feldman, L., Yeh, H.C., & Desai, S.V. (2013, Sep). Residency schedule, burnout, and patient care among first-year residents. *Postgrad Medical Journal*, 89(1055): 495–500.

18 Transue, E. (2006). "Haiku of Residency," in *Body Language: Poems of the Medical Training Experience* (N. Jain, C. Coppock, and S.B. Clark, Eds.). BOA Editions. Used with permission.

19 Nene, Y., & Tadi, P. (2022). Resident Burnout. StatPearls. https://www .ncbi.nlm.nih.gov/books/NBK553176/.

20 Takayesu, J.K., Ramoska, E.A., Clark, T.R., Hansoti, B., Doughberly, J., Freeman, W., Weaver, K.R., Chang, Y., & Gross, E. (2014). Factors associated with burnout during emergency medicine residency. *SAEM*, 21(9): 1031–5.

21 Canadian Medical Association. (2017). National Physician Health Survey. Ottawa.

22 Kelly, E.L. (2005). Coping strategies, depression, and anxiety among Ontario family medicine residents. *Can Fam Physician*, 51: 242–3.

23 Koran, L., & Litt, I. (1988). House staff well-being. *West J Med*, 148: 97–401.

24 Mills, L.D., & Mills, T.J. (2005). Symptoms of post-traumatic stress disorder among emergency medicine residents. *J Emerg Med*, 28: 1–4.

25 Mata, D., et al. (2015). Prevalence of depression and depressive symptoms among resident physicians: A systemic review and meta-analysi. *JAMA*, 314(22).

26 Guille, C., & Sen, S. (2012, Feb). Prescription drug use and self-prescription among trained physicians. *Arch Intern Med*, 172(4): 371–2.

27 Hughes, P.H., Conrad, S.E., & Baldwin, D.C. (1991). Substance use and abuse. *JAMA*, 265: 2069–73.

28 Winkler, A. (2017). Treating physicians for addiction. *Am J. Psychiatry*, 12(4): 6–7.

29 Silver, H.K., & Slicken, A. (1990). Medical student abuse: Incidence, severity, and significance. *JAMA*, 263: 527–32.

30 Anglin, D. (1994). Residents' perspectives on violence and personal safety in the emergency department. *Ann Emerg Med*, 23: 1082–4.

31 Lall, M.D., Bilimoria, K.Y., Lu, D.W., et al. (2021). Prevalence of discrimination, abuse, and harassment in emergency medicine residency training in the US. *JAMA Netw Open*, 4(8). DOI:10.1001/jamanetworkopen.2021.21706.

32 Yaghmour, Nicholas A., Brigham, Timothy P., Richter, Thomas, Miller, Rebecca S., Philibert, Ingrid, Baldwin, DeWitt C. Jr., Nasca, Thomas J. (2017, July). Causes of death of residents in ACGME-accredited programs 2000 through 2014: Implications for the learning environment. *Academic Medicine*, 92(7): 976–83. DOI: 10.1097/ACM.0000000000001736.

33 Ross, M. (1971). Suicide among physicians. *Psychiatry Med*, 2: 189–98.

34 Hochberg, M.S., Berman, R.S., Kalet, A.L., Zabar, S.R., Gillespie, C., & Pachter, H.L. (2013, Feb). The stress of residency: recognizing the signs of depression and suicide in you and your fellow residents. *Am J Surg*, 205(2): 141–6.

35 Knight, J.M. (2013, Jan). Physiological and neurobiological aspects of stress and their relevance for residency training. *Acad Psychiatry*, 37(1): 6–10.

36 Landau, C., Hall, S., Wartman, S.A., et al. (1986). Stress in social and family relationships during medical residency. *J Med Educ*, 61: 654–60.

37 PAIRO study, www.pairo.org.

38 Ly, D.P., Seabury, S.A., & Jena, A.B. (2015). Divorce among physicians and other healthcare professionals in the United States: Analysis of census survey data. *BMJ*, 350: h706. DOI:10.1136/bmj.h706.

39 Reported in *Globe and Mail Report on Business* (1994, June). See also www.ama-assn.org.

40 Sakata, Y., Wada, K., Tsutsumi, A., et al. (2008). Effort-reward imbalance and depression in Japanese medical residents. *J Occup Health*, 50: 498–504.

41 Carius, M. (2001). Avoiding training toxicity. *Ann Emerg Med*, 38: 596–7.

42 Vogel, L. (2019). Growing number of medical trainees named in complaints. *CMAJ*, 191(25).

43 Madsen, T. (2009). A long wait for shorter shifts. *The New Physician*, http://www.amsa.org/AMSA/Homepage/Publications/TheNewPhysician/2009/tnp493.aspx. (link expired).

44 Wells, M.M., Roth, L., & Chande, N. (2012, Aug). Sleep disruption secondary to overnight call shifts is associated with irritable bowel syndrome in residents: A cross-sectional study. *Am J Gastroenterol*, 107(8): 1151–6.

45 Gupta, H.O., Gupta, S., Carter, R.L., Mohammed, A., & Meek, R.M. (2012, Nov). Does orthopaedic surgical training induce hypertension? A pilot study. *Clin Orthop Relat Res*, 470(11): 3253–60.

46 Roberts, M., et al. (2013). Oversight physicians during residency: A cross-sectional and longitudinal study. *Journal of Graduate Medical Education*, 5(3): 205–411.

47   Etzel, S.I., Egan, R.L., & Shevrin, M.P. (1989). Graduate medical education in the United States. *JAMA*, 262(8): 1029–37. http://dx.doi.org/10.1001/jama.1989.03430080049007.

48   *MacLean's*, September 24, 2007, 62.

49   http://www.acgme.org/acWebsite/dataBook/dat_index.asp.

50   Association of American Medical Colleges (AAMC), www.aamc.org.

51   Bickel, J.A. (1990). Women physicians: Change agents or second-class citizens? *Humane Med*, 6: 101–5.

52   Willet, L.L., Wellons, M.F., et al. (2010). Do women residents delay childbearing due to perceived career threats? *Academic Medicine*, 85(4): 640–6.

53   Borsellino, M. (1990, Mar). Female MD time off the job creates uncertainty for manpower planners. *Med Post*.

54   https://jamanetwork.com/journals/jamanetworkopen/fullarticle/2773400.

55   Bartels, C.B., Goetz, S., Ward, E., & Carnes, M. (2008). Internal medicine residents' perceived ability to direct patient care: Impact of gender and experience. *Journal of Women's Health*, 17(10): 1615–21.

56   Franco, K. (1983). Conflicts associated with a physician's pregnancy. *Am J Psychiatry*, 140: 902–4.

57   Davis, J.L., Baillie, S., Hodgson, C.S., Vontver, L., & Platt, L.D. (2001). Maternity leave: Existing policies of obstetrics and gynecology residency programs. *Obstet Gynecol*, 98: 1093–8.

58   Finch, S. (2003). Pregnancy during residency: A literature review. *Acad Med*, 78: 418–28.

59   Barzansky, B. (2002). Educational programs in U.S. medical schools 2001–2002. *JAMA*, 288: 1067–72.

60   Bickel, J.A. (1990). Women physicians: Change agents or second-class citizens? *Humane Med*, 6: 101–5.

61   https://policysearch.ama-assn.org/policyfinder/detail/H-405.960?uri=%252FAMADoc%252FHOD.xml-0-3580.xml.

62   Walsh, A., Gold, M., Jensen, P., & Jedrzkiewicz, M. (2005). Motherhood during residency training. *Can Fam Physician*, 51: 990–1.

63   Alguire, P.C., Whelan, G.P., & Rajput, V. (2008). The international medical graduate's guide to US medicine & residency training. *American College of Physicians*, Philadelphia.

64   https://www.ama-assn.org/education/international-medical-education/international-medical-graduates-img-toolkit-introduction.

65   https://bmjopen.bmj.com/content/11/5/e044321.

66   Etziony, M.E. (1973). *The physician's creed: An anthology of medical prayers, oaths and codes of ethics written and recited by medical practitioners through the ages.* CC Thomas, Springfield, IL, 29–30.

67   *Jerusalem Bible*, Eccles. 38: 1–15.

68   Author unknown.

69   *The Code of Maimonides.* (1949). Yale University Press, New Haven, CT.
70   Planned Parenthood. (n.d.). What does queer mean? Washington, DC: Planned Parenthood. Available from: https://www.plannedparenthood .org/learn/teens/sexual-orientation/what-does-queer-mean.
71   Weinand, J.D., Ehlinger, E.P., Conniff, J.F., Hayon, R.L., & Kvach, E. (2019). Supporting transgender and nonbinary residents. *Transgender Health* 4:1 222–5. https://www.liebertpub.com/doi/10.1089/trgh.2018.0074.
72   Bourns, A., Kucharski, E., Peterkin, A., & Risdon, C. (Eds.). (2022). *Caring for LGBTQ2S people: A clinical guide.* University of Toronto Press, Toronto.
73   https://guides.library.yale.edu/c.php?g=543814.
74   Shehab, S.S. (2018). How do we evaluate doctors with disabilities? [blog] In-house, November 11, 2018. https://in-housestaff.org/how-do-we -evaluate-doctors-with-disabilities-1148.
75   Drolet, B.C., Christopher, D.A., & Fischer, S.A. (2012). Residents' response to duty-hour regulations – a follow-up national survey. *N Engl J Med,* 366(24):e35.
76   https://psychology.berkeley.edu/people/christina-maslach.
77   Hyman, S.A., Michaels, D.R., Berry, J.M., et al. (2011). Risk of burnout in perioperative clinicians. *Anesthesiology,* 114(1): 194–220.
78   Prins, J.T., Gazendam-Donofrio, S.M., Tubben, B.J., van der Heijden, F.M.M.A., van de Weil, H.B.M., & Hoekstra-Weebers, J.E.H.M. (2007). Burnout in medical residents: A review. *Med Educ,* 41: 788–800.
77   Niku, T. (2004). Resident burnout. *JAMA,* 292: 2888–9.
80   McCray, L.W., Cronholm, P.F., Bogner, H.R., et al. (2008). Resident burnout: Is there hope? *Fam Med,* 40(9): 626–32.
81   Low, Z., et al. (2019). Prevalence of burnout in medical and surgical residents: A meta-analysis. *Int. J. Environ. Res. Public Health,* 16(9).
82   Rodrigues, H., et al. (2018). Burnout syndrome among medical residents: A systematic review and meta-analysis. *Plos One.* https://doi.org/10.1371 /journal.pone.0206840.
83   Bouchard, F., & Bélanger, P. (Eds.). (1989). Putting the heat on burnout, health and safety. Committee of the Fédération des infirmières et infirmiers de Québec, Litho Acme, Quebec. https://www .healthlinkscertified.org/uploads/files/2022_11_16_19_56_57_Maslach -burnout-inventory-english.pdf (link expired).
84   Shanafelt, T.D., Bradley, K.A., Wipf, J.E., & Back, A.L. (2002). Burnout and self-reported patient care in an internal medicine residency program. *Ann Intern Med,* 136: 358–67.
85   Mazie, B. (1985). Job stress, psychological health, and social support of family practice residents. *J Med Educ,* 60: 935–41.
86   Hawes, L. (2002). Who is sicker: Patients or residents? Residents' distress and the care of patients. *Ann Intern Med,* 136: 391–3. https://doi .org/10.7326/0003-4819-136-5-200203050-00012.

87 Rudner, H.L. (1988). Work-related stress: A survey of family practice residents in Ontario. *Can Fam Physician*, 34: 577–83.

88 Russell, A.T., Pasnace, R.O., & Taintor, Z.C. (1975). Emotional problems of residents in psyhciatry. *Am J Psychiatry*, 132: 263–7.

89 Ibid.

90 Kobayasi, R. (2018). Gender differences in the perception of quality of life during internal medicine training: A qualitative and quantitative analysis. *BMC Medical Education*, 18, 281.

91 Vogel, L. (2011). Just a little respect, please. *CMAJ*, 183(8): 895.

92 Wright, S., Levine, R.B., Beasley, B., et al. (2006). Personal growth and its correlates during residency training. *Med Educ*, 40: 737–45.

93 Vogel, L. (2011). Just a little respect, please. *CMAJ*, 183(8): 895; AMA News. (2022, Feb). Which factors do applicants weigh most when picking residency programs? www.ama-assn.org/residents-students/residency /which-factors-do-applicants-weigh-most-when-picking-residency -programs (link expired).

94 Fletcher, K.E., Underwood III, W., Davis, S.Q., Mangrulkar, R.S., McMahon Jr., L., & Saint, S. (2005). Effects of work hour reduction on residents' lives: A systematic review. *JAMA*, 294: 1088–100.

95 Puddester, D., Flynn, L., & Cohen, J. (Eds.). *CanMEDS Physician Health Guide: A Practical Handbook for Physician Health and Well-Being*. Royal College of Physicians and Surgeons of Canada; e-book available at www.royalcollege .ca/canmeds (the Royal College of Physicians and Surgeons of Canada CanMEDS Physician Health Guide, adapted with permission).

96 Ibid.

97 Kumar, B., Swee, M., & Suneja, M. (2020). Leadership training programs in graduate medical education: A systematic review. *BMC Medical Education*, 20: 175.

98 Satterfield, J., Swenson, S., & Rabow, M. (2009). Emotional intelligence in internal medicine residents: Educational implications for clinical performance and burnout. *Ann Behav Sci Med Educ*, 14(2): 65–8.

99 Dyrbye, L.N., et al. (2021). Physician's well-being index. *J Gen Intern Med*, 28: 421–7.

100 Brent, D.A. (1981). The residency as a developmental process. *J Med Educ*, 56: 417–22.

101 Lianov, L. (2021). A powerful antidote to physician burnout: Intensive healthy lifestyle and positive psychology approaches. *Am J Lifestyle Medicine*, 15(5).

102 Macedo, P.C.M., Citero, V., Schenkman, S., et al. (2009). Health-related quality of life predictors during medical residency in a random, stratified sample of residents. *Rev Bras Psiquiatr*, 31(2): 119–24.

103 Ratanawongsa, N., Wright, S., & Carrese, J.A. (2008). Well-being in residency: Effects on relationships with patients, interactions with

colleagues, performance and motivation. *Patient Education and Counseling*, 72: 194–200.

104 Seligman, M. (2003). *Authentic Happiness: Using the New Positive Psychology to Realize Your Potential for Lasting Fulfillment*. Free Press, New York.

2 Preventive Medicine

1   Gray, K. (2002, Sep). Critical condition. *Details*, 149.

2   Carek, P.J. (2001). Residency selection process and the match: Does anybody believe anybody? *JAMA*, 285: 2784–5. (This paper is still a classic.)

3   Raff, M.J., & Schwartz, I.S. (1974). An applicant's evaluation of a medical house officership. *N Engl J Med*, 293: 601–5.

4   Van Dyke, A., & Seger, A.M. (2009). Finding, keeping, and revitalizing the meaning in family medicine. *Int'l J Psychiatry in Medicine*, 45(4): 323–31.

5   American Academy of Family Physicians. (2023–24). *Strolling through the Match Guidebook*. The AAFP Students Guide to Residency Selection. https://www.aafp.org/students-residents/medical-students/become-a -resident/match/strolling-through-the-match.html.

6   Contracts: What you need to know: http://www.ama-assn.org/ama/pub /ama-wire/ama-wire/post/7-things-must-before-signing-employment -contract (link expired).

3 Physician Heal Thyself

1   At https://pogoe.org/sites/default/files/hl_physician_guide.pdf (link expired).

2   Colford, J.M., & McPhee, S.J. (1989). The raveled sleeve of care: Managing the stresses of residency training. *JAMA*, 261: 889–93.

3   Leighton, K., & Livingston, M. (1983). Fatigue in doctors. *Lancet*, 1: 1280.

4   Friedman, R.C., Bigger, J.T., & Kornfeld, D.S. (1971). The intern and sleep loss. *N Engl J Med*, 285(4): 201–3.

5   Friedman, R.C., Bigger, J.T., & Kornfeld, D.S. (1973). Psychological problems associated with sleep deprivation in interns. *J Med Educ*, 48: 436–41.

6   Kalter, L. (2019). Residents are sleep deprived. So what's new? AAMC website. https://www.aamc.org/news-insights/residents-are-sleep -deprived-so-what-s-new.

7   Mulenga, A., & Sasangohar, F. (2021). The impacts of sleep deprivation on medical residents: A scoping review of literature. *Proceedings of the human factors and ergonomics society annual meeting*, 64(1): 1898–902.

8   Guraieb-Chahin, P., et al. (2021). Cognitive effects of chronic sleep deprivation in internal medicine residents. *Revisita Mexicana de neurociencia*, 22(2): 51–5.

9   Baba, S., et al. (2021). Impact of sleep on medical residents' emotions. *Fam Med*, 53(4): 275–81.

10   Katz, S. (1989, Oct). Shifting gears: Shift work's assault on our biological rhythms. *Med Post*, 11–12, 48. These findings were replicated in a CIR survey reported in March 2001.

11   Mak, N.T., Li, J., & Wiseman, S.M. (2019). Resident physicians are at increased risk for dangerous driving after extended-duration work shifts: A systematic review. *Cureus*, 11(6): e4843. https://doi.org/10.7759/cureus.4843.

12   Swift, D. (1989, Sep). Humane schedules for residents, interns helps reduce risk of errors. *Med Post*, 47.

13   Ahmed, N., Devitt, K.S., Keshet, I., Spicer, J., Imrie, K., Feldman, L., Colls-Lartigue, J., Kayssi, A., Lipsman, N., Elmi, M., Kulkarni, A.V., Parshuram, C., Mainprize, T., Warren, R.J., Fata, P., Gorman, M.S., Feinberg, S., & Rutka, J. (2014, Jun). A systematic review of the effects of resident duty-hour restrictions in surgery: impact on resident wellness, training, and patient outcomes. *Ann Surg*, 259(6): 1041–53.

14   Veasey, S., Rosen, R., Barzansky, B., Rosen, I., & Owens, J. (2002). Sleep loss and fatigue in residency training: A reappraisal. *JAMA*, 288: 1116–24.

15   Goitein, L., Shanafelt, T.D., Wipf, J.E., & Slatore, C.G. (2005). The effects of work-hour limitations on resident well-being, patient care, and education in an internal medicine residency program. *Arch Intern Med*, 165: 260–6.

16   Desai, S., et al. (2018). Educational outcomes in a duty-hour flexibility trail in internal medicine. *NEJM*, 378: 1494–508.

17   Awan, M., Zagales, I., McKenney, M., Kinslow, K., & Elkbuli, A. (2021, Nov–Dec). ACGME 2011 Duty hours restrictions and their effects on surgical residency training and patients outcomes: A systematic review. *J Surg Educ*, 78(6): e35-e46. DOI: 10.1016/j.jsurg.2021.06.001. Epub 2021 Jun 25. PMID: 34183278.

18   Blum, N.J., & Lieu, T.A. (1992). The effects of paging on pediatric resident activities. *Am J Dis Child*, 146: 806–8.

19   Dinges, D. Cited in *CIR News*. (2001, Dec).

20   Hochberg, M.S., Berman, R.S., Kalet, A.L., Zabar, S.R., Gillespie, C., & Pachter, H.L. (2013, Feb). The stress of residency: recognizing the signs of depression and suicide in you and your fellow residents. *Am J Surg*, 205(2): 141–6.

21   Knight, J.M. (2013, Jan). Physiological and neurobiological aspects of stress and their relevance for residency training. *Acad Psychiatry*, 37(1): 6–10.

22 Bismilla, Z., & Wong, B. (2018). Handover toolkit: A resource to help teach, assess and implement a handover improvement program. Royal College of Physicians and Surgeons of Canada, Ottawa.

23 Marshall, S.A., & Ruedy, J. (2004). *On-call principles and protocols*, 4th ed. Saunders, Philadelphia.

24 Watson, D.T., Long, W.J., Yen, D., & Pichora, D.R. (2009). Health promotion program: A resident well-being study. *Iowa Orthopaedic Journal*, 29: 83–7.

25 Haney, E.M., Stadler, D., & Bliziotes, M.M. (2005). Vitamin D insufficiency in internal medicine residents. *Calcif Tissue Int*, 76: 11–16.

26 Hategan, A., Saperson, K., Harms, S., & Waters, H. (2020). *Humanism and Resilience in Residency Training*. Spring International Publishing, New York.

27 Bong-You, R. (2004). *The residency survival manual*. Morgan Bay Productions, Yarmouth, MA.

28 Patel, H., & Puddester, D. (2012). *The time management guide: A practical handbook for physicians by physicians*. Royal College of Physicians and Surgeons, Ottawa.

29 Borysenko, J. (1988). *Minding the Body, Mending the Mind*. Bantam, New York.

30 Place, S., & Talen, M. (2013). Creating a culture of wellness: Conversations, curriculum, concrete resources, and control. *Int J Psychiatry Med*, 45(4): 333–44.

31 Durso, C., & George, S.C. (1994, Dec). Guns 'n' doctors. *New Physician*. https://www.amsa.org/tnp.

32 Liss G., & McCaskell, L. (1994). Violence in the workplace. *Can Med Assoc J*, 151: 1243–6.

33 Liu, J., Gan, Y., Jiang, H., Li, L., Dwyer, R., Lu, K., et al. (2019). Prevalence of workplace violence against healthcare workers: A systematic review and meta-analysis. *Occup Environ Med*, 76: 927–37.

34 Querin, L, et al. (2021). A qualitative study of resident physician and health care worker experiences of verbal and physical abuse in the emergency department. *Ann Emerg Med*, 79(4): 391–6.

35 Steben, M. (1990). AIDS: Preventing HIV infection in health care workers. *J Fam Pract*, 13–15.

36 Vaillant, G.E. (1992). Physician cherish thyself: The hazards of self-prescribing. *JAMA*, 267: 2773–83.

4 Staying Whole: Maximizing Supports and Finding Balance

1 Rosen, I.M., Christie, J.D., Bellini, L.M., & Asch, D.A. (2000). Health and health care among housestaff in four US internal medicine residency programs. *J Gen Intern Med*, 15(2): 116–21.

2   Weidner, B.C., Dennis, B.M., Ayoub, M.M., Hutchinson, M.B., & Nakayama, D.K. (2014, Mar). Addressing trainees' concerns through a resident advocacy committee. *Am Surg*, 80(3): 307–8.

3   Canadian Mental Health Association. (2018). 5 things to know about peer support. Canadian Mental Health Association. https://cmhawwselfhelp.ca/news/5-things-to-know-about-peer-support/ (link expired).

4   Canadian Medical Association. (2018). https://www.cma.ca/physician-wellness-hub/topics/peer-support (link expired).

5   Butler, R. (1993). Support groups address residents' personal development. *JAMA*, 93: 789–91.

6   Weight, C.J., Sellon, J.L., Lessard-Anderson, C.R., Shanafelt, T.D., Olsen, K.D., & Laskowski, E.R. (2013, Dec). Physical activity, quality of life, and burnout among physician trainees: The effect of a team-based, incentivized exercise program. *Mayo Clin Proc*, 88(12): 1435–42.

7   Pliego, J.F., Wehbe-Janek, H., Rajab, M.H., Browning, J.L., & Fothergill, R.E. (2008). Ob/gyn boot camp using high-fidelity human simulators: Enhancing residents' perceived competency, confidence in taking a leadership role, and stress hardiness. *Simulation in Healthcare*, 3(2): 82–9.

8   Costello, J., Livett, M., Stide, P.J.O., West, M., Premaratne, M., & Thacker, D. (2010). The seamless transition from student to intern: From theory to practice. *Internal Medicine Journal*, 40: 728–31.

9   Laack, T.O., Newman, J.S., Goyal, D.G., & Torsher, L.C. (2010). A one-week simulated internship course helps prepare medical students for transition to residency. *Simulation in Healthcare*, 5(3): 127–32.

10 Bragard, I., & Etienne, A. (2010). Efficacy of a communication and stress management training on medical residents' self-efficacy, stress to communicate and burnout. *J Health Psychology*, 15(7): 1075–81.

11 Satterfield, J.M., & Becerra, C. (2010). Developmental challenges, stressors, and coping strategies in medical residents: A qualitative analysis of support groups. *Medical Education*, 44: 908–16.

12 Howell, J.B., & Schroeder, D.P. (Eds.). (1984). *Physician Stress. A Handbook for Coping*. University Park Press, Baltimore.

13 Levey, R.E. (2001). Sources of stress for residents and recommendations for programs to assist them. *Acad Med*, 76(2): 142–50.

14 Shanafelt, T.D., & Noseworthy, J.H. (2017). Executive leadership and physician wellbeing: Nine organizational strategies to promote engagement and reduce burnout. *MayoClinc Proc* 92(1): 129–46.

15 Shanafelt, T.D. (2005). Finding meaning, balance, and personal satisfaction in the practice of oncology. *J Support Oncol*, 3: 157–64.

16 Van Dyke, A., & Seger, A.M. (2013). Finding, keeping, and revitalizing the meaning in family medicine. *Int'l J Psychiatry in Medicine*, 45(4): 323–31.

17 Beckman, T., Reed, D., & Shanafelt, T.D. (2010). Impact of resident wellbeing and empathy on assessment of faculty physicians. *JGIM*, 52–6.
18 For more useful strategies on coping, maintaining authenticity and "staying human during residency training," a new, excellent reference is *Humanism and resilience in residency training* (2020) by Hategan, A., Saperson, K., Harms, S., & Waters, H. Springer International Publishing.
19 Duckworth, A.L., & Quinn, P.D. (2009). Development and validation of the Short Grit Scale (GritS). *Journal of Personality Assessment*, 91, 166–74. http://www.sas.upenn.edu/~duckwort/images/Duckworth%20and%20Quinn.pdf (link expired). See also Duckworth, A.L., Peterson, C., Matthews, M.D., & Kelly, D.R. (2007). Grit: Perseverance and passion for long-term goals. *Journal of Personality and Social Psychology*, 9, 1087–101. http://www.sas.upenn.edu/~duckwort/images/Grit%20JPSP.pdf (link expired).

5 Protecting and Deepening Personal Relationships

1 Landau, C., Hall, S., Wartman, S.A., et al. (1986). Stress in social and family relationships during the medical residency. *J Med Educ*, 61: 654–60.
2 Smith, M.F., Andrasik, F., & Quinn, S.J. (1988). Stressors and psychological symptoms of family practice residents and spouses. *J Med Educ*, 63: 397–405.
3 Myers, M. (1988). *Doctors' marriages: A look at the problems and their solutions*. Plenum, New York.
4 Leining, M. (2006). "October 1st," in *Body Language: Poems of the Medical Training Experience* (N. Jain, C. Coppock, and S.B. Clark, Eds). BOA Editions. Used with permission.
5 Guldner, G.T. (2001). Long-distance relationships and emergency medicine residency. *Ann Emerg Med*, 37: 103–6.
6 Sargent, M.C., Sotile, W., Sotile, M.O., Rubash, H., & Barrack, R.L. (2012, Oct). Quality of life during orthopaedic training and academic practice: Part 2: Spouses and significant others. *J Bone Joint Surg Am*, 94(19): e145(1–6).
7 Math, K. (2013). *Surviving residency: A medical spouse guide to embracing the training years*. Champagne and Bonbons Press.
8 Jaco, J.M. (1989). *Can we live with this job?* PAIRO, Toronto.
9 Myers, M. (2002). Medical marriages and other intimate relationships. *MJA*, 181: 392–3.
10 Sangi-Haghpeykar, H., Ambani, D.S., & Carson, S.A. (2009). Stress, workload, sexual well-being, and quality of life among physician residents in training. *Int J Clin Pract*, 63: 462–7.

11 Adapted from La Puma, J., & Preist, E. (1992). Is there a doctor in the house? An analysis of the practice of physicians treating their own families. *JAMA*, 267: 1810–12.
12 Dempsey, L., & Ecker, J. (1994, Nov). Understanding the dating guidelines. *CPSO Members' Dialogues*, 9–11.

6 Keeping Professional Relationships Healthy

1   Mitchell, R., et al. (2014). The ABC of health care team dynamics: Understanding complex affective, behavioral, and cognitive dynamics in interprofessional teams. *Health Care Manage Rev*, 39(1): 1–9.
2   Lencioli, P. (2002). *The five dysfunctions of a team: A leadership fable*. Jossey-Bass, New York.
3   Jellinek, M.S. (1985). Recognition and management of discord within resident teams. *JAMA*, 256: 754–5.
4   Alexander, M., et al. (2013). The hateful resident. *J Grad Med Educ*, 5(4): 547–9.
5   American Medical Association. (2019). https://www.ama-assn.org/residents -students/resident-student-health/physician-well-being-developing -culture-wellness.
6   Canadian Medical Association Physician Wellness Hub, https://www.cma .ca/physician-wellness-hub.
7   Edmondson, E., Kumar, A, & Smith, S. (2018). Creating a culture of wellness in residency. *Academic Medicine*, 93(7): 966–8.
8   Adapted from Goldman, L., Lee, T., & Rudd, P. (1983). Ten commandments for effective consultation. *Arch Intern Med*, 143: 1753–5.
9   Tokarz, J.P., Bremer, W., & Peter, K. (1979). *Beyond survival: A book prepared by and for resident physicians to meet the challenge of the impaired physician and to promote well-being through medical education*. AMA Press, Chicago.
10 Srivastava, A. (2018). Impaired physicians: Obliterating the stigma. *American Journal of Psychiatry Residents' Journal*, 13(3): 4–6.
11 Edwards, J.C., & Marier, R.L. (1988). *Clinical teaching for medical residents: Roles, techniques and programs*. Springer, New York.
12 Morrison, E.H. (2000). Yesterday a learner, today a teacher too. *Pediatrics*, 105: 235–43.
13 Smith, C., & Ricotta, D. (2016). The resident as teacher. NEJM Knowledge+. https://knowledgeplus.nejm.org/blog/resident-as-teacher/.
14 Wigle, R.D., & Eisenhauer, E.E. Queen's University. Reprinted with permission.

15 Patterson, F., Knight, A., Stewart, F., & MacLeod, S. (2013). How best to assist struggling trainees? Developing an evidence-based framework to guide support interventions. *Education for Primary Care*, 24: 330–9.

16 College of Physicians and Surgeons of Ontario. (2021). Professional Responsibilities in Medical Education. https://www.cpso.on.ca/en /Physicians/Policies-Guidance/Policies/Professional-Responsibilities -in-Medical-Education.

17 Berlin, R.M. (2006). "The Hotseat," in *Body Language: Poems of the Medical Training Experience* (N. Jain, C. Coppock, and S.B. Clark, Eds.). BOA Editions, Rochester, NY. Used with permission.

18 CMPA. (2022). Team communication. https://www.cmpa-acpm.ca /serve/docs/ela/goodpracticesguide/pages/communication/Team _Communication/importance_of_teamwork-e.htmls (link expired).

19 Winter, R.O., & Birnberg, B. (2002). Working with impaired residents: Trials, tribulations, and successes. *Fam Med*, 34: 190–6.

20 Villafranca, A., et al. (2021). Disruptive behaviour in the perioperative setting: A contemporary review. *Can J Anes*, 64: 128–40.

21 Institute of Medicine (US) Committee on Quality of Health Care in America. (2001). *Crossing the quality chasm: A new health system for the 21st century*. National Academies Press (US), Washington, DC.

22 The Arnold P. Gold Foundation. https://www.gold-foundation.org/resources.

23 Elwyn, G., et al. (2012). Shared decision making: A model for clinical practice. *J Gen Intern Med*, 27(10): 1361–7.

24 Hickson, G., et al. (2007). A complementary approach to promoting professionalism: Identifying, measuring and addressing unprofessional behaviour. *Acad Med*, 82: 1040–8.

25 CMPA. (2022). Respecting boundaries. https://www.cmpa-acpm.ca /serve/docs/ela/goodpracticesguide/pages/professionalism/Respecting _boundaries/preventing_boundary_issues-e.html.

26 Brook, G., et al. (2019). UK national guideline for consultations requiring sexual history taking. https://www.bashhguidelines.org/media/1239/2019 -sexual-history-guidelines-final.pdf.

27 From Members' Dialogue (CPSO). (1993, Nov). Reprinted with permission.

28 French P. (2007). BASHH National guidelines – Consultations requiring sexual history taking. *Int J STD AIDS*, 18(1): 17–22. http://dx.doi. org/10 .1258/095646207779949989.

29 Peterkin, A.D. (1989, Sep). Encouraging empathy. *Curr Ther (Med Post Suppl)*, 6, 8, 34.

30 Bellini L.M., Baime, M., & Shea, J.A. (2002). Variation of mood and empathy during internship. *JAMA*, 287: 3143–6.

31   Peterkin, A.D. (2012). Getting the real story from your patient: Practical strategies for practicing a more narrative-based medicine. *Canadian Family Physician*, 58(1): 63–4.
32   National Institute of Mental Health, https://www.nimh.nih.gov/health /statistics/mental-illness#part_2539.
33   Peterkin, A.D. (2010, May). Using reflective writing with students: Ten tips. *CAME Newsletter*, 6, 12.
34   Royal College of Physicians and Surgeons. (2014). Mental Health Competencies for Physicians.
35   Kopacz, D. (2006). "I Remember," in *Body Language: Poems of the Medical Training Experience* (N. Jain, C. Coppock, and S.B. Clark, Eds.). BOA Editions. Used with permission.

7 Whiz Kids: Teaching, Learning, Doing Research, and Leading with No Time

1   Ellaway, R. (2011). eMedical Teacher. *Medical Teacher*, 33: 258–60.
2   Audet, N. (Sep. 1995). How to manage CME reading time efficiently. *Can J CME*, 83–8.
3   Mazmanian, P.E. (2002). Continuing medical education and the physician as learner: Guide to the evidence. *JAMA*, 288: 1057–60.
4   AMA Policy Statement 300.988; www.ama-assn.org
5   Transue, E. (2006). "Haiku of Residency," in *Body Language: Poems of the Medical Training Experience* (N. Jain, C. Coppock, and S.B. Clark, Eds.). BOA Editions. Used with permission.
6   Thomson, P. (2009). Medical education vs. medical educators. *The New Physician*. http://www.amsa.org/AMSA/Homepage/Publications /TheNewPhysician/2009/tnp479.aspx.
7   Snell, L. (1994, Sep). How to give an effective audiovisual presentation. *Can J CME*, 1–3.
8   Tomlinson, C., Labossiere, J., Rommens, K., & Birch, D.W. (2012, Aug). The Canadian general surgery resident: Defining current challenges for surgical leadership. *Can J Surg*, 55(4): S184–90.
9   Taylor, B. (2010). *Effective Medical Leadership*. University of Toronto Press, Toronto.
10   Wear, D., & Skillicorn, J. (2009, April). Hidden in plain sight: The formal, informal, and hidden curricula of a psychiatry clerkship. *Academic Medicine*, 84(4): 451–8.
11   https://pubmed.ncbi.nlm.nih.gov/9580717/.

8 The Medical Humanities/Health Humanities and Narrative-Based Medicine

1   Evans, M. (2002, July). Reflections on the humanities in medical education. *Medical Education*, 36(6): 508–13.
2   https://www.acgme.org/globalassets/PDFs/commonguide/IVA5e
     _EducationalProgram_ACGMECompetencies_Professionalism
     _Explanation.pdf.

9 Not Just a Job

1   Royal College of Physicians and Surgeons of Canada, https://www
     .royalcollege. ca/canmeds.
2   Ibid.
3   Ibid.
4   Eno, C., et al. (2020). Milestones Guidebook for Residents and
     Fellows. https://www.acgme.org/globalassets/pdfs/milestones
     /milestonesguidebookforresidentsfellows.pdf.
5   NEJM Knowledge+. (2017). Exploring the ACGME core competencies:
     Part 7. https://knowledgeplus.nejm.org/blog/acgme-core-competencies
     -professionalism/.
6   American Board of Internal Medicine, https://www.abim.org.
7   https://abimfoundation.org/wp-content/uploads/2015/12/Medical-
     Professionalism-in-the-New-Millenium-A-Physician-Charter.pdf.
8   Crawshaw, R., Rogers, D.E., Pellegrino, E.D, et al. (1995). Patient-
     physician covenant. *JAMA*, 273: 1553. Reprinted with permission.
9   Ibid.
10   Jacobson, J.A., Tolle, S.W., & Stocking, C. (1989). Internal medicine
     residents' preferences regarding medical ethics education. *Acad Med*,
     64: 760–4.
11   Hong, D.Z., Goh, J.L., Ong, Z.Y. et al. (2021). Postgraduate ethics training
     programs: A systematic scoping review. *BMC Med Educ*, 21, 338. https://
     doi.org/10.1186/s12909-021-02644-5.
12   Pourbairamian, G., Bigdeli, S., Arabshahi, S., Yamani, N., Sohrabi, Z.,
     Ahmadi, F., & Sandars, J. (Accepted/In press). Hidden curriculum in
     medical residency programs: A scoping review. *Journal of Advances in
     Medical Education and Professionalism*.
13   Hundert, E.M., Hafferty, F., & Christakis, D. (1996). Characteristics of the
     informal curriculum and trainees' ethical choices. *Acad Med*, 71: 624–42.

14 Bennett, N., Lockyer, J., Mann, K., Batty, H., LaForet, K., Rethans, J.J., et al. (2004). Hidden curriculum in continuing medical education. *J Contin Educ Health Prof*, 24(3): 145–52.

15 Lempp, H., & Seale, C. (2004). The hidden curriculum in undergraduate medical education: Qualitative study of medical students' perceptions of teaching. *BMJ*, 329(7469): 770–3.

16 Farrell, C., & Hayward, B. (2022). Ethical dilemmas, moral distress, and the risk of moral injury: Experiences of residents and fellows during the COVID-19 pandemic in the United States. *Academic Medicine*, 97(3S): S55–S60. DOI: 10.1097/ACM.0000000000004536.

17 Shreves, J.G., & Moss, A.H. (1996). Residents' ethical disagreements with attending physicians: An unrecognized problem. *Acad Med*, 71: 1103–5.

18 Thoma, H., Meador, K., Payne, K., & Drohte, B. (2021). Interdisciplinary ethics certificate program for graduate medical education trainees. *J. Grad Med Educ*, 13(6): 863–7.

19 Jonsen, A.R., Siegler, M., & Winslade, W.J. (2010). *Clinical ethics: A practical approach to decisions in clinical medicine*, 7th ed. McGraw-Hill, New York.

20 Canadian Medical Protective Association. (2022). "Informed consent." In *The good practices guide*. https://www.cmpa-acpm.ca/serve/docs/ela /goodpracticesguide/pages/communication/Informed_Consent/three_key _elements-e.html (link expired).

21 Beauchamp, T.L., & McCullough, L.B. (1984). *Medical Ethics: The Moral Responsibilities of Physicians*. Prentice-Hall, Englewood Cliffs, NJ; CMPA, Ottawa, 2008.

22 https://www.canada.ca/en/health-canada/services/medical-assistance -dying.html.

23 https://www.cmpa-acpm.ca/en/advice-publications/browse-articles/2011 /end-of-life-care-support-comfort-and-challenging-decisions.

24 https://www.choosingwisely.org.

25 https://www.ama-assn.org/delivering-care/ethics/code-medical-ethics -financing-and-delivery-health-care.

26 https://www.acgme.org/what-we-do/diversity-equity-and-inclusion/. (link expired).

27 https://www.who.int/news-room/fact-sheets/detail/patient-safety.

28 Curtis, E., Jones, R. Tipene-Leach, D., Walker, C., Loring, B., Paine, S.-J., & Reid, P. (2019). Why cultural safety rather than cultural competency is required to achieve health equity: A literature review and recommended definition. *International Journal for Equity in Health*, 18: 174. https://doi.org /10.1186/s12939-019-1082-3.

29 Howard, F., McKneally, M., & Levin, A.V. (2010). Integrating bioethics into postgraduate medical education: The University of Toronto model. *Acad Med*, 85(6): 1035–40. DOI: 10.1097/ACM.0b013e3181dbebb8.

30 Evans, K.G. (1990). *Summary of Federal Legislation and Laws Enacted in the Province of Quebec*. CMPA, Ottawa.
31 Ellaway, R. (2010). eMedical teacher: Digital professionalism. *Medical Teacher*, 32(8): 705–7.
32 Hutchison, R. (1990). Do not resuscitate – The writing of no-code orders. *Humane Med*, 6: 135–7.
33 CMA. (2004). Code of Ethics. Canadian Medical Association, Ottawa.
34 https://www.ama-assn.org and https://www.ama-assn.org/system/files/a22-502.pdf.
35 Crosbie, C., McDougall, A., Pangli, H., Abu-Laban, R.B., & Calder, L.A. (2022, Jan). College complaints against resident physicians in Canada: a retrospective analysis of Canadian Medical Protective Association data from 2013 to 2017. *CMAJ Open*, 10(1): E35-E42. DOI: https://doi.org/10.9778/cmajo.20210026.
36 Emson, H. (1989, Sep). Testifying. Courtroom etiquette. Here comes the judge – are you ready? *Curr Ther (Med Post suppl)*, 25–7.
37 (1990). Oath for new doctors. *The New York Times*.

10 Taking Care of Business: Managing Your Finances

1 MD Management Ltd. Guide to Establishing a Medical Practice. Ottawa. (Much of this chapter is reprinted with permission from this guide.)

11 Knowledge Is Power: Social Media Guidelines and Helpful Resources

1 CMA. (2012). Social Media and Canadian Physicians: Issues and Rules of Engagement. CMA, Ottawa.
2 AMA Policy Finder, https://policysearch.ama-assn.org/policyfinder.
3 Canadian Medical Association, https://www.cma.ca/virtual-care-playbook-canadian-physicians.
4 Excerpted from Dermer, M. (2020, March). *Virtual care playbook*. CMA, Royal College, CFPC. https://www.nygh.on.ca/sites/default/files/documents/2020-07/-virtual-care-playbook_cma-cfpc.pdf.

12 I'm Finally Done: Now What? Thoughts on Transitioning into Practice

1 https://www.royalcollege.ca/ca/en/health-policy/building-medical-workforce-data-evidence/employment-study.html.

2   Souba, W., & Tsai, A. (2019). Beyond better, safer, cheaper health care: What's ultimately at stake? *Academic Medicine*, 94(11): 1679–84.

3   Dickson, G., & Aerde, J. (2018). Enabling physicians to lead: Canada's LEADS framework. *Leadership in Health Services*, 31(2): 1751–879.

4   https://www.aamc.org/news-insights/five-emerging-medical-specialties -you-ve-never-heard-until-now.

5   Pololi, L. (2006, Jan). Career development for academic medicine – A nine step strategy. *BMJCareers*, 38–9.

6   For an overview on health systems worldwide, see Woo, S. (2008, Dec). How health care works in other countries, *The New Physician*.

7   https://quotefancy.com/quote/1353799/William-Osler-The-practice-of -medicine-is-an-art-not-a-trade-a-calling-not-a-business-a.

Index

CPI Group (UK) Ltd, Croydon, CR0 4YY
16/04/2025